BROWN

HBJ SCIENCE
—Nova Edition—

Elizabeth K. Cooper
formerly Coordinator
of Teacher Training
University of California

Paul E. Blackwood
formerly Specialist for
Science Education
U.S. Office of Education

John A. Boeschen
formerly Science Teacher
Pinole, California

Morsley G. Giddings
Professor of Education
Brooklyn College, City University
of New York

Arthur A. Carin
Professor of Elementary and
Early Childhood Education and
Director of Environmental Education
Queens College
City University of New York

Biology and Ecology
Garrett Hardin
Emeritus Professor of
Human Ecology
University of California
Santa Barbara, California

Cooperative Learning
David W. Johnson
Professor of Educational
Psychology
College of Education
University of Minnesota
Minneapolis, Minnesota

Roger T. Johnson
Professor of Curriculum
and Instruction
College of Education
University of Minnesota
Minneapolis, Minnesota

Biology and Genetics
Richard C. Lewontin
Professor, Harvard University
Cambridge, Massachusetts

Geology and Earth Science
Alistair W. McCrone
Professor of Geology
Humboldt State University
Arcata, California

Physics
Franklin Miller, Jr.
Emeritus Professor of Physics
Kenyon College
Gambier, Ohio

Astronomy and Science Education
Fletcher G. Watson
Emeritus Professor
Harvard University
Cambridge, Massachusetts

Advisory Board

Judy H. Dennison
Coordinator of
Elementary Science
Fulton County Schools
Atlanta, Georgia

Kathleen Donnellan
Elementary Science
Resource Teacher
Springfield Public Schools
Springfield, Massachusetts

Iris Maney
Title II Staff
Development Specialist
Orleans Parish
New Orleans, Louisiana

Dale Rose
Supervisor of Science
Hampton School
Administration Center
Hampton, Virginia

LaWanna S. White
Science Supervisor
Cleveland Public Schools
Cleveland, Ohio

 HBJ

HARCOURT BRACE JOVANOVICH, PUBLISHERS
Orlando   San Diego   Chicago   Dallas

Reviewers

Frances M. Culpepper
Instructional Services Center
Science Coordinator, K-12
Atlanta, Georgia

Robert W. Deem
Former Coordinator of Science,
    Health and Outdoor Education
School District 446
Elgin, Illinois

Marjorie Slavick Frank
Adjunct Faculty
School of Education
Manhattan College
Bronx, New York

Sister Anna Marie Goetz, R.S.M.
St. Maurice School
Pittsburgh, Pennsylvania

Deborah G. Gozzard
Science Teacher
Lynnhaven Junior High School
Virginia Beach, Virginia

Darlene Harmon
Clausell Elementary School
Jackson, Mississippi

Ernestine Hightower
Whittier Elementary School
Lawton, Oklahoma

Janet Iona
Adams County School District #12
Northglenn, Colorado

Patricia C. Manning
Professor, College of Education
University of Central Florida
Orlando, Florida

Thomasena Woods
Science Supervisor
Newport News Public Schools
Newport News, Virginia

PICTURE CREDITS

KEY: (t) top, (b) bottom, (l) left, (r) right, (c) center.

Cover: J. Brownlie/Bruce Coleman, Inc..

Contents pages: iii(t), Marty Stouffer/Animals Animals, (c) George Holton/Photo Researchers, (b) David Pollack/Stock Market; **iv**(t), William Koplitz/DPI, (c) Marvin Newman/DPI, (b) Ned Haines/Photo Researchers; **v**, Craig Aurness/Woodfin Camp.

ILLUSTRATORS: Graphic Ideas, Inc., Mulvey Associates, Ruth Soffer, Phillip M. Veloric, Lloyd Birmingham.

UNIT 1: Pages; **viii**(l), Breck Kent/Earth Scenes, (tr) DPI, (br) Charles G. Summers, Jr./DPI; **1**(t), Ron Karten/Omni-Photo Communications, (b) Robert C. Fields/Animals Animals, **2**, Alex Langley/DPI; **3**(l), Oxford Scientific Films/Animals Animals, (r) W. H. Hodge/Peter Arnold; **4**(t), Granger Collection, (b) Ken Lewis/Earth Scenes; **6**(both) HBJ; **7**(all), Clara Aich; **8**(t), Lizabeth Corlett/DPI, (b) Clara Aich; **9**(l), Hilary Masters/Image Bank, (r) Lizabeth Corlett/DPI, **10**, Chris Reeberg/DPI; **11**, Ruth Dixon; **12**, Lynn M. Stone/Bruce Coleman; **13**(t), Leonard Lee Rue III/Animals Animals, (b) K. Preston Mafhan/Animals Animals; **15**(both) Marty Stouffer/Animals Animals; **16**(tl), Ethan Hoffman/Archive Pictures, (tr) Lawrence Migdale/Photo Researchers, (b) Terrence Moore/Woodfin Camp & Assoc.; **18**(t), Frank E. Toman/Taurus, (b) Michael Habicht/Animals Animals; **19**(t), Oxford Scientific Films/Animals Animals, (bl) Sven Olaf/DPI, (br) Stephen J. Krasemann/Peter Arnold; **21**(t), Z. Leszczynski/Animals Animals, (r) Laura Riley/Bruce Coleman; **22**, Grant Heilman; **23**(l), Mono Lake Committee, (r) Grant Heilman; **24**, Alex Langley/DPI; **25**(l), Andrew Odum/Peter Arnold, (r) J. C. Stevenson/Animals Animals; **26**, Simon Trevor/Bruce Coleman; **27**, Clara Aich; **28**(l), Z. Leszczynski/Animals Animals, (r) Leonard Lee Rue III/Animals Animals; **29**, Scripps Institute of Oceanography; **30**(t), Mark Schorr, (b) Grant Heilman; **31**(t), Bill Dyer/Photo Researchers, (b) Dave Woodwark/Taurus; **32**(tl), M. Austerman/Animals Animals, (tr) Breck P. Kent/Earth Scenes, (tr) D. Lyns/Bruce Coleman; **33**(t), Dale & Marion Zimmerman/Bruce Coleman, (b) Dave Penland; **34**(l), Eric V. Grave/Photo Researchers, (r) Russ Kinne/Photo Researchers; **35**(l), Ann Hagen-Griffiths/Omni-Photo Communications, (r) Vince Strebno/Bruce Coleman; **37**, Clara Aich; **38**, Lester Tinker/Taurus; **39**, Charles Schmidt/ Taurus; **41**(t), Latham/Monkmeyer, (b) Breck P. Kent/Earth Scenes;
UNIT 2: **42**(l), George Holton/Photo Researchers, (tr) J. & C. Kroeger/Animals Animals, (br) Kojo Tanaka/Animals Animals; **43**(t), Greenpeace/Sygma, (c) Carl Roessler, (b) Byron Crader; **44**(t), Jacques Jangoux/Peter Arnold, (bl) Richard Wiers/Peter Arnold, (br) Ted Levin/Earth Scenes; **45**(l), Leonard Lee Rue III/DPI, (r) Leonard Lee Rue III/Animals Animals; **46**(t), Bjorn Bolshad/Peter Arnold, (b) John Shaw/Bruce Coleman; **47**(t), Hans Reinhard/Bruce Coleman, (bl) Jerry De Camp/Taurus, (br) Z. Leszczynski/Animals Animals; **48**(t), Tony Fiorio/DPI, (b) Charlie Ott/DPI; **49**(t), The Stone Flower Studio/DPI, (c) W. H. Hodge/Peter Arnold, (b) Charlie Ott, DPI; **50**(tl), Leonard Lee Rue III/Bruce Coleman, (r) S. Moxes/Animals Animals, (bl) M. Stouffer Productions/Animals Animals; **51**(all), Peter Menzel; **52**(t), G. Ziesler/Peter Arnold, (b) Phil Dotson/DPI; **53**(l), Jerry Frank/DPI, (tr) James H. Carmichael/Bruce Coleman, (br) Grant Heilman; **54**(tl), Stephen Krasemann/Photo Researchers, (tr) Breck P. Kent/Animals Animals, (bl) DPI, (br) Frederick J. Dodd/Peter Arnold; **55**, Clyde H. Smith/Peter Arnold; **56**, Culver Pictures; **58**(t), Peter Arnold, (bl) Grant Heilman, (br) Stephen J. Krasemann/Peter Arnold; **59**(t), E. R. Degginger/Animals Animals, (bl) Mickey Gibson/Animals Animals; **60**(l), Charlie Ott/DPI, (r) Panuska/DPI; **61**(t), Stephen J. Krasemann/Peter Arnold, (b) Tom Brakefield/Taurus; **62**(tl), Stephen J. Krasemann/Peter Arnold, (tr) Panuska/DPI, (c) Joe McDonald/Animals Animals; **63**(both), Environmental Research Lab/Univ. of Arizona; **64**, G. Scott Mills; **65**, Charlie Ott/DPI; **66**(tl), Hal McKusick/DPI, (tr) Leonard Lee Rue III/DPI, (b) Bob & Clara Calhoun/Bruce Coleman; **67**(t), Stouffer Productions/Animals Animals, (b) Jerry Hout/Bruce Coleman; **68**(both), Clara Aich; **69**, Jeff Rotman/Peter Arnold; **70**(t), Delmar Lipp/DPI, (bl) Earl Roberge/Photo Researchers, (br) Joan Menschenfreund/International Stock Photo; **73**(t), Keith Gillett/Earth Scenes, (b) NASA; **74**(l), Phillip A. Harrington/Peter Arnold, (r) Manfred Kage/Peter Arnold; **75**(l), Manfred Kage/Peter Arnold, (r) Grant Heilman; **76**(tl), Robert P. Carr/Bruce Coleman, (bl) DPI, (r) Clyde H. Smith/Peter Arnold; **77**(tl), Bob Evans/Peter Arnold, (tr) Grant Heilman, (c) John McGregory/Peter Arnold, (b) Taurus; **78**(tl), Z. Leszczynski/Animals Animals, (tr, cr) Grant Heilman, (cl)

(continued on page 405)

Contents

BROWN

HBJ
—Nova ✳ Edition—
SCIENCE

Living Things – Interdependence

These people are hard at work. Shortly they will stop to eat. They may have their favorite foods. Perhaps they like to eat chicken or pasta. People like many different foods.

A giraffe is drinking water from a small pool. Soon it will stretch its long neck to reach its favorite food—tender leaves from a nearby tree.

In the forest the air is alive with the sounds of animals. However, this barn owl is fast asleep. The owl is a creature of the night. Only then does it seek its favorite food—field mice.

The people, the giraffe, and the barn owl all have something in common. They could not live without green plants. In fact, all animal life would die off without green plants. Are you surprised? Continue reading to find out why.

1

1 ▶ Living Things Need Each Other

Early one Saturday morning Jeff hears his friends call to him. "Let's get going," they shout. Suddenly he remembers. Today is the day they promised to clean up the old lot near school. Jeff knows he should have breakfast first, but he's late. "Just this one time I'll skip breakfast," he says to himself.

In a few hours Jeff begins to tire. His stomach has begun to send him an urgent message. He's hungry. Jeff needs food. Why? Food contains the energy his body requires. In that, Jeff is certainly not alone. Everyone needs food for energy. So do animals and plants. However, the way in which people and animals get food is different from that of plants.

Animals cannot make their own food. Green plants can. Green plants, then, are food **producers.** Other living things are dependent on the food produced by green plants.

Producers

These African elephants are feeding on grass. ■ Elephants are among the largest land animals to ever live. You can imagine how much food they must eat.

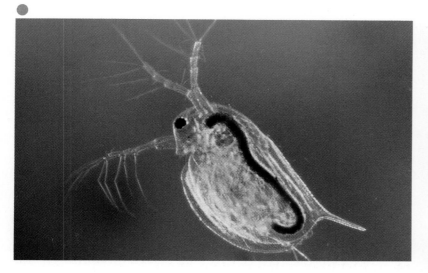

Tiny animals also need food. The *daphnia*, or water flea, lives in the water. ● It cannot be seen easily with the eye alone. In its microscopic world, the daphnia eats tiny green plants to survive. The largest and the smallest animals are all dependent on food-producing green plants for their energy.

Some plantlike organisms are not green. They cannot make their own food. They are not food producers. This mushroom is growing on a tree. ▲ To get its food, the mushroom breaks down the matter of the tree. So nongreen, plantlike organisms are also dependent on green plants for energy. Are you beginning to see why most life on Earth depends on green plants?

It may seem as if green plants produce food for the convenience of the animals in the world. Not so. Green plants make food for their own use. We happen to benefit from the process. If there were no animals, the green plants would still continue to produce food.

Green plants cannot produce food all on their own. They must obtain the basic building blocks from the soil, air, and water. To produce food, they need energy as well. So green plants are also dependent. How do green plants depend on their environment?

Photosynthesis

In ancient times the Egyptians worshipped the Sun. They believed it was the source of life. They built statues of the Sun god. ■

Today we know the Sun is just one of countless stars in the sky. The Sun is by far the closest star to Earth. It provides our planet with light energy. Green plants use light energy to make food in a process called **photosynthesis** (foh-toh-SIN-thuh-sis). In fact, photosynthesis means just that. *Photo* refers to light and *synthesis* to making food. Imagine for one moment just how remarkable that really is. Light energy produced in the Sun travels over 150 million kilometers to the Earth. There some of it is captured and changed into energy green plants can use.

Green plants can convert light energy into the energy of food. In a way, the ancient Egyptians were right. The Sun is the source of energy for life on Earth.

Food-Making in a Leaf

Since green plants perform photosynthesis, you might guess that it is the *green* part of the plant that does this important job. You would be right. When you think of the green part of most plants, you probably think of the leaf first. ● So let's look at food-making in the leaf. However, keep in mind that the other green parts of the plant can also perform photosynthesis.

Study the structure of a typical leaf. ▲ The first layer of cells on the top and bottom are clear. They do not perform photosynthesis. Fortunately, light passes easily through these layers. Inside the leaf are many cells that contain a green substance called **chlorophyll** (KLOR-uh-fil). It is chlorophyll that captures light energy from the Sun.

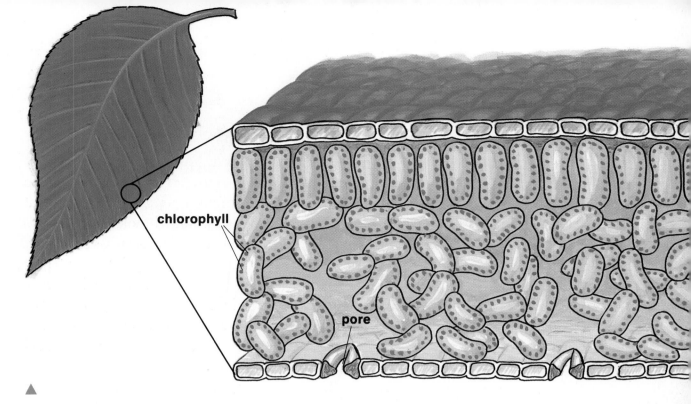

chlorophyll

pore

▲

You probably know that plants take in water through their roots. Some of the water travels to the leaf. Gases in the air can also enter the leaf. One gas in the air is *carbon dioxide*. Carbon dioxide enters the leaf through pores in the leaf's outer layer.

In photosynthesis, plants use the light energy from the Sun, along with water and carbon dioxide, to make food. The food produced is a sugar called **glucose** (GLOO-kohs). During photosynthesis, oxygen is released. The whole process is very complex. Scientists still do not completely understand how photosynthesis works. However, we can describe photosynthesis in simple terms:

$$\text{water} + \text{carbon dioxide} \xrightarrow[\text{energy}]{\text{light}} \text{glucose (sugar)} + \text{oxygen}$$

Most of the oxygen produced during photosynthesis leaves the plant through pores in its leaves. Remember that carbon dioxide enters the leaf through these same pores. *ACTIVITY*

Carbon Dioxide and Green Leaves

You can use: bean seeds, 4 small pots, potting soil, petroleum jelly

1. What might happen if the pores in leaves were closed? To find out, first soak the bean seeds for several hours.

2. Fill the flower pots with soil. Label the pots *A*, *B*, *C*, and *D*. Plant several seeds in each pot, about one centimeter below the soil. Place the pots where they will get plenty of sunlight. Keep the soil in the pots slightly moist.

3. Let the plants grow about 7 centimeters high. Then select four plants that are about the same size, one plant from each pot. Carefully remove all the other plants. Leave the remaining plants in pots *A* and *B* alone. Spread petroleum jelly thinly on all the leaves of the plants in pots *C* and *D*. ■ Make sure you cover the tops and bottoms of the leaves. Keep all the pots in the same place.

4. Observe the plants for two weeks. This is what one person saw at the end of that time. ● Compare the growth of the coated plants and uncoated plants. Were the plants with the coated leaves able to make food? Explain.

Storing Energy in Foods

Taste a piece of fruit. ■ You can tell that there is sugar in the fruit, can't you? The energy in the sugar can be used by the plant for growth and repair. But the plant doesn't use all the energy in the sugar at once. So the plant stores some of the energy. Green plants, then, are not only food-energy producers. Green plants are also energy storers.

Now taste a potato. It doesn't taste as sweet as the fruit. The potato contains a lot of starch. Starch is made up of a chain of sugar molecules. Some of the sugar in plants is changed to starch. Plants such as corn and beans also store energy in starch. Here are some common foods that contain starch. ●

Some of the sugar in plants is changed to fats. Plants also store energy in fats. The peanut is a plant that contains a great deal of stored fats. Many foods, such as olives, contain liquid fats. We often call such fats vegetable oils. ▲

You have probably never tasted a blade of grass or the bark of a tree. Yet somehow you know that they are not sweet. Plants can combine sugar with substances from the soil and water to build other parts of the plant. Some of the blades of grass and bark of the tree are made of compounds that were formed from sugar. ■

Using the Energy Stored in Foods

Plants store a great deal of energy in sugars, starches, and fats. But plants do not use the energy while it is stored in these foods. To release the energy, plants must break down stored foods. During this process, plants use oxygen. Plants can take in oxygen from the air. The oxygen passes through the pores in the leaves of the plant.

Breaking down food to release energy is called **respiration** (res-puh-RAY-shun). During respiration, carbon dioxide and water are given off by the plant. So we can write respiration like this:

sugar + oxygen ⟶ carbon dioxide + water + energy

Now compare the equations for respiration and photosynthesis.

Green plants obtain their energy through photosynthesis and respiration. Where do animals get energy? You know the answer. Animals and people eat green plants. You eat stems, leaves, seeds, roots, and fruits of plants. ● You eat celery, peas, potatoes, and strawberries. You also eat animals that eat plants. ▲ In this way, the energy stored in plants is passed on from one living organism to another. Because animals cannot make their own food but must eat it instead, we call them food **consumers.** Nongreen, plantlike organisms are also consumers.

Once an animal has eaten food, it must be able to break down the food through respiration. Animals also use oxygen in respiration. Remember Jeff, the boy who skipped breakfast to work in the lot? When he finally ate lunch, his body broke down the food. Only then could Jeff obtain the energy from food.

Where do animals get the oxygen to use during respiration? Where do you get your oxygen? If you're not sure, take a deep breath and think again.

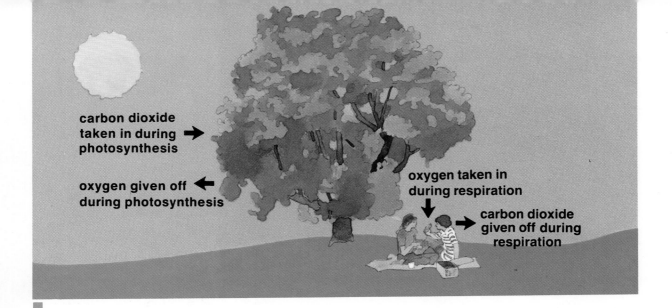

carbon dioxide taken in during photosynthesis →

oxygen given off during photosynthesis ←

oxygen taken in during respiration ↓

carbon dioxide given off during respiration →

The Cycles of Life

During photosynthesis, plants take in carbon dioxide. They release oxygen. You might think that eventually all the carbon dioxide in the world would be used up. Then the air would be full of oxygen only. Yet this doesn't happen. Why? During respiration, plants and animals take in oxygen and release carbon dioxide. For example, when you breathe in you take in oxygen. When you breathe out, you release carbon dioxide. There is a natural cycle of carbon dioxide and oxygen. ■ Neither is used up. Neither becomes too plentiful. What might happen to plants and animals if this cycle were changed?

What happens to the matter that makes up plants and animals? All living things die. Is the matter lost forever? If that were so, we would have run out of important substances needed for life millions of years ago. Instead, dead plant and animal matter is broken down. ● That is the job of **decomposers.** The most common decomposers are decay bacteria. Mushrooms that live on dead trees are also decomposers. Like animals, decomposers are consumers. They use dead matter as food. Then they return some of the matter to the Earth.

On a separate sheet of paper, write each statement with the best ending.

1. The substance in plants that captures light energy from the Sun is
   a. carbon dioxide b. chlorophyll
   c. sugar

2. The gas produced during photosynthesis is
   a. nitrogen b. oxygen
   c. carbon dioxide

3. Green plants are food
   a. consumers b. producers
   c. decomposers

4. Plants and animals break down stored foods for energy through
   a. photosynthesis b. respiration
   c. decay

5. The statement that fits the *main* concept of this section is:
   a. The Sun is the source of energy only for green plants.
   b. The Sun is the source of energy for all living things on Earth.

YOU CAN DISCOVER

Water in the air falls to the Earth as rain and snow. ▲ Water in lakes and oceans evaporates into the air. The water in plants and animals is returned to the Earth when they die. In this way water is not lost. It is used over and over again. See if you can discover more about the water cycle. You may want to write a short report. Then discover if there are any other important cycles on Earth.

▲

The matter of the Earth has been used over and over again. The matter in a tree may once have been part of an octopus, or even a dinosaur. The carbon dioxide you breathe out may be used by a plant to make sugar. Perhaps you will one day eat the plant that used the carbon dioxide you breathe out.

The relationships between plants, animals, and their environment is probably much more complicated than you might have thought. Scientists have a name for the study of the relationship between living things and the nonliving environment. They call it **ecology** (i-KOL-uh-jee).

The Food Chain

This bird is a turkey vulture. ■ Circling high in the sky, the vulture searches for food. Yet it is not looking for living plants or animals. Vultures are **scavengers** (SKAV-in-jurs). At least part of a scavenger's food comes from dead plant and animal matter. In this way some of the food energy stored in a dead organism is passed on to the living vulture.

A **food chain** describes how food energy is passed from one organism to another. Green plants are food producers. They are always the first link in the food chain. Many animals eat plants for their food energy. They include deer, sheep, squirrels, and a great many insects. ● Animals that eat only plants form the second link in the food chain. They are called *first-order consumers*.

Some animals, like dogs, lions, and otters, eat other animals. ▲ Animals that eat other animals, or a combination of plants and animals, form the next link in the food chain. They are *second-order consumers*. The turkey vulture, then, is a second-order consumer. Of course, second-order consumers still depend on green plants. Why?

A simple food chain can begin with a corn plant. The corn is a producer. It is the first link in the chain. A chicken eats the corn. The chicken is a consumer, a first-order consumer. We can draw this simple food chain like this:

Corn ⟶ Chicken

Now, suppose the chicken is raised on a chicken farm. It is sent to market and sold. A family eats the chicken. People are second-order consumers. They use the first-order consumer as food. We can complete our food chain like this:

Corn ⟶ Chicken ⟶ People

Food chains are found in water as well as on land. On and near its surface, the ocean is filled with tiny green plants called plankton. These green plants are the first link in this ocean food chain. ■ You can see that tiny, microscopic organisms eat the plankton. They are eaten, in turn, by small fish. Then the small fish are eaten by larger fish, which are eaten by even larger fish. Perhaps the largest fish in this food chain will be caught and eaten by people.

Now, the tiny green plankton may not seem so important. But think about this. Suppose the plankton were destroyed? What would happen to the first-order consumers? Then what would happen to the other links in the food chain? Let's look at what can happen when a food chain is broken.

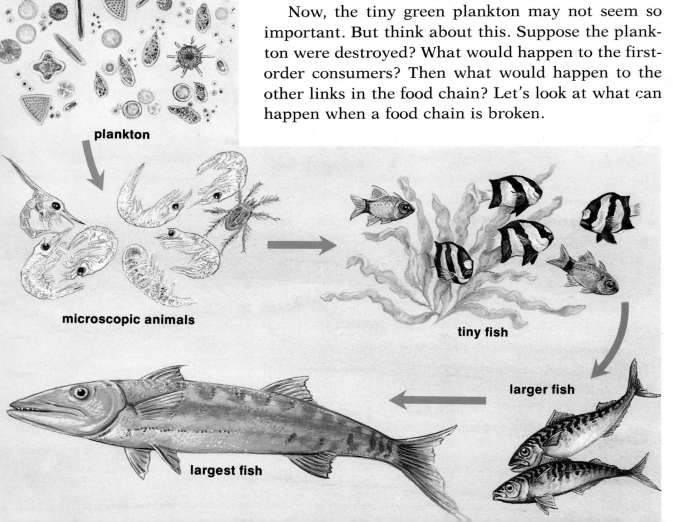

plankton

microscopic animals

tiny fish

larger fish

largest fish

Breaking a Food Chain

The giant panda is one of the world's most popular animals. ● Its delightful coloring and playful looks make it irresistible. Even with so much attention, almost one fourth of all the world's pandas have died in the past few years.

Aside from the few pandas in zoos, all pandas live in isolated mountain regions of China. There they feed on the umbrella bamboo and fountain bamboo plants. ▲ The pandas live in balance with their environment. The bamboo supplies their energy needs and the pandas eat little else. However, once every hundred years, these bamboo plants blossom. The bamboo plants produce seeds and then die.

The death of the bamboo plants breaks the panda's food chain. The new seeds take several years to grow. In the meantime, many of the pandas cannot find another source of food and starve to death.

Today Chinese and American scientists are determined to solve the problem. However, studying pandas in their isolated environment is not easy. Scientists attach radio transmitters to the pandas so that they can follow their movements. They hope to find another source of food until the bamboo grows back. Will they succeed? Or will the break in the food chain mean that the pandas may be lost forever?

EXPLORING SCIENCE AND TECHNOLOGY

Growing Vegetables Without Soil

Have you ever wondered how people who will some-day live in space will grow their food? Most spaceships or space stations will not be large enough to store all the soil necessary to grow plants for large groups of people.

Today, scientists are experimenting with an entirely new way to grow plants. They are learning to grow vegetables without soil. This new technology is called *hydroponics* (hy-druh-PAHN-iks). Scientists are growing green plants in water solutions containing all the nutrients that growing plants need.

In one method of hydroponic farming, plants are supported above a screen while their root systems dangle below in water enriched by nutrients. ■ Scientists also use conveyer belts to rotate vegetables through a hydro-ponic bath. ● Some researchers are growing vegeta-bles on A-frames or on poles to save space. Hydroponics will make it possible for space travelers to grow food in outer space. ▲

How do you think hydroponics will help people on Earth?

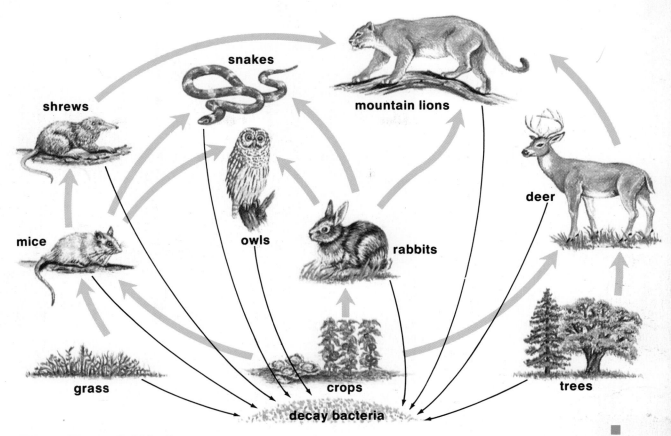

The Food Web

Food chains are a good way to show how food energy moves in an environment. Yet plants and animals do not always fit into any one food chain in an orderly way. For example, crops on a farm may be eaten by a rabbit. Then the rabbit may be eaten by an owl. The crops, the rabbit, and the owl form a food chain. But a snake eats rabbits, too. So the crops, rabbit, and snake form another food chain. Also, rabbits aren't the only animals to eat crops on a farm. A deer might wander into the pasture and eat some crops. The deer and crops would form yet another food chain. You can see that in most environments there are a great many possible food chains. A **food web** can show all these food chains.

In this food web, which organisms feed on the crops? ■ Which feed on the rabbit? This food web even includes decomposers such as decay bacteria.

Interdependence

Animals depend on green plants for food energy. They also depend on the oxygen given off by plants during photosynthesis. It may not seem as if green plants depend on animals, but they do. Green plants use the carbon dioxide given off by animals to make food. Plants depend on animals for other reasons as well. The bee, for example, helps some flowering plants reproduce by carrying pollen from one plant to another. ■

Everywhere you look, living things appear to depend on other living things. Living things need other living things. They are **interdependent.** The robin feeds on the earthworm. ● The worm feeds on decayed leaves in the soil. These leaves were once the green leaves of a plant. Suppose something accidentally destroys the decay bacteria. What will happen to the leaves, to the earthworm, and finally to the robin?

Yes, plants and animals are interdependent. Yet the environment is made up not only of living things. It also is made up of the things that living things need. To survive, living things need more than each other—they need the right environment. You know, for example, that a seed will not grow by itself. Give the seed air as well as sunlight. Water it. Then the seed will grow. In time, the plant may have flowers—then, more seeds. The cycle of life will continue when the environment is right.

What is true of plants is true of animals. Animals are also dependent on the right environment. They need food for energy. They need warmth, oxygen, water, and shelter too. Rattlesnakes, rabbits, pelicans, and tigers—each must have the right environment. The environment gives them the substances they need for growth and activity. This leads us to a most important concept: **Plants and animals are interdependent with one another and with their environment.**

On a separate sheet of paper, write each statement with the best ending.

1. The study of the relationship between living and nonliving things is called
   a. photosynthesis   b. ecology
   c. cycle of life

2. The turkey vulture is a
   a. producer   b. decomposer
   c. scavenger

3. A person eats a hamburger. The person is a
   a. first-order consumer
   b. producer
   c. second-order consumer

4. The first link in an ocean food chain is often
   a. tiny fish   b. plankton
   c. large fish

5. The statement that fits the *main* concept of this section is:
   a. Animals are dependent on green plants for food.
   b. All living things are interdependent with one another and their environment.

YOU CAN DISCOVER

How many food chains can you find here? ■ What are they?

Let us visit a forest. It is cool and very quiet under the tall trees. From a small pond we hear a soft "plop." There is a frog staring at us—its head just above water. ● The frog feeds on insects it finds near the pond. It also depends on the air, water, and sunlight in its environment.

You read that the living and nonliving things in an environment are interdependent. This relationship is called an **ecosystem** (EE-koh-sis-tum). An ecosystem, then, includes both the living and nonliving things in a given area. An ecosystem may be as small as a drop of water or as large as planet Earth.

This frog's ecosystem—a pond—is part of a forest. In a tall tree is a woodpecker. ▲ Like the frog, the woodpecker eats insects. The woodpecker doesn't find its insects in the pond. It finds insects in the tree. The tree is the woodpecker's ecosystem.

The ecosystem of the frog is part of the forest. The ecosystem of the woodpecker is also part of the forest. There are many other ecosystems in the forest. In fact, all the animals and the plants of the forest make up one great ecosystem—the forest ecosystem.

21

Now let's look into another ecosystem. We will see what can happen when the balance of living and nonliving things is changed.

An Ecosystem in Danger

Mono Lake is in California. ■ The Sierra Nevada Mountains in the background help form a beautiful, natural setting. Streams formed by melting mountain snows supply the lake with water. In the past, many kinds of plants grew along these streams. Yet now only desert sagebrush grows in the lake ecosystem. People used to enjoy the lake. Boating and swimming were once popular, but no more. Today scientists warn that the lake may be slowly dying. Its ecosystem may be destroyed.

Within Mono Lake are two small islands. Each year seagulls nest on these islands. ● In the summer of 1981 many of the baby seagulls were found dead. That seemed rather unusual in an ecosystem that supported the seagull population for many centuries.

People began to investigate. Strangely enough, they discovered that the death of the baby seagulls may have been caused by actions far from the lake itself. For years mountain streams kept the amount of water in the lake the same. Then some of the water from the streams began to be used for drinking and for other purposes. Less and less water reached the lake each year.

There is salt in Mono Lake. Year after year the lake had about the same amount of salt. But as the water level dropped, the same amount of salt was dissolved in less water. The concentration of the salt increased. How could this affect the seagull population? The seagulls, and a great many other birds, feed on tiny brine shrimp in the lake. ▲ However, brine shrimp cannot survive in water that is too salty. As the concentration of salt increased, it kept the baby brine shrimp from developing. As the number of brine shrimp decreased, many of the baby seagulls starved to death. If the salt concentration continues to increase, in time the brine shrimp and the birds that feed on them will all be gone.

There is yet another reason the birds are endangered. The islands where the gulls nest are not far from shore. In the past, the water protected them from animals such as coyotes. As the water level dropped, however, the coyotes were able to swim to the islands. They killed many of the seagulls.

At first, the people who took water from the streams had no idea that their actions could damage Mono Lake. They learned a hard lesson. Ecosystems, in one way, are like living organisms. They are very delicate. When you change one thing somewhere, you may affect living and nonliving things far away. If the balance between living and nonliving things is changed, the results can be serious.

Populations and Communities

What kinds of animals do you see on this African plain? ■ There is a group of zebras. Another group is made up of impalas. On the African plain, and in all ecosystems, groups of living things live together. In an ecosystem, a group made up of one kind of living thing is called a **population.** The zebras living

together in this ecosystem are a population. The impalas are another population. Even the grass growing on the plain is a population. How many other populations can you find?

Groups of populations in an ecosystem form a **community.** A community includes all the living things in an ecosystem. The populations and communities in an ecosystem depend on the environment of that ecosystem. For example, you are not surprised to find this boa constrictor in the rain forest of South America. ● You would not expect to find one in the park near school, though. For the boa constrictor, the rain forest is the right environment. The park near school is not. The environment of an ecosystem helps determine which organisms can live there.

Competition in an Ecosystem

The capybara live in the Andes Mountains of South America. ▲ They eat the plants that grow in this ecosystem. Animals that use plants as food are called **herbivores** (HUR-buh-vohrs). Since there is only a certain amount of plant life, there is usually competition for food among the herbivores. Organ-

25

isms compete when they try to get the same material they need for life. Animals, for example, may compete for food, water, and shelter. The capybara must compete for the limited amount of green plants.

Some animals, like these lions, eat only other animals. ■ They are **carnivores** (KAHR-nuh-vohrs). There is often competition for food among carnivores, too.

Animals that eat both plant and animal life are **omnivores** (AHM-ni-vohrs). There is competition among omnivores as well. Finally, although you probably haven't thought of it, there is also competition among the decomposers in an ecosystem. After all, there is only so much dead matter at any one time. Decomposers compete for the food energy from dead matter. How fast can decomposers break down dead matter? *ACTIVITY*

Decomposers in the Soil

You can use: string, digging tools, dead vegetation, old panty hose, plastic bag, plastic bag with holes

1. Place equal amounts of dead vegetation (leaves, grass clippings, discarded lettuce leaves) into each of the three bags: panty hose, plastic bag, and plastic bag with holes. ■ Tie the top of each bag tightly with string.

2. With your teacher's help, dig a hole in the school-yard large enough to hold all three bags. Place the bags in the soil. Keep the bags separated from each other by shoveling soil between each bag.

3. Wait four to eight weeks. Dig up the bags. In which bag were decomposers in the soil most active? Least active? How can you explain your results?

Some Other Relationships

Competition is not the only relationship in an ecosystem. Some organisms help each other. Many large crocodiles live in the Nile River in Africa. ■ Sometimes tiny leeches attach themselves to the gums of a crocodile. Leeches live on the blood they take from other organisms. When the Nile crocodile opens its mouth, a small bird called the Egyptian plover actually lands in the opened jaws of the crocodile. However, the crocodile does not harm the plover. The plover eats the leeches attached to the crocodile. The plover gets food. The crocodile gets its teeth and gums cleaned. Both animals benefit from this relationship.

This wart hog lives in the forests of Africa. ● Very often ticks and other tiny organisms may be found on its hide. The ticks live on the blood of the wart hog. A tiny bird sits on the back of the wart

■

●

28

hog, too. This tickbird clings to the wart hog with its sharp claws. It feeds on the ticks. In this way the tickbird gets a meal and the wart hog gets a good cleaning.

Here is an interesting relationship that was just discovered. These giant tube worms live deep in the sea near vents, or breaks, in the ocean floor. ▲ The vents release hot water from inside the Earth. In the hot water are chemical compounds containing sulfur. The tube worms have no eyes, no stomach, not even a mouth. How do they get food in their dark, under-water ecosystem? One section of the tube worm is packed with many tiny bacteria. The bacteria can take sulfur from the water. They use sulfur instead of sunlight to obtain their energy. With this energy, they can make food from carbon dioxide gas in the water. Both the bacteria and the tube worm use the food. The relationship between the tube worm and the bacteria is one of the most unusual in nature.

Balance in an Ecosystem

Competition is still the most important relation-ship in an ecosystem. Living things that compete successfully survive. Those that do not, die off.

There is usually a balance between competing organisms and their food supply. If the balance is changed, the whole ecosystem is affected. For example, in one area there may be many deer that eat plants for their food energy. There may also be wolves that use the deer for food. ■ If you remove the wolves, would you help the deer survive? Without the wolves to kill some deer, the deer population would grow larger each year. In time there would not be enough plant life to feed them all. The plants would soon be eaten and the deer would starve. By changing the balance in the ecosystem, we may kill off all the deer, the plants, and the wolves.

Niches in an Ecosystem

Three different kinds of warblers live in this spruce tree. ● All the warblers eat insects. ▲ Do you expect the three types of warbler to be competing for food? They are not. Why? Each type of warbler nests and feeds in a different part of the tree. One lives among the lower branches. One lives in the middle branches. The third lives near the top of the tree. Each warbler fills a different role in the spruce tree ecosystem. The role an organism plays in its environment is called its **niche** (NICH). The area an organism lives in and how it obtains food is part of its niche.

Plants, too, may fill different niches in an ecosystem. One plant may grow best on the shady side of a hill. For that plant, its right environment is in the shade. Another plant may grow best with more direct sunlight. Its niche would be the sunny side of the hill. Each plant lives in the hill ecosystem, but they do not compete.

In most ecosystems there are many niches to be filled. Organisms in the ecosystem that fill different niches live in harmony. Those that fill the same niche must compete.

An Ecosystem for People

Plants and animals fill a niche in their ecosystem. Move them to another ecosystem or destroy their niche and they may die. However, people have used their brains to live in almost every ecosystem on Earth. For example, few organisms can live in the very bottom of the ocean, or in the very top of the atmosphere. People, however, can go underwater and into space provided they take the right environment with them. ◆

There is another way in which people are different. Other living things do not change their environment the way we do. True, some animals, such as beavers, can build dams. ■ They can change the flow of rivers. Yet even this change is fairly simple. Compare it with changes we make. ● We change the environment in complex ways. Sometimes the change is not for the better. We can damage our ecosystem in many ways. ▲

Of course, people often do change the ecosystem for the better. They change it not just for themselves, but for other living things as well. Now read about one way people made a change in an ecosystem for the benefit of a small bird.

Changing an Ecosystem

Peregrine falcons make their nests high on steep cliffs. ◆ From there they can spot the small birds that make up their main food source. Then, with ease and grace, they swoop down in a power dive that has been timed at over 320 kilometers per hour. Peregrine falcons have few natural enemies. They are at the top of their food chain. Once you could see peregrine falcons in the skies over much of our country, but no more. There are few falcons left. In the eastern part of the country they almost disappeared.

People are the main reason the falcons nearly died off. For many years people used a substance called DDT to kill insects that damaged food crops. Insects ate the plants treated with DDT. Often these insects were eaten by small birds. A bird must eat a lot of insects for energy. So the tiny amount of DDT in the insects built up in the small birds. The falcons that used the small birds as food took in larger amounts of DDT. The DDT damaged the shells of their eggs. Few new falcons were born. When people realized the danger and stopped using DDT, it was too late. Most of the falcons were gone. Could anything be done?

This time the answer was yes. Farms were set up to breed falcons. Then the new young falcons had to be returned to the wild. Special nests were set up for the baby falcons. Some were on cliffs in National Parks. Others were on tall towers built especially for the falcons along the coast of New Jersey. Still others were set up in cities, such as high atop the Smithsonian Castle in Washington, D.C. ★

Many of the falcons did not survive. Others, though, were able to hunt and find food. They raised young of their own. Each year the number of falcons has increased. The falcons are not out of danger yet, but with the help of people falcons may return. Today, if you are lucky and keen-eyed, you may spot a peregrine falcon soaring high above a city skyscraper.

CHECK-UP TIME: Vocabulary . . . Facts . . . Concepts

On a separate sheet of paper, write each statement with the best ending.

1. People are
   a. carnivores   b. omnivores
   c. herbivores

2. All the living things in an ecosystem make up its
   a. community   b. population
   c. environment

3. The living and nonliving things in a given area make up
   a. an ecology   b. a community
   c. an ecosystem

4. The role each plant or animal plays in an ecosystem is its
   a. life cycle   b. environment
   c. niche

5. The statement that fits the *main* concept of this section is:
   a. All living things in an ecosystem are in competition with each other.
   b. Living things that fill the same niche are in competition with each other.

YOU CAN DISCOVER

A parasite is an organism that lives on or in a host organism. ■ As the parasite takes its food, it harms the host. All living things can have parasites. Find out what kinds of parasites harm people. How are they introduced into the body of a human?

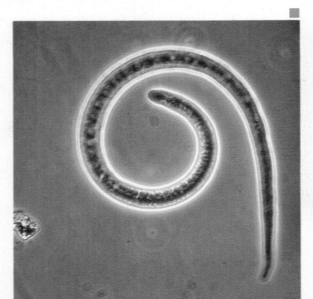

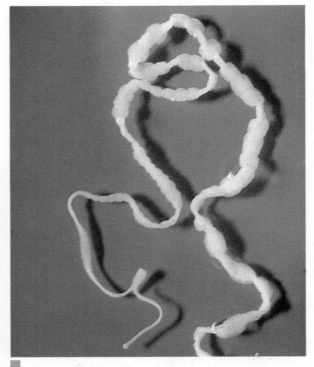

Learning to Think Like a Scientist

SCIENCE AND YOUR CAREER

You may not ever become a scientist. Yet even now you are an apprentice scientist. Do you know what the word *apprentice* means? It means anyone who is a learner, a beginner. ■ In one way you will be an apprentice all your life. For all your life you will learn. ● From this book you will learn many things about stars, light, atoms, and someone very important—you.

You will also learn how a scientist learns. You will learn the *processes* of a scientist. You will need these processes as you do the activities in this book. You will use such processes your entire life.

Observing and Measuring

In your activities you will use many tools of a scientist. The first tool you will use is yourself. In observing, you use your senses—sight, hearing, touch, smell, and taste. These are the scientist's most important tools. However, our senses may fool us. Also, we may need more accurate information than our senses can provide. So, often it is better to use additional tools for observing.

Some tools are used for a special kind of observing known as measuring. For example, scientists use the metric ruler to measure length. They use a platform balance to measure mass. They use a Celsius thermometer to measure temperature.

Recording

There are other tools that we must not forget—paper and pencil. Whenever you do an activity, never trust your memory. Keep a record in a notebook. Write down your plans, your observations, and your results.

As you continue your study of science, you will learn more about how scientists investigate. You will learn to *interpret* your observations. You will learn something scientists keep in mind each and every time they do an investigation. Your observations can be entirely correct; your thinking can be extremely logical—and you can still be completely wrong. Here's an example.

Controlling Variables

A simple question occurs to you. Will mold grow better in the light or the dark? This, you decide, calls for an investigation. So you divide a slice of bread in half and place each in a jar. You add ten drops of water to each jar and cap tightly. You put one in a dark closet. You keep the other one in the light. In a few days, you make an observation. You observe that the mold in the light is growing better than the mold in the dark. ▪

From this observation, you infer that mold grows better in light. You are sure of your answer. After all, the evidence seems clear. Yet, in truth, scientists know that light has no effect on the growth of mold. Why, then, did the investigation make it seem as though mold grows better in the light?

Think a moment. Because the amount of light varied, we say that light was a **variable.** Since light was the only

variable considered, you assumed that it was the light that affected the growth of the mold. Was light the only variable you changed? Or could you have changed another variable without realizing it?

What about temperature? Suppose that the temperature of the mold in the light was higher. Then it is possible that the higher temperature, not the light itself, caused the growth. Whenever you do an investigation, there may be several possible variables. If you wish to see the effects of changing one variable, such as the amount of light, then you must make sure all the other possible variables remain the same. That is, you must **control** the other variables.

In this investigation, to control the variable temperature, you must keep the temperature the same for the mold in the light and the mold in the dark. If you had done so, you would have discovered that the mold grew just as well in the dark closet. However, even then you could not be sure of your conclusion. The investigation must be repeated many times. After all, what happens once can be an accident. Scientists don't base their conclusions on one trial. They repeat the investigation again and again and again.

The rest of this year you will be an apprentice. You will be an investigator. You may even decide one day to become a scientist.

✓ On a bright, clear day sunlight streams onto the Earth. ■ Some of the light is captured by the chlorophyll of green plants.

✓ Chlorophyll is an amazing substance. It can use the Sun's energy to make photosynthesis possible. No other substance can do that.

✓ In order to survive, green plants also need air, water, and soil. Given the right environment, green plants will make food.

✓ Green plants are the food producers for the world. They form the first link in the food chain. Wherever you find animals alive, you find food. You can trace this food to green plants. ●

✓ We have come then to an important concept:

The capture of the Sun's energy by green plants is basic to the growth of living things.

✓ Animals that depend on green plants directly for their food are first-order consumers. Animals that depend on other animals, or a combination of plants and animals, for their food are second-order consumers.

✓ Nongreen, plantlike organisms and decomposers are consumers.

✓ All living things, including people, depend on their environment for life. We must be wise managers of our environment. We must conserve our environment. If we destroy the green plants, all living things will die.

✓ We have come then to yet a second important concept in science:

All living things are interdependent with each other and with their environment.

A. CHOOSE THE BEST ANSWER.

1. Since mushrooms have no chlorophyll, they cannot carry on
   a. growth   b. photosynthesis   c. respiration

2. A food substance that does not come from light energy captured by green plants is
   a. sugar   b. iron   c. starch

3. Two different organisms live in the same tree and eat the same food. They share the same
   a. niche   b. population   c. life cycle

4. The gas given off during photosynthesis is
   a. carbon dioxide   b. nitrogen   c. oxygen

5. A starch is a chain of
   a. sugar molecules   b. fat molecules
   c. oil molecules

6. To describe many food chains we can use the
   a. ecosystem   b. food web   c. community

7. Mono Lake may be dying because of
   a. added salt   b. added water   c. less water

8. Plants store energy in
   a. fats   b. starches   c. both of these

9. Animals that eat only other animals are
   a. omnivores   b. carnivores   c. herbivores

10. The statement that fits the *main* concept of this unit is:
    a. Green plants are a major resource of the world ecosystem.
    b. People, unlike other animals, do not depend on green plants.

40

B. ANSWER THESE QUESTIONS.

1. In what ways are green plants dependent on animals? On the nonliving environment?

2. Why is the Sun the source of all food energy on Earth?

3. What would happen to life on Earth if there were no decomposers? Explain.

4. During photosynthesis, plants take in carbon dioxide and release oxygen. How is it their supply of carbon dioxide has not run out?

Find Out More

1. How does a fire destroy a forest ecosystem? ■ How can ecologists help restore the ecosystem after a forest fire? How long do you think it will take?

2. Oil is pouring into the ocean from a leak in an undersea oil well. How is the oil spill damaging part of the ocean? How can people conserve the ocean ecosystem?

3. Find one way in which an ecosystem in your area is being destroyed. How can you help conserve that ecosystem?

Challenge Your Thinking

These are the remains of an animal that once lived in an ancient ocean. ● However, it was found on dry land far from any ocean. How can that be?

The Earth's Biomes

If you traveled to Australia, you might see animals that do not live in the United States. For example, koalas rest in the upper branches of a eucalyptus tree. Kangaroos, some of nature's greatest jumpers, live on the plains.

The cold, barren continent of Antarctica is home for other animals. However, it is much too cold for organisms to live inland. So the penguins and large seals live near the shore.

In the Pacific Ocean off South America, still other animals exist. In the Galapagos Islands, for example, a giant tortoise moves along inland. On the shore, a marine iguana clings to the jagged rocks as fierce waves pound against it.

The Earth is not the same all over. There are many different kinds of places where plants and animals can live. Let's look at a few of them. As you read the next pages, think what life would be like for you in the different places that are described.

1 ▶ The Forest Biomes

It is the middle of winter in the Everglades of Florida. The Sun is shining brightly. Palm trees sway in warm breezes. The air is filled with the scents of flowers. In the swamp, tall grasses and mangroves seem to grow right out of the water. ■ You may spot herons with long legs wading through the swamp. ● Alligators lie in the Sun near the water's edge. Perhaps a wildcat may pass by, looking for food. In the warm water, manatee swim peacefully among the many fish.

In the forests of the northern United States and Canada it is also winter. Snow covers much of the ground. The lakes and ponds are frozen. Although the Sun shines throughout the day, it seems as if it will never be warm again. All around, trees such as these red maple and hemlock grow. ▲ There are few green plants growing close to the ground. If you look

carefully, however, you may spot a deer searching for plants under the snow. ◆ Perhaps a fox is hunting for small animals. ★

Winter in the Everglades and in the northern forests is quite different. How many differences can you see? Are you surprised to find that different plants and animals live in each ecosystem? Probably not.

On the other hand, you might expect similar plants and animals to live in similar environments. Scientists use the word **biome** (BY-ohm) to describe areas that have similar geography and climate. Some of the most common biomes are the forests, the grasslands, the deserts, and the tundra. Of course, there are no sharp borders between most biomes. Instead, each biome gradually blends into the other.

Most plants and animals can only live in one type of biome. That biome is the right environment for them. Some plants and animals can live in more than one biome. One living thing can be found in all the biomes. Do you know which it is? Look in the mirror for your answer.

The Deciduous Forest

Much of the eastern half of the United States is a deciduous forest biome.  Deciduous trees, like maple, beech, oak, and hickory are common in the forests.

In the deciduous forest the climate changes throughout the year. Summers are generally hot, while the autumn is mild. Winters can be very cold. The following spring will probably be mild.

Rainfall in the deciduous forest is plentiful all year round. In the winter, of course, the rain may fall as snow. However, snow in the deciduous forest usually melts soon after it falls.

Life in the Deciduous Forest

Sunlight falls onto the tops of the trees in the deciduous forest. Much of it is captured by the leaves of tall trees, but the rest filters to the Earth below. In the lower levels of the forest grows a variety of smaller trees, shrubs, and grasses. Wildflowers like the marigold are common as well. ● You can see that there are many food producers living in the deciduous forest.

Animal life is abundant, too. Deer, raccoon, rabbits, and even some bears roam the forest searching for food. In the trees, squirrels hunt for nuts. Beneath the forest floor are worms and burrowing animals like this mole. ▲ Frogs and salamanders may live in ponds or rivers.

If you have ever visited a deciduous forest, you know that insects are plentiful. You may have been bitten by mosquitoes in the summer, for example. Where you find insects you will find animals that eat insects. Thus many insect-eating birds make their nests in the deciduous forest.

Deciduous trees grow new leaves each spring. In the autumn, the leaves change color. ◆ Red, yellow, and orange leaves fall to the ground. Seeds, nuts, and berries also fall to the ground. These materials are a rich supply of food for the forest animals. Because this supply will soon be gone, some animals store food for the cold winter months ahead. Other animals such as the woodchuck will fatten up on food. ★ Then the woodchuck will find a place to **hibernate,** sleep through the cold winter. What other animals do you know that hibernate?

▲

★

◆

47

The birds in the forest do not hibernate. However, if you walk through the forest in the winter, you will not see many birds. Most of them have flown south to warmer climates. ■ These birds and other animals **migrate.** They move from one area to another. The birds that migrate south in the winter return north in the spring.

The Coniferous Forest

Go north from the deciduous forests. The trees change to pine, hemlock, and spruce. You have entered the coniferous forest. ● Coniferous forests form a wide band across much of North America, particularly Canada.

Like the deciduous forests, coniferous forests go through four seasons. However, the summers are shorter and less hot. The winters are longer and quite cold. Snow may often fall in the coniferous forests. Much of the snow does not melt until the warm spring arrives.

A great deal of the coniferous forest area was once covered by icy glaciers. ▲ The glaciers have long since gone, but they left behind many lakes and ponds.

Life in the Coniferous Forest

There are some deciduous trees in the coniferous forest. But by far the most common trees are conifer trees. They include spruce, fir, and pine trees. These trees produce cones. ◆ Most conifers are evergreens. They have long leaves, like needles. Since they are green all year, you might think that evergreens do not shed their leaves. Actually, evergreens shed their leaves all year round, but replacement leaves grow back quickly. The floor of the coniferous forest is always covered with needles.

Conifers usually grow close together. Little light reaches the lower levels of the forest. Yet a few shrubs, like the blueberry, do grow in clearings on the forest floor. ★ Also, mosses often cover the forest floor and grow on the side of trees.

Many of the consumers in the coniferous forest live on the food produced by trees. Insects that attack trees are very common. If you walk through the forest, you may find birds eating seeds from the cones of conifers. Squirrels feed on the long needles. It is not unusual to find a porcupine nibbling on the bark of a tree. ■

Larger animals like wolves, foxes, weasels, and moose find food and shelter in the forest. ● Deer feed on any small shrubs they find. During the winter, elk and caribou come to the forest from the colder regions to the north.

Winter in the coniferous forest is long and cold. However, this hare is well suited to the winter. ▲ With its broad feet like natural snowshoes, the hare can walk easily over the snow. Other animals, like the ground squirrel, will hibernate through the winter. Most birds will migrate south.

Sealed in Biosphere II

There is a special place in the Arizona desert called Biosphere (BY-uh-sfeer) II. ■ Biosphere II is a miniature Earth, smaller than two football fields, built under glass, where you can find a series of different biomes. One day soon, Biosphere II will be sealed. Inside, eight people, called Biospherians, will live for two years. They will receive no supplies from the outside world. Instead, they will have to provide for all of their own needs. They will learn how to farm, to keep animals and fish, to make rain, and to recycle water. ● They will recreate the food chains and ecosystems that exist on Earth.

What people learn from Biosphere II will help change how and where people live in the future. It will prepare scientists and engineers to build space stations. ◆ If the Biospherians can live sealed up in Biosphere II for two years, then it is likely people will be able to live in a similar Biosphere on the Moon or on Mars for the same length of time.

Now that you know about Biosphere II, what do you think you know about Biosphere I?

The Tropical Rain Forest

Although it is only early morning in the tropical rain forest, the temperature has begun to rise. You feel uncomfortable as you walk past the tall trees of the forest. ■ Above you monkeys fill the air with their constant chattering. Suddenly the forest is pierced by the howl of a leopard. ● The other animals become silent, waiting for a sign of the big cat's movements. You, too, stop and listen.

In the tropical rain forest you are near the equator. It is warm all year round. The temperature often changes more between day and night than between summer and winter.

Rain is plentiful, too. Almost every day there may be a short but powerful rainstorm. So much sunlight and rain makes the tropical rain forest the ideal location for many plants and animals. In fact, there may be more kinds of plants and animals in a few acres of rain forest than there are in all of Europe.

Life in the Tropical Rain Forest

If you flew over a tropical rain forest, you would be able to see only the tops of tall trees. There are hundreds of different kinds of trees in the rain forest. Long vines hang from many of the trees. Climb down one of these vines and you find smaller trees. The farther you go, the darker it gets. Less and less light is able to get through. Very little light actually reaches the forest floor. As you might expect, then, few plants grow there.

Trees are not the only plants in the rain forest. Some plants attach themselves to the branches of tall trees. Perhaps the most beautiful of these is the orchid.  Another plant that uses trees in this way is the bromeliad.  The bromeliad's leaves form a cup that collects rainwater.

At almost every level of the rain forest we can find animals in search of food. Above the trees, bats and birds hunt for insects. In the upper branches, parrots, opossums, and monkeys eat leaves and fruit.

Climbing up and down the tree trunks are lizards and snakes hunting for food. On the floor of the rain forest large cats, such as the panther, and wild pigs search for food. ■ Since there are many insects, animals like the anteater are at home in the tropical rain forest. ●

In no other biome do so many animals live and feed. It is not uncommon to find larger versions of animals here than in other biomes. For example, moths with a wingspan of almost 30 centimeters live in the rain forest. ▲ This spider is so large it can feed on small birds. ◆

On a separate sheet of paper, write each statement with the best ending.

1. Trees that grow new leaves each spring and lose them in the fall are
   a. conifers   b. evergreens
   c. deciduous

2. The word used to describe areas that have similar geography and climate is
   a. ecosystem   b. biome
   c. forest

3. Trees that shed their leaves all year long are
   a. evergreen   b. deciduous
   c. hardwood

4. When animals travel to warmer places in winter, they are
   a. migrating   b. hibernating
   c. respiring

5. The statement that fits the *main* concept of this section is:
   a. We find the same organisms in forests throughout the world.
   b. The geography and climate of a forest play an important role in determining what organisms live there.

YOU CAN DISCOVER

The grizzly bear lives in some forests in the United States. ★ This animal and many others are in danger of dying out. What other animals are endangered?

★

2 ▶ Grassland and Desert Biomes

This is a grassland in Oklahoma in the 1920's. ■ About fifteen years later the same area had become a "dust bowl." ● How can such a thing happen so quickly? In the grasslands, the roots of the grass hold the soil in place during high winds and strong rains. However, farmers often removed the grasses and plowed the soil. Cattle and sheep herders allowed their animals to eat too much of the grass too quickly. Without the grass to hold it down, the soil simply blew away in the wind. People had learned another important lesson. Biomes change, just as the Earth does. Usually the changes are very slow, but the actions of people can change a biome very quickly.

Grasslands

Much of the midwestern region of the United States is grassland. Grasslands are flat, open areas. In some places you can stand and look in any direction without seeing a tree or tall bush. The grasslands in this country are often called the Great Plains.

Like the deciduous forest, grasslands have four seasons. Also, sunlight is just as plentiful as in the forest biomes. However, rainfall in the grasslands varies throughout the year. It is difficult to predict when it will rain.

At one time, almost half of all the land on Earth was grassland. Today much of that grassland has become farmland. Farms in the grasslands supply us with most of our corn, wheat, and other grains.

Life in the Grasslands

Most of the plant life in the grasslands consists of different grasses. ■ The grasses grow all summer long, providing an abundance of food. A few trees may grow in the grasslands, but only near streams where they get a constant supply of water. Some small shrubs and bushes also grow in the grasslands. Close to the ground, a variety of wildflowers may flourish.

At one time, vast herds of bison roamed freely across the grasslands of this country. Most were killed by hunters. Today it is more common to see herds of sheep and cattle grazing on the tall grasses. There are many other consumers in the grasslands. Grasshoppers and crickets can be found in most fields of grass in the midwest. Insect-eating birds like the meadowlark are common. ● Hawks and owls hunt small mice and other animals for food. This mound is the home of a prairie dog. ▲ Prairie dogs use their underground homes for shelter. Although wolves are no longer a common sight, coyotes still prowl the grasslands as they did hundreds of years ago. ◆

The Desert

When you think of the desert, you may think of far-off lands where people ride camels and live in tents. ★ Yet there are deserts in this country, too. In fact, almost one fifth of all the land in the world is desert.

All deserts have one thing in common. They are dry most of the year. They get little rainfall. Many deserts are extremely hot during the day. The plants and animals that live in deserts are quite varied. Let's look at a hot, dry desert of the United States.

★

Plants in the Desert

Plants that grow in the desert must be able to live in a dry environment. You probably know one common kind of desert plant already—the cactus. This saguaro cactus is one of the world's largest. ■ It can grow up to 15 meters high. The saguaro stores water in its thick green stem. After a heavy rain it can absorb enough water for an entire year.

There are many kinds of cactuses in the desert. Some cactuses have spines instead of leaves. Most plants lose a lot of water through their leaves. If the cactus had broad leaves, it would lose too much water. The cactus would die. The spines of the cactus do not carry on photosynthesis. How might they help the plant?

The mesquite bush is another plant that survives in the dry desert. ● The mesquite has a deep root system. Its roots may go down as far as 30 meters until they reach water beneath the surface of the desert. Usually you will never see two mesquite bushes growing near one another. Can you explain why this is so?

Cactuses can store water and survive in the desert all year round. During the rainy season, the cactuses may produce beautiful flowers and the seeds from which new cactuses will grow. There are also other kinds of flowering plants in the desert. ▲ Most cannot store large amounts of water. The seeds of these plants may lie on the hot desert floor for months. Then after a heavy rain, the seeds sprout. The plant quickly grows and produces flowers. It forms new seeds that fall to the desert floor. Soon the flowering plant will die, but its seeds will remain on the desert floor until the next heavy rain. Is it strange that a plant will live and die in such a short time? Do you think such plants are fitted to survive in the desert?

Animals of the Desert

If you walk through the desert during the hot day, you might think that no animals live there. However, if you look carefully, you might see a lizard or snake moving through the sand in search of food. ◆ You

might spot a tortoise munching on a desert plant, or a scorpion about to attack a small insect. ■ The roadrunner is another animal you might spot during the day. ● Most desert animals, however, stay out of the hot Sun. Where do the animals hide?

A skunk, a coyote, or a jack rabbit may lie in the shade of a bush or cactus. Smaller animals may hide under a rock. The tiny kangaroo rat lives underground. The temperature in its burrow just below the surface of the hot desert soil can be quite cool. The kangaroo rat survives on a diet of dry seeds. It can go without water for long periods of time.

Some animals have found unusual ways to live and reproduce in the desert. For example, normally it takes several months for an adult toad to develop from an egg. Now look at a desert variety—the spadefoot toad. ▲ The toad lays its eggs in a mud puddle after a heavy rain. The eggs then hatch and develop from tadpole to adult toad in less than ten days. The entire process is completed before the mud puddle dries up.

Growing Food in the Desert

It is hard to farm in the desert. In a climate as dry as a desert, fruits and vegetables need a lot of fresh water. But fresh water is scarce and very expensive to use to irrigate desert farms. Many deserts, especially coastal deserts, are near seawater. Unlike fresh water, seawater is plentiful and very salty.

In Puerto Peñasco, in the Sonoran Desert near the coast of Mexico, there is an experimental farm where crops are irrigated with seawater. ■ Here scientists are growing plants that can tolerate salt. Salt-tolerant plants are called *halophytes* (HAL-uh-fyts). Scientists have found some halophytes that might feed many people and animals in the future.

The scientists began their experiment in Puerto Peñasco by testing seeds from plants growing naturally in seawater along the coast. ● One early success was *Distichlis palmeri* (dis-TICK-lis pahl-MER-ee), or saltgrass, that has wheat-like seeds local Indians have used to make into bread. The major halophyte crop at Puerto Peñasco is *Salicornia* (sa-lee-KOR-nee-UH). ◆ Its rich seeds are ground to make a vegetable oil that compares with safflower oil. The rest of the plant, high in protein, is used to feed livestock. The yield of *Salicornia* per acre is greater than the average produced by wheat, barley, or corn.

Every year the population of the Earth increases. Finding ways to grow food in the Earth's abundant deserts may be one solution to the world's hunger problems.

On a separate sheet of paper, write each statement with the best ending.

1. Grasslands are usually
   a. flat and open   b. mountainous
   c. flat with many tall trees

2. In the grasslands, rainfall is
   a. difficult to predict
   b. very heavy   c. very light

3. Most desert cactuses have
   a. broad leaves
   b. thick leaves
   c. no leaves

4. An animal that lives in an underground desert burrow is the
   a. desert toad   b. kangaroo rat
   c. coyote

5. The statement that fits the *main* concept of this section is:
   a. An animal or plant that can live in the harsh desert can live anywhere.
   b. Plants and animals are adapted to live in their particular environment.

YOU CAN DISCOVER

This hedgehog cactus is one of many plants now in danger of dying out. See if you can find out why. Then try to find out what other plants are endangered in this country.

64

3 ▶ The Tundra Biome

Now let us visit a land in the far north. A land that is cold all year round. This strange land is called the tundra. In the tundra the winter days are short and there is little sunlight. Even in the summer when the days are long, the tundra is still cold. The warmest days of summer are only a little above freezing. There is little rain in the tundra at any time of the year.

Most of the soil of the tundra remains frozen throughout the entire year. This frozen soil is called the **permafrost.** In the summer the snows of the tundra melt, but the ground remains frozen solid. So the melting snow cannot seep into the ground. Instead, it forms small lakes and marshes. The tundra is filled with these lakes for the two months of summer.

The shift from summer to winter is very rapid. Soon the lakes and ponds freeze. High winds sweep across the frozen soil. You can see that the tundra is a difficult place for life to exist in the winter. ● Yet in the summer months, many organisms make the tundra their home.

Life in the Tundra

If you visited the tundra, perhaps the first thing you would notice is that there are no trees. The frozen soil and harsh weather make it very difficult for any tall plants to grow. Most of the plants that do survive in the tundra are grasses and small shrubs such as the dwarf willow. Even these plants must produce all their food for the entire year in the two short months of summer.

In the summer the tundra is filled with animal life. Insects seem to be everywhere. Flocks of birds swarm to the lakes and ponds to feed their young. If we could sneak up to a lake unnoticed, we would see many kinds of geese. ■ Grazing animals such as the caribou abound. ● Rabbits, wolves, foxes, mice, and snowshoe hares are among the smaller animals that live in the tundra. This tiny animal is the lemming. ▲ If you look carefully, you may find it running among the plants during the summer.

The tundra in winter is another story. Since food is scarce, many animals migrate to other biomes. The caribou and foxes leave the tundra for the coniferous forests farther south. Many water birds fly south. Some animals do stay in the tundra. However, you will not find them easily in winter. This ptarmigan is one bird that stays in the tundra. ◆ In the summer it is brown, but it turns white in the winter. Why is changing color an advantage for a bird that remains in the tundra?

Another animal that stays all year long is the lemming. The lemming burrows under the snow in a sheltered spot. It feeds on roots and seeds stored during the summer. Ground squirrels also burrow underground. The ground squirrel hibernates through the cold winter. There is one animal that faces the weather above ground. These musk oxen live in the open all year round. ★ They find food by uncovering plants buried under the snow. How do the musk oxen keep from freezing during the cold tundra winter? The musk oxen have a thick fur. The fur insulates the oxen from the cold. *ACTIVITY*

Keeping Out the Cold

You can use: mixing bowl, plastic or metal containers, insulating materials (paper, wool, leather, Styrofoam, aluminum foil), thermometer, gelatin, large container to hold ice (ice chest), ice cubes

1 Set one container aside. Then wrap each of the other containers with one layer of insulating material. ■ Use paper, wool, aluminum foil, or any material you choose.

2 Mix the gelatin and water. Fill each container, including the unwrapped one, with equal amounts of gelatin.

3 Place each container in the ice chest. Add ice up to the tops of the containers. Keep track of the temperature in the chest with a thermometer. ● If the temperature goes above 5 degrees Celsius, add more ice. Do not allow the ice cubes to go over the edge of the containers.

4 Which container of gelatin freezes first? Second? Last? Make a record of your results. Which material provided the best insulation? Why?

On a separate sheet of paper, write each statement with the best ending.

1. A biome that is cold all year round is the
   a. deciduous forest   b. tundra
   c. coniferous forest

2. The frozen soil beneath the tundra is called
   a. bedrock   b. topsoil
   c. permafrost

3. During the summer, lakes and marshes in the tundra are formed by
   a. heavy rains   b. melting snow
   c. beaver dams

4. An animal that migrates during the tundra winter is the
   a. lemming   b. musk ox
   c. caribou

5. The statement that fits the *main* concept of this section is:
   a. Even in the harsh tundra biome, many plants and animals find a home.
   b. Animals survive the tundra winter by moving south to warmer biomes.

YOU CAN DISCOVER

You have studied the forest, grassland, desert, and tundra biomes. There are other biomes on Earth as well. Find out what they are. This photo might give you one hint. ■ What plants and animals live in this biome?

69

Forester

We get wood for building from forests. We get paper and fuel and many other products as well. The forests are home for many plants and animals. People, too, enjoy the pleasures of the forest. ■ In order for us to use and enjoy our forests, they must be properly managed. The people who manage and develop our forests are the foresters.

Foresters have many duties. Some make maps that show how many trees there are and how many can be cut down at one time. Foresters know that trees must be protected from people who would cut down too many too fast. Often they help in the planting of new trees to replace those that are cut down. ●

Some foresters work in parks where they supervise campers and help manage the wildlife. They may teach courses about camping and the proper use of our forests. Some search out and protect trees that are threatened by disease or harmful insects. ▲ Foresters must be aware of the dangers of forest fires. If you like working with your hands in the outdoors, then forestry may be a career for you.

70

✓ There are a great many ecosystems in the world. Ecosystems with similar geography and climate are grouped into biomes.

✓ The Earth's biomes include the forests, grasslands, deserts, and tundra. ■

✓ Many different kinds of plants and animals fill a role, or a niche, in each biome. Organisms that are well-fitted to the biome are usually successful.

✓ A change in a biome can result in changes in the kinds of organisms that live there.

✓ You have come to another important concept in science:

Successful organisms are well fitted to their biome. If the biome changes, the organism may no longer be able to survive.

■ Tundra
■ Coniferous Forest
☐ Grassland
■ Tropical Rain Forest
■ Deciduous Forest
☐ Desert

A. CHOOSE THE BEST ANSWER.

1. The most complex ecosystem is in the
   a. deciduous forest   b. grasslands
   c. tropical rain forest

2. Most animals search for food at night in the
   a. desert   b. grassland   c. tundra

3. An animal that sleeps through the cold winter
   a. migrates   b. respires   c. hibernates

4. During the tundra winter, the ptarmigan turns
   a. brown   b. black   c. white

5. The tree that is *not* deciduous is
   a. beech   b. spruce   c. oak

6. A plant that forms a cup to capture rainwater is the
   a. saguaro cactus   b. bromeliad   c. marigold

7. The tree that is *not* coniferous is
   a. hemlock   b. pine   c. hickory

8. A desert plant with a deep root system is the
   a. mesquite bush   b. dwarf willow
   c. marigold

9. Musk oxen are protected from the cold by their
   a. high body temperature
   b. insulating feathers   c. thick fur

10. The statement that fits the *main* concept of this unit is:
    a. An organism can survive anywhere it can find food and water.
    b. Organisms survive in biomes for which they are well-fitted.

B. ANSWER THESE QUESTIONS

1. How can animals live in a hot, dry biome like the desert?
2. Explain the differences between the three forest biomes: deciduous forests, coniferous forests, and tropical rain forests.
3. Why do we find few tall plants in the tundra?

Find Out More

Tropical rain forests contain more types of organisms than any biomes on Earth. ■ Tropical rain forests, for example, contain the widest variety of trees. While the largest tropical rain forests are found in South America, there are also large rain forests in Africa and much of Asia. However, each year vast areas of tropical rain forests are destroyed by people. Find out what is being done to save the rain forests. ■

Challenge Your Thinking

This area was once visited by a famous Viking. ● Do you know where it is?

A System of Classification

Just think. Almost 2 million kinds of living things have been discovered! You may wonder how anyone can put all these living things into any order. Fortunately, there are certain likenesses that allow scientists to sort out, or *classify,* living things.

For many years scientists tried to fit all organisms into a system of classification divided into the **Plant Kingdom** and the **Animal Kingdom.** In time they saw that some organisms did not seem to fit. Some organisms shared likenesses with both plants and animals. Others did not appear to be like either. To classify these puzzling organisms, the **Protista Kingdom** was proposed.

Since Protista means "the very first," let us begin our investigation into classification with this kingdom.

Protista

Most **protists** (PROH-tists) are single-celled. They are very small. However, they are among the most common organisms on Earth. We can divide the protists into several smaller groups.

In a drop of water, you may see members of the *Protozoans.* The foot-shaped protozoan is a paramecium. This ameba is another protozoan.

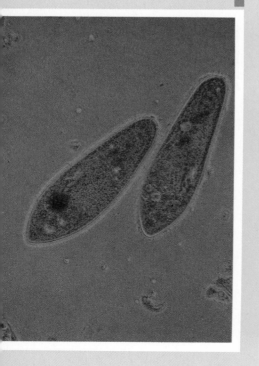

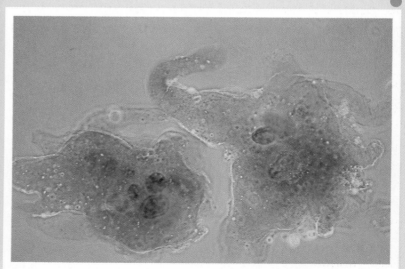

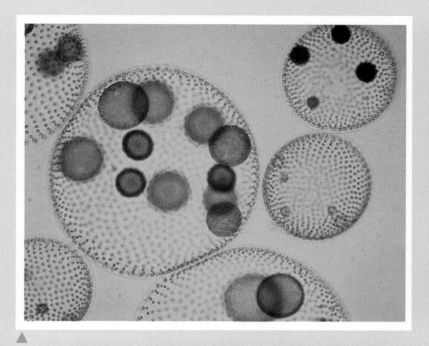

▲

Bacteria form a second group of protists. You have already read about one kind of bacteria—the decay bacteria. In the next unit you will learn how these important protists can be both a friend and an enemy to people.

A third group of protists are the *algae.* Algae have chlorophyll and carry out photosynthesis. However, in many algae the green chlorophyll is masked by other pigments, ranging from blue-green to red. Algae, along with green water plants, are the main food producers in our oceans. A few kinds of single-celled algae group together to form colonies. Can you see the individual cells of algae in this volvox? ▲

Fungi are a fourth group. One type of fungi includes the molds such as those that grow on bread. Mushrooms, shelf fungi, and puffballs are other kinds of fungi. ◆ Yeasts are fungi, too. These different types of fungi share at least one likeness. They do not have chlorophyll. They must get their food from an outside source. Many grow on dead matter. They are decomposers. Other fungi grow on living things. They can cause disease, like athlete's foot.

Now let's carry our investigation further—into the Plant Kingdom.

Plants

All plants share certain likenesses. For example, plants have chlorophyll. They make their own food through photosynthesis. Plants have many cells, and the cells have specialized functions. That is, different cells do different jobs.

We can divide the Plant Kingdom into two main groups. In the first group are the *mosses* and the *liverworts.* These plants do not have any tubes that can transport water through the plant. For this reason, they grow in moist locations. Also, they cannot grow tall, since without tubes water could not reach the top of the plants. Mosses play an important role in nature. In some areas they are often the first plants to grow. ■ When they die, their matter can form the rich soil in which other plants may grow.

The most common plants with water tubes are the *flowering plants.* ● Flowering plants reproduce from seeds formed within the flower. Another plant, the *conifer,* produces seeds, but no flowers. Conifers produce seeds inside cones. *Ferns* also have tubes, but they do not produce seeds. ▲

Scientists use two important likenesses to classify plants: whether they have water tubes and how they reproduce. Now let us look into some of the likenesses scientists use to classify animals.

76

Animals

Like plants, animals are made up of many cells with specialized functions. Unlike plants, animals cannot make their food. We can divide animals into two groups: **vertebrates** (VUR-tuh-brayts), animals with backbones; and the **invertebrates** (in-VUR-tuh-brayts), animals without backbones.

In the invertebrate group there are many smaller groups. For example, the sponges are animals that filter food particles out of the water. ◆ Different kinds of worms are invertebrates. Clams, oysters, snails, squid, and the octopus are soft-bodied animals that form another group of invertebrates. ★ By far the largest group of invertebrates are animals with segmented bodies covered by a tough, outer skeleton. They include the lobster, shrimp, and the over 600,000 kinds of insects. ▫

You probably know most of the main groups of vertebrates. The *fish* such as trout, bass, and salmon have gills to breathe underwater. ◎ *Amphibians* spend part of their life in water and part on land. Some common amphibians include frogs, salamanders, and toads. Animals that often look similar to amphibians are the *reptiles.* However, reptiles are suited to a life on land. Unlike

amphibians, reptiles usually have dry, scaly skin. Lizards, snakes, and turtles are reptiles. ■ Another group of vertebrates are the *birds.* Birds share some likenesses with reptiles. For example, their legs are covered with scales. However, most of the bird's body is covered with feathers. ● Many birds, of course, can fly. Most fish, reptiles, amphibians, and birds lay eggs.

The last group of vertebrates are the *mammals.* All mammals have hair or fur. Most give birth to live young. Female mammals feed their young milk produced in their bodies. We can divide the mammals into smaller groups. For example, some mammals such as the shrews and moles are insect-eaters. The armadillo is a toothless mammal. ▲ The camel, elk, and rhinoceros have hoofed feet. ◆ Some mammals, such as the orangutan, have flexible hands and feet. ★ These are but a few of the many kinds of mammals in the world.

The three kingdom system—Protista, Plants, and Animals—is the one used in this and many other books. It is not the only system. Some scientists still classify living things as only plants or animals. Others use systems with four or five kingdoms. Classification is a tool of the scientist. Any system that orders living things in a logical way is useful.

Now try a project. Plan your very own system of classification. First, pick four nonliving objects. Divide the objects into two groups according to their likenesses. These two groups will be your first two kingdoms. Here is what one student chose. ☐ She placed the blue chalk and blue ball into the Blue Kingdom. The wooden pointer and wooden globe were placed into the Wood Kingdom. She then divided each kingdom into smaller groups. ⚪ Can you think of another way to group these four objects?

Each week for the next two months "discover" two more members for your classification system. The new objects may share some likenesses with the objects already in your system. In that case they may fit into your system easily. If not, they may form an entirely new kingdom.

You may find that you have to change your entire system to fit the new objects. Scientists must do the same when they discover a new kind of living thing. In the end, you should have at least 20 objects divided into no more than 5 kingdoms. Each kingdom will be divided into groups. The groups will be further divided into smaller groups, until you finally have each item in a group by itself. Do you now have some idea of how difficult it is to classify several million kinds of living things?

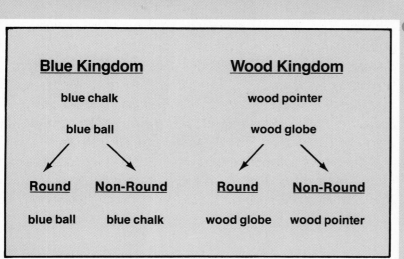

Blue Kingdom		**Wood Kingdom**	
blue chalk		wood pointer	
blue ball		wood globe	
Round	**Non-Round**	**Round**	**Non-Round**
blue ball	blue chalk	wood globe	wood pointer

Bacteria and Viruses

In 1980, Mount St. Helens, in Washington, erupted. The volcano sent out tons of hot ash and rocks, destroying all crops and animals in a wide area. Not long after, scientists found one kind of organism that had already begun to thrive.

You can see that the environment in Antarctica is far from inviting. Temperatures often fall well below 0° C. However, one kind of organism can survive and even grow here.

The hot springs are in Yellowstone National Park. The water in the springs gets very hot, in fact too hot for people, or for plants and animals. Yet there is one kind of organism that can live in the hot springs.

Now imagine that you are 10,000 meters below the surface of the ocean. The water pressure is so great that most life would be crushed in seconds. Still, one kind of organism can survive.

What kind of organism can live where no other can? Read on to find out.

▶ **Bacteria**

Certain organisms are found just about every-where on Earth. Some live in soil. Some live in water. Still others are carried in the air by winds. Wherever you find living things, you will find them. They live and grow in your body. Some can make you sick but most do us no harm. In fact, some do a great deal of good. These organisms are **bacteria.** (The singular is *bacterium.*)

Bacteria are the most numerous organisms on Earth. Pick up a handful of soil. You have probably also picked up several million bacteria. Why do you suppose you can't see the bacteria?

The Size of Bacteria

Bacteria are among the smallest of all living things. In fact, you could fit over 250,000 average-sized bacteria on the period at the end of this sentence. Look at the palm of your hand. ■ It looks clean, doesn't it? Yet there are bacteria on your hand right now.

You *can't* see a single bacterium with your eyes alone. However, when bacteria grow and reproduce, they form a group called a **colony.** There are millions of bacteria in a colony. You *can* see colonies of bacteria. These colonies are being grown on specially prepared dishes in the laboratory. ●

To see a single bacterium you have to use a microscope. As you know, a microscope magnifies objects. It makes them look many times larger. Organisms, like bacteria, that can be seen only with a microscope are called **microorganisms** (my-kroh-AWR-guh-niz-ums). For you to see one clearly, a microorganism on your hand must be made about 400

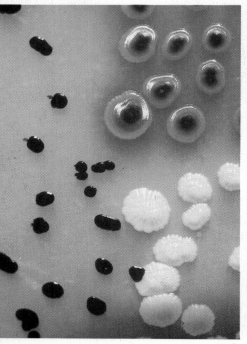

times larger. A high-powered microscope, similar to the ones you may have in school, magnifies about that much. You can get some idea of what this means if you just imagine that you are magnified 400 times. You would be as tall as a small mountain!

The Shapes of Bacteria

There are many, many different kinds of bacteria. However, if you could examine bacteria under a microscope, you would find something surprising. You would see just three main shapes.

These bacteria are rod-shaped. ▲ Rod-shaped bacteria are called **bacilli** (buh-SIL-y). (The singular is *bacillus*.) This photograph of bacilli was taken through a high-powered microscope. Sometimes scientists need to study bacteria in even more detail. ◆ They use the most powerful of all microscopes—the electron microscope. An electron microscope can magnify objects a million times or more.

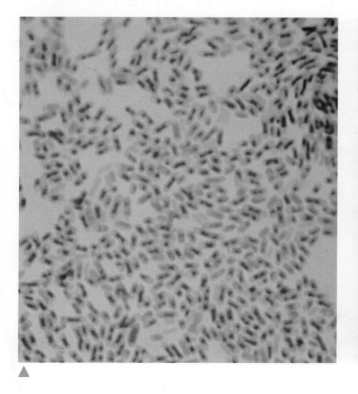

▲

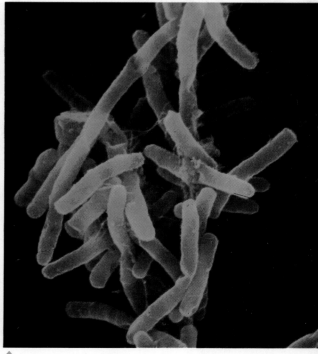

◆

Some bacteria are sphere-shaped. They are called **cocci** (KAHK-sy). (The singular is *coccus*.) Look at the cocci under a high-powered microscope and an electron microscope. ■ ●

Other bacteria are corkscrew-shaped. They are called **spirilla** (spy-RIL-uh). (The singular is *spirillum*.) Can you see the corkscrew shape under the high-powered microscope? ▲

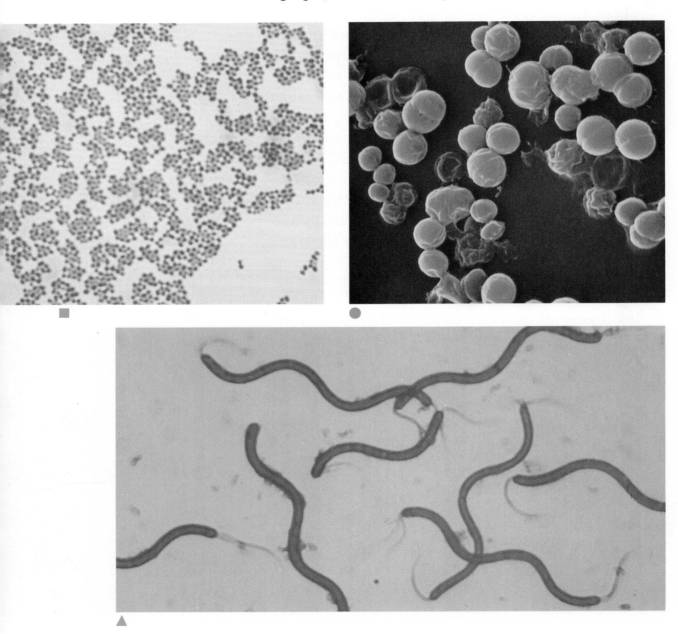

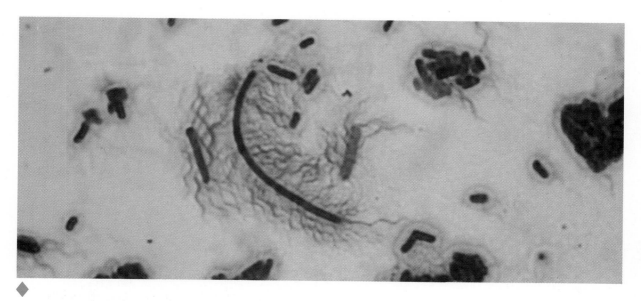

A few bacteria have one or more tiny, hairlike **flagella** (fluh-JEL-uh). ◆ The bacteria beat the flagella like a whip. In this way they can move quite rapidly through water. Most other bacteria, on the other hand, cannot control their own movement. They are often carried by air or water currents.

The Environment for Bacteria

You know that plants and animals need the right environment to live and grow. So do bacteria. You learned that some bacteria are found in hot springs; others in the cold Antarctic. Yet each is in the right environment. If we were to switch their environments, they would no longer be able to grow. Temperature, then, is one important factor in the environment of bacteria.

All bacteria also need water. Of course, different kinds of bacteria need different amounts of water. Also, while some bacteria grow in a salt-water environment, others live in fresh water. You might guess that, like plants and animals, bacteria need oxygen. You would only be partly right. Many bacteria do need oxygen, but many others do not.

The right environment must also give bacteria a source of food. A few bacteria can carry out photosynthesis. They use sunlight to make their own food. The bacteria that live within the giant tube worms make their own food from chemicals in the water. However, most bacteria cannot make their own food. They are food consumers. Many are decay bacteria. Others live off living plants and animals. Often, these bacteria cause illness.

Bacteria Reproduce

In the right environment, all living organisms reproduce. One bacterium reproduces by dividing in two. How does this come about? First, the bacterium grows larger. Then the wall around the bacterium begins to pinch in the middle. ■ The pinched part becomes narrower until the two new bacteria separate. Some organisms reproduce quickly and some slowly. You may be surprised how quickly bacteria can reproduce. One kind of bacterium, for example, can reproduce every 11 minutes! *ACTIVITY*

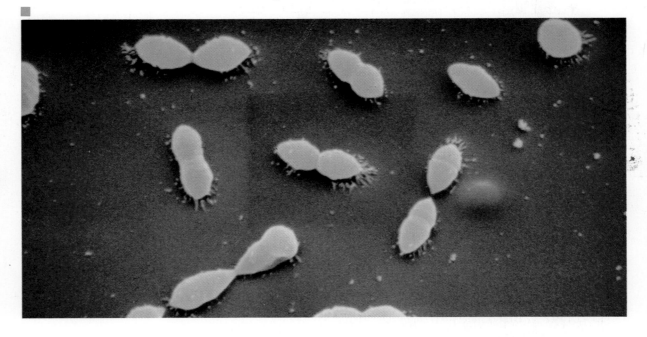

Calculating Bacteria Growth

You can use: Pencil and paper

1 When bacteria reproduce, one bacterium divides to make two. The two bacteria divide into four. The four divide into eight, and so on. ■ Different bacteria reproduce at different rates. How quickly they reproduce often depends on the environment. Now calculate how many bacteria will form under various conditions.

2 In the Sun, one bacterium will reproduce every 20 minutes. How many bacteria will there be after an hour? After two hours? After six hours? Can you calculate how many there will be after an entire day? ●

3 The same bacterium at room temperature reproduces once every 40 minutes. How many will there be after an hour? After two hours? After six hours? Again, try to calculate how many there will be after an entire day.

4 When we place the same bacterium in the refrigerator, it reproduces once every three hours. Calculate how many bacteria there will be after an hour, two hours, and six hours. Now it may be easier to find how many there will be in a day.

■

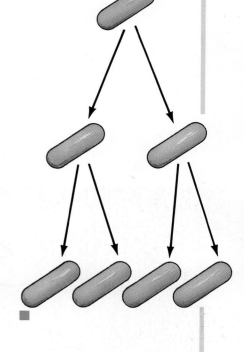

87

EXPLORING SCIENCE AND TECHNOLOGY

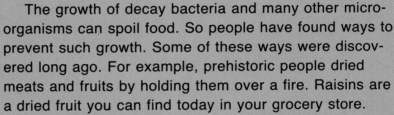

Preserving Foods

The growth of decay bacteria and many other microorganisms can spoil food. So people have found ways to prevent such growth. Some of these ways were discovered long ago. For example, prehistoric people dried meats and fruits by holding them over a fire. Raisins are a dried fruit you can find today in your grocery store.

Salt also slows the growth of bacteria. This wall painting from ancient Egypt is 3,000 years old. Yet we see people drying fish and storing them in salt-filled containers. Today, chemical forms of salt are used to preserve foods.

Ancient Romans carried ice and snow to the city to help cool and preserve foods. Today, we use a refrigerator to slow the growth of bacteria. To preserve foods even longer, we freeze them. Two modern methods of preserving food combine drying and freezing. In *freeze-drying,* foods are dried after they are frozen, which makes them light and airy. In *dehydrofreezing* (dee-HY-droh-freez-ing), fruits and vegetables are dried before freezing, which makes them smaller and easier to pack.

Many foods can be preserved by canning. First, foods are sealed in an air-tight can. Bacteria and oxygen cannot reach the food. Then the food is heated until all the bacteria inside the can are killed. Food that is properly canned can last a year or more without spoiling. Some people can food at home.

One modern method of food preservation, *irradiation,* slows the growth of bacteria by exposing foods to rays from radioactive elements. This method is entirely new and still being tested.

88

Nature Uses Bacteria

Bacteria! Somehow the word immediately makes people think of organisms that produce disease. Some do, it's true. Yet bacteria are an important part of our marvelously complex ecosystem. On Earth, living things depend on one another. Without bacteria, life would be difficult, if not impossible.

You already know one important way bacteria help all living things. Decay bacteria break down dead plant and animal matter. Decay bacteria allow substances to be used again and again.

To grow, green plants need nitrogen. Our air contains almost 80 percent nitrogen. You would think the plants could get all they need. However, plants cannot use nitrogen gas in the air. So nature uses bacteria to help the plants. **Nitrogen-fixing bacteria** take nitrogen gas in the air and combine it with other substances. In this way the nitrogen is made available in a form green plants can use.

Many nitrogen-fixing bacteria live in soil. They help keep the soil rich with nitrogen compounds. Some live in the roots of plants, particularly those of the pea family. Farmers know how important nitrogen is for their crops. Every few years they may plant a crop of soybeans with nitrogen-fixing bacteria in their roots. ■ In this way they put back into the soil the nitrogen the plants used. Can you see the swellings containing nitrogen-fixing bacteria on the roots of this soybean plant? ●

Other kinds of bacteria normally live in your digestive system. These bacteria do not make you ill. Instead, they help your body by producing some of the B vitamins you need.

People Use Bacteria

Long before people knew about microorganisms, they had learned how to use them in their daily life. Over 5,000 years ago, people in Babylon used bacteria to convert the sugars in certain fruits into vinegar. People have used bacteria to help change certain dairy products for thousands of years as well. Yogurt, for example, contains bacteria. By controlling the growth of bacteria, we can make buttermilk from regular cow's milk. Many cheeses are also produced with the aid of bacteria. ■

Industry uses bacteria in a great many ways. Some bacteria are used to remove waste products from sewage. ● Other kinds of bacteria can help clean polluted streams and rivers. Bacteria have medical uses, too. Some bacteria can be made to produce the vitamins people may add to their diet. Some bacteria can even produce medicines that are used to kill other disease-causing bacteria. Can you see why bacteria are among the most useful and important organisms on Earth?

On a separate sheet of paper, write each statement with the best ending.

1. To see a single bacterium, you must use
a. your eyes alone   b. a telescope
c. a microscope

2. Rod-shaped bacteria are called
a. cocci   b. bacilli   c. spirilla

3. Some bacteria move with the help of hairlike
a. rods   b. flagella
c. chromosomes

4. All bacteria need
a. oxygen   b. high temperatures
c. water

5. The statement that fits the *main* concept of this section is:
a. Bacteria can grow in just about any environment.
b. Bacteria, like all other living things, can live and grow only in an environment suited to their needs.

YOU CAN DISCOVER

These ancient bakers are using a microorganism to bake bread. ▲ Today bakers use the same microorganism. Find out what it is. *Hint:* It's not a bacterium.

▲

As you know, bacteria need the right environment to live and grow. For some bacteria the right environment is inside another living organism. An invasion by harmful bacteria or other microorganisms is called an **infection.** Bacteria can infect plants. ■ They can infect animals. Bacteria can often infect people, too.

Bacteria, of course, are all around us. We cannot avoid them. But we can try to avoid disease-causing bacteria. This scientist is taking a sample of soil on a farm. ● He knows that a few bacteria will not cause much harm to crops. However, whole colonies of bacteria might. How do scientists count bacteria? *ACTIVITY*

Bacteria Invade the Body

When bacteria invade the body, they soon begin to feed and grow. As you will read, the body has many defenses against bacteria. The body wins most of its battles against bacteria. Some battles are lost. Others take time to win. While the battle goes on, the bacteria continue to grow. They reproduce. The body is infected. Diseases caused by bacteria include tetanus, diphtheria, whooping cough, and tuberculosis. Just how do bacteria make us sick? There is more than one way.

Some bacteria attack body cells for food. The healthy body cells are destroyed. You become sick. Other bacteria produce a poison called a **toxin** (TAHK-sin). For example, you may have had "strep" throat. In this case, a bacterium called streptococcus infects your throat. The streptococcus produces a toxin. The toxin makes you sick.

Taking a Sample

You can use: meter stick, bean seeds, tape, wire mesh (one decimeter square)

1 Imagine that bacteria are the size of bean seeds. Mark off an area one meter square. Ask a friend to sprinkle a number of bean seeds into the marked area.

2 Get a piece of wire mesh one square decimeter in size. Throw the wire mesh anywhere in the area. Count and record the number of beans under the mesh. ■ Repeat this four more times.

3 Add up the total number of beans you counted. Divide this number by five to find the average. Now multiply this number by 100. Why? (*Hint:* there are 100 square decimeters in one square meter.) This answer should be close to the actual number of beans in the square. Is it?

4 Can you invent a way for scientists to count a large number of bacteria? ● Must they count each one? Explain.

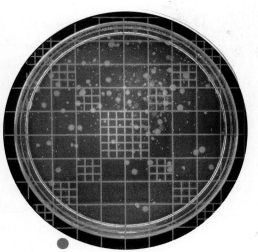

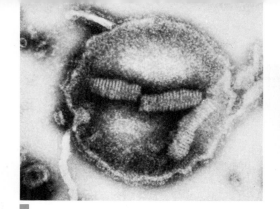

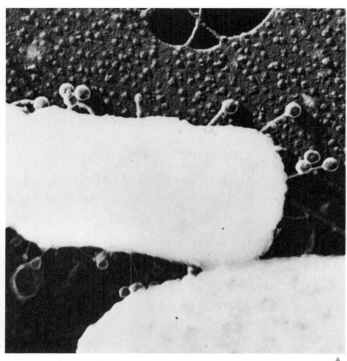

Viruses

Have you ever had a cold? Colds can be a real bother. People believe that damp weather, or a poor diet, or being overtired can cause a cold. All of these things may help lead to a cold. However, the real culprits are **viruses.** When you have a cold, viruses are attacking your body. Viruses also cause other diseases including chicken pox, measles, and mumps. This round-shaped virus causes influenza, the "flu," in people. ■

Like bacteria, viruses cause disease in plants and animals as well. For example, this tobacco plant has been infected by a virus. ● In other ways viruses are nothing like bacteria. Bacteria are one-celled organisms. A virus is not a cell. Viruses are much smaller than bacteria. They are so small they can only be seen through the powerful electron microscope. Notice how large the rod-shaped bacterium looks next to the ball-shaped viruses. ▲

Many people think that viruses are not living organisms. After all, they are not made up of cells. Also, viruses cannot grow or reproduce on their own. However, other people group viruses with living things. They argue that viruses act like living things when given the right environment. What is the right environment for a virus?

Viruses in the Cell

There are many kinds of viruses. Yet they all have one thing in common. They infect living cells. For a virus, then, the right environment is inside the cell of another organism. This illustration shows a virus attached to the outside of a bacterial cell. ◆ Yes, even bacteria can be infected by viruses.

When a virus enters a cell, it takes control of the cell. It uses the energy produced by the cell. It uses the food in the cell. Then the virus multiplies. A great many viruses form. ★ In time, the cell will be destroyed and the new viruses will spill out, ready to infect nearby cells. □ The viruses that make you sick infect your cells in much the same way this virus infected the bacterial cell.

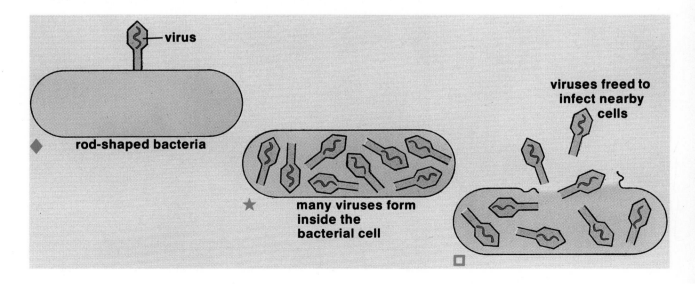

virus

viruses freed to infect nearby cells

◆ rod-shaped bacteria

★ many viruses form inside the bacterial cell

□

So you see, outside a living cell viruses do not appear to be alive. Yet inside a cell they can grow and reproduce. Are viruses alive? Scientists still cannot agree. However, one thing is sure. Living or not, viruses, along with bacteria, cause a great deal of human suffering. How can we prevent such suffering? One way is to learn how disease-causing organisms are spread.

How Diseases Spread

How do diseases spread? Often we become infected when we come in contact with someone who already has a disease. You may be sitting on a crowded bus. The person next to you sneezes. ■ You see that she has not held her hand or a tissue over her face. What you cannot see are the disease-causing microorganisms being sent out into the air. You, or anyone else on the bus, can breathe in the air with the microorganisms. You may become ill.

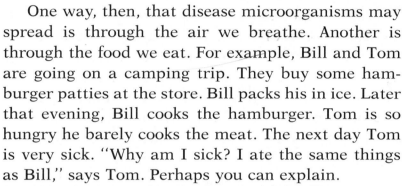

One way, then, that disease microorganisms may spread is through the air we breathe. Another is through the food we eat. For example, Bill and Tom are going on a camping trip. They buy some hamburger patties at the store. Bill packs his in ice. Later that evening, Bill cooks the hamburger. Tom is so hungry he barely cooks the meat. The next day Tom is very sick. "Why am I sick? I ate the same things as Bill," says Tom. Perhaps you can explain.

Millions of people around the world become sick each year from disease microorganisms in foods. Many millions more are infected by microorganisms in the water they drink. To stop the spread of such diseases, cities purify water to kill microorganisms in it. The government inspects meat and fish to get rid of any infected food. The places where foods are handled and packaged are also inspected. ● The government requires refrigeration of foods that spoil quickly. However, no one can make sure that foods are handled and cooked properly once they leave the store.

Some microorganisms that cause disease are spread to people by animals. The bite of an insect, for example, might allow a bacterium or virus to get into the blood. *Rocky Mountain spotted fever* is a disease spread through the bite of a certain tick. ▲

Rabies is a very serious disease caused by a virus. The rabies virus can be spread through the bite of an infected animal, such as a wild squirrel or raccoon. ■ Pets that can carry rabies are usually protected in this country through rabies shots. ●

An Epidemic

Our knowledge of how some diseases are spread has been gained through years of study. We have been able to slow the spread of many diseases. It was not always so. About 600 years ago, a disease called the Black Death swept through Europe. A certain kind of bacterium causes the Black Death. However, 600 years ago people did not know that bacteria caused disease. Still, even without any knowledge of bacteria, people might have been able to control the Black Death if they had known the way it was spread.

The bacterium causing Black Death was carried from town to town by infected rats. Fleas picked up the bacterium when they bit the infected rats. After the infected rats died, the fleas often found a human to live on. When the fleas bit the human, the human became infected. So the Black Death was spread by rats to humans through tiny fleas. If people had known how the disease was spread, they could have destroyed the infected rats and their fleas. However, they did not. Instead the Black Death killed one fourth of all the people in Europe!

A disease that spreads rapidly and affects many people is called an **epidemic.** The Black Death was just one of the many epidemics that have occurred throughout history. Some have been eliminated. For example, epidemics of smallpox, cholera, influenza, and typhoid were once common. People were forced to take unusual measures to protect themselves. ▲ Today, epidemics of many of these diseases do not happen in countries with modern health practices. Of course, some epidemics still occur. Every few years you may read about an influenza epidemic. For this reason, doctors are always on the alert for diseases that may affect large numbers of people. Their knowledge of the ways diseases spread often helps them slow down an epidemic—or prevent one.

▲

On a separate sheet of paper, write each statement with the best ending.

1. An invasion of the body by harmful microorganisms is called
   a. a virus   b. a colony
   c. an infection

2. All of these diseases are caused by bacteria except
   a. tuberculosis   b. tetanus
   c. a cold

3. Any disease that spreads rapidly and affects many people is
   a. a toxin   b. an epidemic
   c. an infection

4. Viruses appear alive in
   a. water   b. a living cell
   c. the wind

5. The statement that fits the *main* concept of this section is:
   a. Diseases may be spread in many different ways.
   b. Diseases are usually spread from person to person.

YOU CAN DISCOVER

In some parts of the world a disease called *malaria* kills a great many people. Malaria is caused by a microorganism spread through the bite of a certain mosquito. The microorganism causing malaria is not a bacterium or virus. ■ Find out what it is. Then find out what other kinds of microorganisms can cause disease in people.

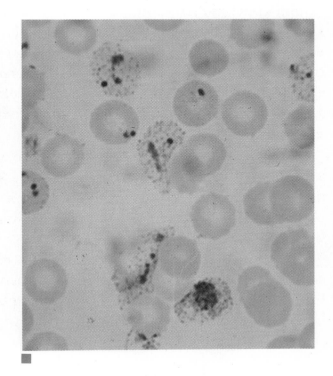

3 ▶ Your Body's Defenses

Bacteria are everywhere in the environment—even in places that are kept very clean, such as hospitals. Of course, in a hospital operating room there are probably very few bacteria on the instruments. The room and the instruments are kept as clean as possible. Still, everywhere around you there are bacteria. Why, then, aren't you always ill? One reason is that your body is on the defense against bacteria—all the time.

First-Line Defenses

How do you keep rain from getting inside your house? With a protective covering, of course—a roof and walls. When there is a break in the window or a hole in the roof, the rain gets in. So can certain living things—insects, for instance.

Look around you. Are people like houses in a way? Do they have a protective covering? You know they do. It's their skin. When it is unbroken, your skin forms a barrier against organisms of infection, such as bacteria. It's like a shield you carry with you at all times.

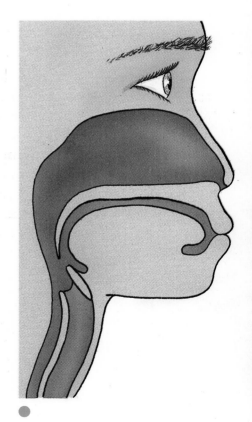

Your skin helps form your first line of defense against infection, but it is not alone. Wash your hands until they are very clean. Then feel the inside of your cheek. It is covered with moist saliva. Saliva contains water and a sticky fluid.

This sticky fluid is **mucus** (MYOO-kus). Special cells that line the mouth, nose, and other places in the body give off mucus. ● Mucus traps invading bacteria. In the mucus is a chemical that helps kill some bacteria.

101

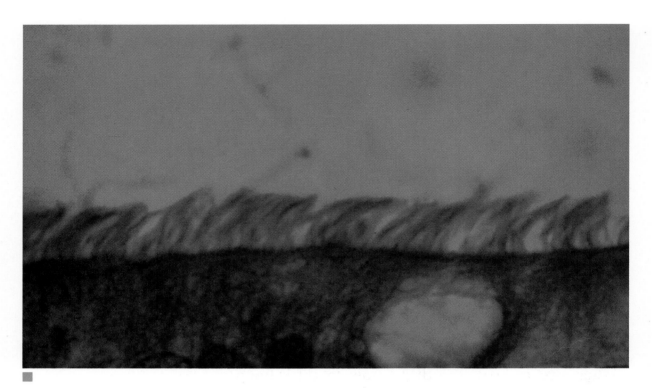

Inside the passages in the nose are tiny hairs called **cilia** (SIL-ee-uh). The cilia help mucus trap bacteria, as well as any dirt particles, you breathe in. Of course, bacteria may slip past the defenses in your nose and mouth. They may reach your windpipe. However, the windpipe is also coated with sticky mucus.

If you could look at the lining of the windpipe under a microscope, you would see more tiny cilia. ■ These cilia can move in a special way. They sweep the mucus and trapped bacteria out of the windpipe and back into the throat. Usually they are quickly swallowed. But sometimes the body removes mucus and trapped bacteria by coughing or sneezing.

When you swallow mucus, the trapped bacteria reach your stomach. Other bacteria reach your stomach when you swallow your food. Don't worry. You have protection there, too! Certain cells in your stomach produce digestive juices. Digestive juices kill many of the bacteria that you swallow.

Your Immune System

Suppose you fall and cut yourself. Sometimes harmful bacteria get into an open wound. Your first line of defense has failed. What happens next? The bacteria may reproduce. They may even be spread through your bloodstream. You are infected.

Your body can recognize these invading microorganisms and fight off the infection. This ability of your body is called **immunity** (i-MYOO-ni-tee). It is the job of your immune system. Without immunity you could not live in a world filled with disease-causing microorganisms.

Let us return to the cut in your skin to see how your immune system helps you. However, keep in mind that your immune system is working throughout your body, wherever microorganisms infect you. When you are cut, the blood flow to the damaged area increases. If we stain a drop of blood and place it under the microscope, it would look like this. ● The round objects are red blood cells. The larger objects are **white blood cells.** White blood cells are a part of your immune system.

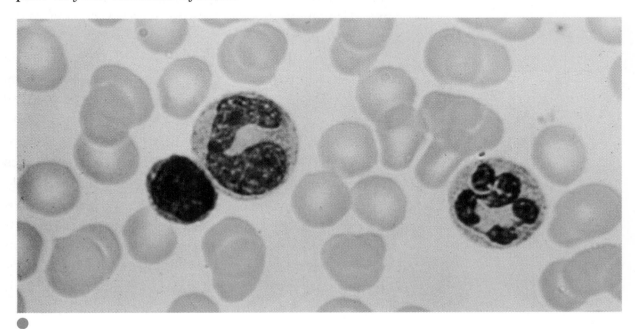

Your white blood cells defend you in an amazing way. They attack bacteria before an infection can become serious. They "swallow" the enemy whole! First a white blood cell is carried by the blood to the bacteria. ■ It surrounds the bacteria. ● Then it destroys the bacteria with special chemicals. ▲ Have you ever seen an infected cut? You may have noticed its yellow-white color. This color means that many white blood cells are destroying bacteria.

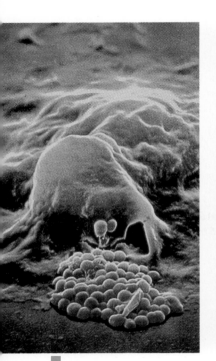 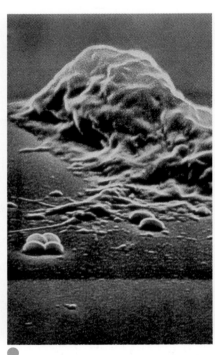 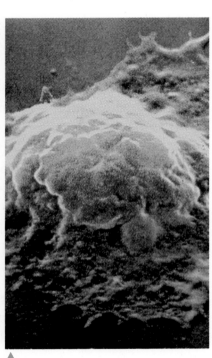

■   ●   ▲

Antibodies

White blood cells kill many bacteria in your body. However, they cannot always defeat a bacterial infection on their own. Also, they are of little help against invading viruses. So the body often calls upon another part of the immune system to protect it.

Suppose, for example, the virus that causes measles gets into a person's body. The virus enters a living cell. It multiplies. The person has measles. In time, the body reacts to the virus. Special cells begin to make substances called **antibodies.** The measles antibodies help the body destroy the measles virus. ◆ The person gets better. Yet, even after the person recovers from the disease, the measles antibodies usually stay in the blood. Then we say the person has immunity against measles, or is **immune** to measles.

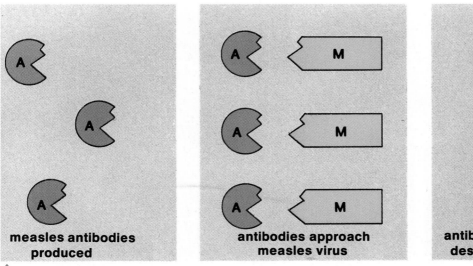

measles antibodies
produced

antibodies approach
measles virus

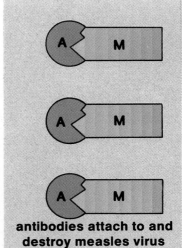

antibodies attach to and
destroy measles virus

◆

So people who have had measles and recovered have antibodies against measles in their blood. They are immune to measles. They will not get measles again. However, the measles antibodies will not protect that person from another disease. A different type of antibody is usually needed to fight each different kind of disease.

The body always produces antibodies when it is invaded by disease microorganisms such as bacteria or viruses. Often, as with measles, the antibodies give you lifetime immunity against the same disease. Other times the immunity does not last. For example, you know that a bacterium causes strep throat. The body produces antibodies to help fight the infection. However, they do not provide lasting immunity. You can get strep throat again and again.

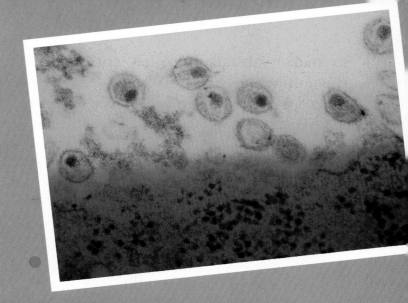

EXPLORING SCIENCE AND TECHNOLOGY

Preventing the Spread of AIDS

Ever since the discovery of Acquired Immune Deficiency Syndrome (AIDS) in 1981, scientists and researchers have been working hard to prevent the spread of the disease. 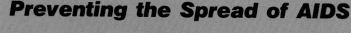 They are also searching for ways to treat and cure AIDS. As of yet, there is no known cure for the disease, and there is no AIDS vaccine. However, this does not mean that scientists have not made any progress toward conquering the disease. As a matter of fact, they have made more gains in less time than they have for any other dangerous disease.

Here are some of the advances scientists and researchers have already made:

1. They have identified the virus that causes AIDS.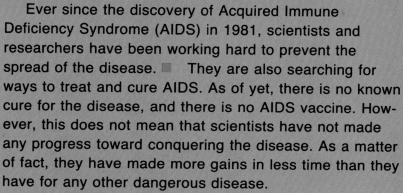

2. They have developed and continually improve upon blood tests to diagnose AIDS.

3. They have provided for safe blood transfusions that are free of the AIDS virus.

4. They are progressing in their search for an AIDS vaccine.

5. They are experimenting with possible treatments for those already infected with AIDS.

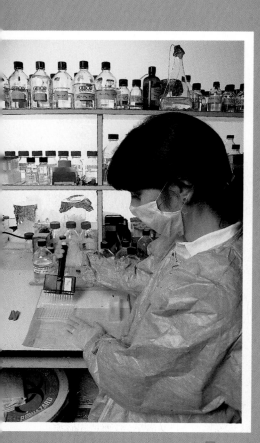

Many scientists and researchers believe that as they learn more about AIDS, they are also getting closer to a vaccine to prevent cancer. The war against AIDS is one of the best examples of science and technology working together to improve people's lives.

On a separate sheet of paper, write each statement with the best ending.

1. The body's first line of defense against invading bacteria includes
   a. blood   b. skin   c. antibodies

2. Blood cells that destroy bacteria are
   a. red blood cells
   b. white blood cells
   c. red and white blood cells

3. The body can help rid itself of bacteria in a
   a. yawn   b. cough   c. shiver

4. The ability of the body to fight disease is called
   a. immunity   b. infection
   c. antibody

5. The statement that fits the *main* concept of this section is:
   a. The body has many ways to protect itself from infection.
   b. Once an infecting bacteria gets past the first line of defense, the bacteria will be able to grow and reproduce with little trouble.

YOU CAN DISCOVER

1. This girl has spent her entire life in a special environment. ■ Her body cannot fight off dangerous microorganisms. Try to explain why, using what you know about the immune system.

2. In some parts of the country, there may be a great deal of pollen in the air at various times of the year. The weather report may give the *pollen count.* See if you can find out how the pollen count is measured. What is a high pollen count? What is a low pollen count?

4 ▶ Helping Your Body's Defenses

It often takes time for your body to fight off an infection. While the battle is going on you may feel very sick. ■ Also, there are some disease microorganisms your body cannot defeat easily. So doctors look for ways to help your body's defenses.

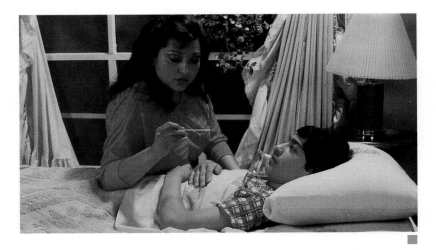

Antiseptics

Imagine once again that you cut yourself. Bacteria enter the cut. Surely, the best way to help your body is to destroy the bacteria before they can grow and infect you. Scientists know many ways to destroy bacteria. They know that extreme heat will kill bacteria. They know that strong acids and other powerful chemicals can kill bacteria. They know that a part of the Sun's radiation called ultraviolet radiation can kill bacteria. However, they cannot use any of these methods on your cut.

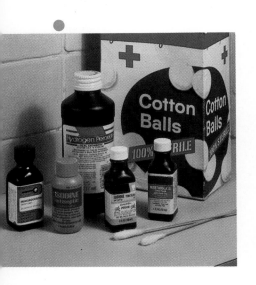

There are some things you can do to stop infection in a cut. First, you can use soap and water to clean an open cut. Then you can use an **antiseptic.** ● An antiseptic is one kind of substance that stops or slows down the growth of bacteria. *ACTIVITY*

Antiseptics and Bacteria

You can use: 2 Petri dishes with covers, a package of plain gelatin, a bouillon cube, bottle of antiseptic

1 First, you must make a place for bacteria to grow where they can find food. Sprinkle gelatin into ¼ cupful of cold water. Stir until well mixed. Add the bouillon cube to ¾ cupful of boiling water. Stir until the cube dissolves. Then pour the gelatin into the bouillon. Stir well. While the mixture is still warm, pour it into two Petri dishes to a depth of about ½ centimeter. Expose the dishes to the air for several hours.

2 Boil more water and allow it to cool. To one dish of gelatin, add boiled water about halfway to the top.

3 Add a few drops of antiseptic to the other dish. Then add boiled water about halfway to the top of the dish.

4 Label the dishes. Cover them and place them in a warm, dark spot. Observe the dishes for several days. Here are the results of one trial after several days. Antiseptic was added to this dish. ■ No antiseptic was added to this dish. ● How do you explain these results?

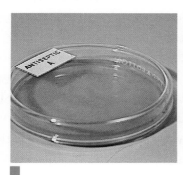

■

●

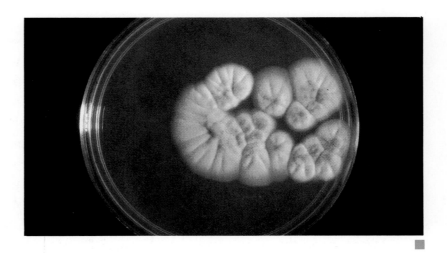

Antibiotics

Moldy meat, moldy cheeses, even moldy breads were once used to heal wounds. Sometimes these remedies worked. No one knew why.

Then in 1928 a scientist, Sir Alexander Fleming, made an interesting discovery. At first Fleming was angry. He was trying to grow bacteria in a Petri dish. However, a mold had contaminated his dish. What Fleming saw looked much like this. ■ Many scientists had similar experiences. Most threw their dishes away and started again, but not Fleming. He was a true scientist—an observer. Fleming noticed that there were no bacteria in the area where the mold grew. He suspected that something produced by the mold would stop bacteria from growing.

Fleming was right. The mold produced a substance he named *penicillin*. Penicillin was the first **antibiotic** discovered. Doctors use antibiotics to treat diseases, such as pneumonia, caused by bacteria.

Today modern medicines, such as antibiotics, have helped us conquer most diseases caused by bacteria. However, antibiotics work mainly against bacteria. Suppose the disease is caused by viruses, which antibiotics cannot usually attack. Is there another way to help the body fight infection?

Vaccines

In 1962 almost 500,000 people in this country became ill from measles. Most recovered. They would probably never get measles again since their bodies produced antibodies against the measles virus. Yet not everyone was so fortunate. Measles can be a serious disease. It can even cause death. However, by 1968 the situation had changed completely. Only about 22,000 people got measles. Today, doctors hope to eliminate measles in this country.

What brought about such a change? It was the discovery of the measles **vaccine.** A vaccine contains dead or weakened bacteria or viruses. For example, weakened measles viruses may be injected into the body. They do not harm the person. However, the body still produces antibodies against the measles virus. The antibodies destroy any measles viruses that enter the body in later years. The person is immune to measles without ever having the disease.

You probably don't remember when you were vaccinated. Before you were two years old you had vaccinations against whooping cough, diphtheria, tetanus, and polio. ● Most children are also vaccinated against measles, rubella (German measles), and mumps. Some vaccinations, like those for measles and mumps, may give you lifetime immunity. Others will not last that long. For example, you may need a *booster shot* to be protected against tetanus.

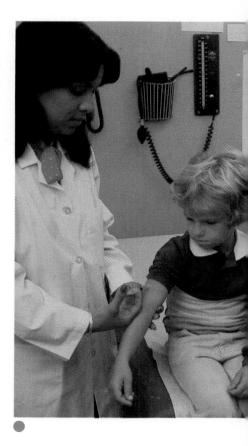

Vaccines have been of enormous help in our continued struggle to help the body fight disease. At one time almost everyone expected to get the measles or mumps. Today the number of people who get these "childhood" diseases is small.

Because of the great success of vaccines in eliminating certain diseases, some people no longer feel they need vaccinations against these diseases. You know that these people are very wrong!

On a separate sheet of paper, write each statement with the best ending.

1. A substance the body makes to destroy invading bacteria is an
   a. antibiotic   b. antiseptic
   c. antibody

2. Penicillin is an example of an
   a. antiseptic   b. antibiotic
   c. antibody

3. Antibiotics work mainly against
   a. bacteria   b. viruses
   c. bacteria and viruses

4. A substance containing weak or dead bacteria injected into the body is
   a. an antibiotic   b. a vaccine
   c. an infection

5. The statement that fits the *main* concept of this section is:
   a. In the end, the growth of disease organisms cannot be controlled.
   b. Substances produced by the body, along with various methods of helping the body's defenses, have made it possible for people to survive many dangerous diseases.

YOU CAN DISCOVER

Alexander Fleming, the discoverer of penicillin, also discovered a useful substance in the human body. ■ Fleming experimented with the substance. He learned it could lyse (dissolve) bacteria. Fleming named it lysozyme.

Lysozyme is an *enzyme*. There are many important chemical substances in your body that are also enzymes. Find out what enzymes do.

5 ▶ Health—A Personal Concern

Up to now, your family has worried about your health. They have planned your diet, taken care of your aches and pains, and watched your growth. They have seen that you had regular medical and dental checkups. Your teachers and the school also have been interested in your health.

Soon your health will be your own responsibility. As an adult, you must be ready to look after your health yourself. You should do everything possible to keep yourself in the finest health. The human body is a marvelous machine. Its care and upkeep are not hard—if you know what you are doing.

Keeping Clean

In the mid-1880's, in Vienna, a doctor named Ignaz Semmelweis saw a serious problem. More than one out of every ten women who came to the hospital to give birth died from a disease. After making many observations, Semmelweis had an idea. He believed that doctors themselves were spreading the disease. He urged doctors to clean their hands before every operation. That seems logical to you, of course. But times were different then. People laughed at Semmelweis. His advice was ignored. Sadly, in the year he died the first antiseptic operation was performed. Semmelweis was finally proven right.

Today all operating rooms are antiseptically clean. ● However, keeping clean is not just for doctors in hospitals. It's necessary for everyone's health. Keeping clean helps us avoid dangerous bacteria. People who stay clean feel good—and they look good, too. So it's important for you to have good cleaning habits throughout your life.

What are good cleaning habits? To start with, bathe or shower regularly. For most people, soap and water are all they need to keep their skin clean. Also, a mild shampoo can help keep your hair looking its best. ■ Aside from your regular shower or bath, there are special times when you should make an effort to wash up. It is important to wash your hands before you eat. Can you explain why? You should also wash your hands before and after using the bathroom.

Make sure you keep all cuts and scratches clean. Remember, a cut in your skin is an open door inviting bacteria to enter. An adhesive bandage will help keep an open cut free from dirt and bacteria. Show any serious cuts to a parent or school nurse.

Taking Care of Teeth

Perhaps you have heard these words before: "If you don't want cavities, don't snack on candy, soda, or other sweet foods." Your teeth are covered with **enamel,** the hardest substance in your body. How can sugary foods destroy the hard enamel and give you a cavity?

On the enamel is a sticky, colorless substance called **plaque** (PLAK). Plaque is made up mainly of saliva and dead cells from the lining of your mouth. In the plaque grow certain bacteria. ● For these bacteria, the mouth is the right environment. They

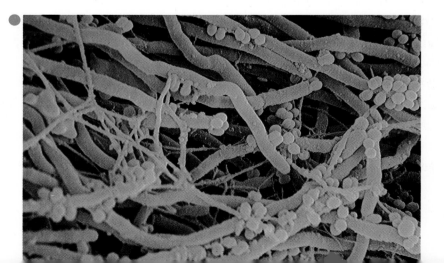

live on the sugars and starches left in your mouth after you eat. As they use foods, the bacteria produce an acid. The acid can break down the enamel covering of your teeth. It takes time, of course. However, after a while a cavity forms. You have tooth decay.

Scientists are working on a vaccine against the bacteria that cause tooth decay. So someday people may no longer have cavities. Until then, the best way to avoid tooth decay is to keep your mouth as clean as possible. You should always brush your teeth and gums in the morning and at night before going to bed. ▲ If possible, brush after every meal as well.

A dentist or school nurse can show you the best way to brush. They can show you how to use dental floss as well. ◆ Using dental floss properly is just as important as brushing. Dental floss removes food that may be caught between your teeth. Make regular visits to the dentist—at least twice a year. The dentist will check your teeth for cavities and clean any plaque or foods left after brushing. Try to avoid sugary snacks. Snack on fresh fruits, vegetables, cheeses, or nuts.

Would you like to see how well you brush your teeth? *ACTIVITY*

How Well Do You Brush?

You can use: disclosing tablets, toothbrush, mirror

1 After dinner, brush your teeth. Then chew a disclosing tablet. ■ (You can get these from a dentist or druggist.) Swirl it around your mouth for thirty seconds. Then look at your teeth in a mirror.

2 Do you see any red spots on your teeth? These spots show where your teeth are not completely clean. Here's what one person saw. ● How well did she brush her teeth? How about you? Remember, on every red spot may be bacteria producing acid.

3 If you saw many red spots in your mouth, you are not doing a good enough job of keeping your teeth clean. Learn the proper way of brushing your teeth. Then try the activity again. This time use dental floss as well. Will you see as many red spots? What is your prediction?

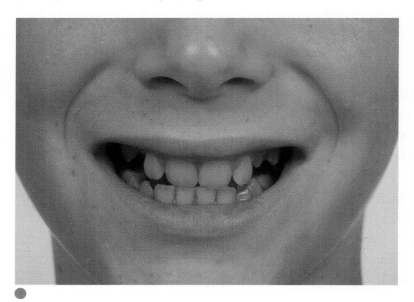

Other Important Health Habits

There are a few other health habits you should follow. They will help you avoid disease-causing organisms, and help you get better faster when you do get sick. Keep away from people who have colds or other diseases that can spread. If you don't feel well, tell your parents or school nurse. Don't hide an illness and hope it will get better.

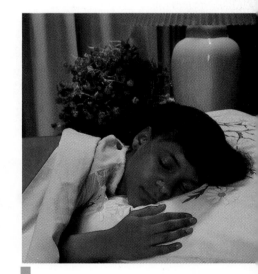

Find out about your health history. Have you had all the available vaccines? Sometimes people are tested in school for diseases such as tuberculosis. If you are absent when the test is given, make sure you tell the school nurse.

If you have been sick recently, your body may not be as able to fight disease as it usually is. A weakened body is a good environment for a disease organism to infect. So eat well and get a lot of rest for a while.

Remember, you should follow one simple rule. **Take an active interest in your health.** ■

On a separate sheet of paper, write each statement with the best ending.

1. The hardest substance in the body is
   a. muscle   b. enamel   c. skin

2. A sticky substance made up of saliva and dead cells from the lining of your mouth is
   a. mucus   b. starch   c. plaque

3. For their food supply, bacteria in your mouth use
   a. plaque   b. saliva   c. sugar

4. For good dental care, you should do the following *except*
   a. use dental floss
   b. eat sugary snacks
   c. visit the dentist regularly

5. The statement that fits the *main* concept of this section is:
   a. A good way to help stay healthy is to keep clean.
   b. No one ever prevented a disease by keeping clean.

YOU CAN DISCOVER

The person who performed the first antiseptic operation was Sir Joseph Lister. ■ Lister changed surgery in several important ways. Find out and report about this amazing man of medical science.

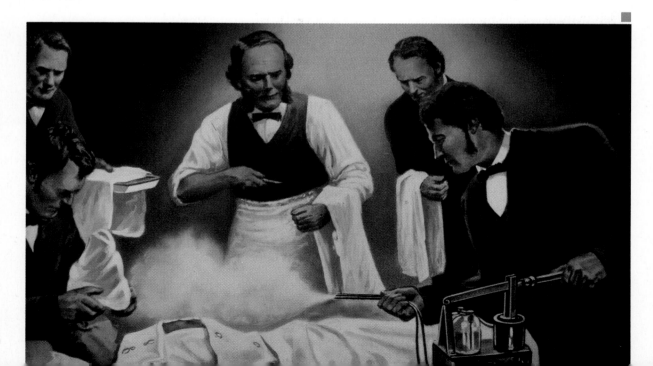

Food Inspector

Have you ever seen the blue stamp on meat in the supermarket? ■ The stamp shows that the meat was inspected. It is safe for people to eat. It is the job of the food inspector to check meats, poultry, and fruits and vegetables.

Food inspectors make sure foods have correct labeling. They check if food is spoiled by bacteria or other microorganisms. ● They look for polluting chemicals in foods. They check if conditions are sanitary in places where foods are handled. So to do their job, food inspectors must go to places where foods are produced, processed, stored, and finally marketed.

Some food inspectors check food products from other countries. Fruits and vegetables, for example, may have disease organisms that can infect crops in this country. So cars, trains, airplanes, and boats carrying foods are inspected.

In these ways and more, food inspectors make sure that the foods we eat are as safe as possible.

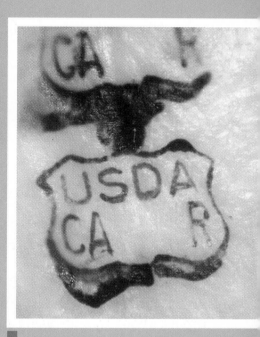

119

✓ Bacteria are an important part of the world eco-system. Decay bacteria, for example, break down dead plant and animal matter.

✓ Nitrogen-fixing bacteria take nitrogen from the air and combine it with other substances. In this way, the nitrogen is made available in a form green plants can use.

✓ Some bacteria, of course, are harmful. Bacteria may feed on animals, plants, and even humans. They cause disease.

✓ All bacteria share one thing in common. They are dependent on their environment. This leads us to a further understanding of an important concept:

All living things need the right environment to grow and reproduce.

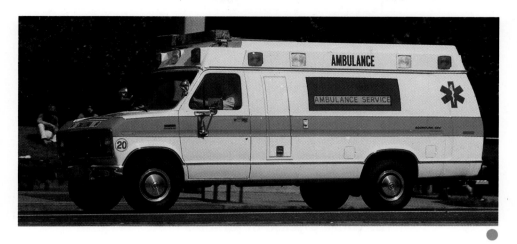

✓ Your body has ways to fight infection from bacteria and viruses. Skin, mucus, and cilia help keep such organisms out of the body. White blood cells may attack invading organisms. Sometimes you may need the help of antibodies produced by the body.

✓ We can also help the body fight disease. ■ We have discovered antibiotics and vaccines. Through science we have learned to control and even wipe out some diseases. ●

✓ We now know it is also important to make our environment a safer place. For instance, there are health laws that require school children to be vaccinated against polio and measles.

✓ We still have much more to do in our search for a longer, more healthful life. In many parts of the world diseases for which the cause and prevention are well known still kill many people. So we must also find better ways to use our knowledge for the good of all.

A. CHOOSE THE BEST ANSWER.

1. Living things that can be seen only with a microscope are called
   a. blood cells   b. viruses   c. microorganisms

2. A group of many bacteria living together is
   a. a colony   b. an environment   c. plaque

3. Most bacteria
   a. are harmless   b. cause disease in people
   c. cause disease in animals

4. Sphere-shaped bacteria are called
   a. bacilli   b. spirilla   c. cocci

5. Corkscrew-shaped bacteria are called
   a. spirilla   b. bacilli   c. cocci

6. Of the following diseases the one *not* caused by viruses is
   a. whooping cough   b. chicken pox   c. mumps

7. A sticky fluid produced in the mouth and nose is
   a. cilia   b. white blood cells   c. mucus

8. The person who first discovered antibiotics was
   a. Semmelweis   b. Fleming   c. Lister

9. Vaccines work mainly against
   a. bacteria   b. viruses   c. bacteria and viruses

10. The statement that fits the *main* concept of this unit is:
    a. The best thing science could do would be to destroy all the bacteria on Earth.
    b. Although some bacteria cause disease, many other bacteria are useful to nature and to people.

B. ANSWER THESE QUESTIONS.

1. A farmer grows the same crops year after year. Then she notices that fewer plants seem to grow strong and healthy. What sort of crop would you advise her to use to enrich the soil? Why?

2. Bacteria multiply very quickly. How is it that they do not overrun the entire Earth?

3. Discuss three ways people preserve food to prevent the growth of bacteria.

4. People who have had measles will probably not get them again. Why?

5. Discuss three ways disease-causing organisms can be spread.

Find Out More

Without water neither plants, animals, nor people could live. Yet disease-causing bacteria also live in water. In this country, many cities and towns purify their drinking water when necessary. How is the drinking water in your community kept clean? ■ Find out.

Challenge Your Thinking

This person is taking a vaccine developed by Dr. Albert Sabin. ● Unlike others, this vaccine is taken through the mouth, not through an injection. From what disease will the Sabin vaccine protect the boy?

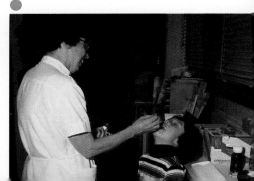

Electric Energy

It was a typical autumn evening on the east coast of the United States. Wide highways and narrow roads shone like ribbons of color as people drove to the comforts of home. Great cities and small towns sparkled as one home after another lit up with signs of life. A chill would keep many people indoors. They watched television, listened to the radio, or perhaps read a book. Some were doing their homework. Everything seemed normal.

Then without warning, the lights went out. Televisions and radios went dead. Appliances stopped running. In an instant the skyline of New York became dark. All electric power along the entire east coast was out.

Eventually, of course, power returned. People joked about how they got through the "Great Blackout." However, everyone had learned a valuable lesson. In one long night, people realized how much they depend on electricity—and how little they knew about it.

125

◣ ▶ Electric Charge

Over two thousand years ago, a man named Thales lived in Greece. One day he received a gift of several pieces of amber. Amber is formed from the hardened sap of certain trees. Because of its attractive color, amber was considered valuable.

Thales polished his gift to make it shine. He rubbed the amber with a cloth. He was certainly not the first person to do so. However, Thales was a scientist—an observer. He noticed something very interesting. When he placed the amber near some thread, the thread stuck to it. ■ He tried the same thing with bits of straw and feathers. Again the objects stuck to the amber, as if attracted to it.

Thales realized that by rubbing the amber with the cloth, he had changed it in some way. How was the amber changed? Thales could not answer the question. Today you can. *ACTIVITY*

Attract or Repel

You can use: 2 balloons, string, scissors, marking pen, 2 wool cloths, bits of paper and other materials

1 Mark a small X on each balloon with the marking pen. Then blow up the balloons and tie them with string. Leave about ½ meter of string attached to each balloon.

2 Have a classmate hold a balloon from the end of the string. With the wool cloth, carefully rub the part of the balloon marked with an X. Then hold the wool cloth close to the balloon. Here's what one student saw when she tried it. ■

3 Now have your classmate hold both balloons by their strings so that the X's on each balloon are opposite each other. Then rub each X with a wool cloth. This is what one student saw when he took the cloths away. ●

4 Once again rub one balloon with the cloth. This time see if other materials are attracted to the balloon. Will bits of paper, for example, stick to the balloon? What about bits of rubber eraser, or metal paper clips, or cloths made out of materials other than wool?

127

Charged Particles

When you rub a balloon with the wool cloth, they stick to each other. They are *attracted* to each other. When two balloons rubbed with wool seem to move away from each other, they *repel* each other. How can we explain what happened? Let's look into the nature of the atom.

Look at the simple model of the atom. ■ In the center is the *nucleus*. Whirling around the nucleus are **electrons** (i-LEK-trahns). Each electron carries a bit of electricity—an **electric charge.** The charge is negative and is written with a minus (−) sign.

Within the nucleus of an atom are other kinds of particles—the **neutrons** (NOO-trahns) and the **protons** (PROH-tahns). Neutrons do not carry bits of electricity. They have no charge. Protons do have a charge, but it is different from the electron charge. The protons have a positive charge. A positive charge is written with a plus (+) sign.

In general, an atom contains the same number of electrons and protons. ● It has the same number of positive and negative charges. Because the charges seem to cancel each other, most atoms are neutral.

Scientists now believe that another particle, a *quark* (KWAHRK), may also be found in the nucleus of an atom. In fact, some scientists believe that quarks make up neutrons and protons. Research is still being conducted to discover more about quarks.

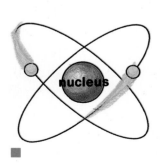

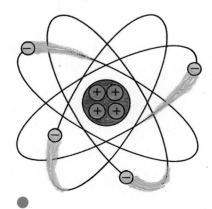

128

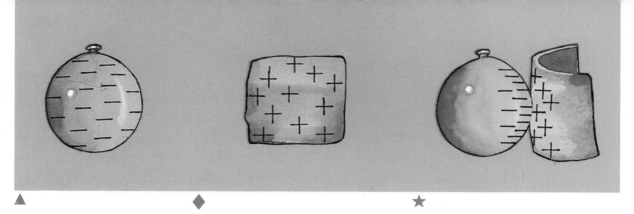

Rubbing off Electrons

The atoms of a balloon and a cloth are neutral. Something happens to the atoms when you rub the balloon with wool, however. Some of the electrons of the wool rub off and collect on the balloon. The balloon gains electrons. These extra electrons give the balloon a negative charge. ▲ At the same time, the wool loses some electrons. Since it now has more positive than negative charges, it gains a positive charge. ◆ You know what happens next. The balloon and the wool stick together. ★ You have discovered an important concept about charge: **Objects that have opposite charges attract each other.**

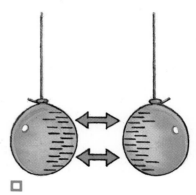

When you rub two balloons with wool, each balloon gains electrons. Each balloon has a negative charge. Now the two balloons are not attracted to each other, are they? They repel each other. ☐ You have discovered a second concept about charges: **Objects with the same charge repel each other.** This is true when both objects have a positive charge or when they both have a negative charge.

We began this unit with a story about Thales. Thales could not know about charge. He could not know that by rubbing the amber he was changing its electric charge. The science of Thales' day was unable to provide him with an answer to his problem. It is interesting to note, however, that the Greek word for amber is *elektron*. Thales' investigation led the way for future scientists. Such is the nature of science.

Static Electricity

An object with extra electrons gains a negative charge. An object that loses electrons gains a positive charge. The charge that builds up on an object is called **static electricity.** The term static means *not moving.* Static electricity, then, is a charge that stays in one place.

Like other forms of energy, static electricity can cause objects to move. You saw the balloon move toward the wool cloth, for example. So static electricity must have provided a force which moved the objects—an *electric force.* The electric force can make objects become attracted or repelled, depending on their charge. However, in each case the charge itself does not move.

Can a charge ever move from one place to another? That is, is all electricity static electricity? What is your prediction?

Shock, Crackle, and Spark

Try this on a dry day. Scuff your feet on a carpet. Don't touch anything with your hands. Continue scuffing for 15 seconds. Then touch your finger to your friend. What do you both feel?

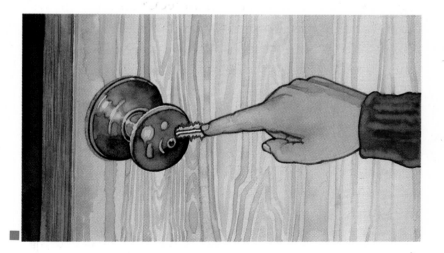

Now try it again in a dark room. Instead of your friend, touch a metal doorknob. What do you observe? ■

Have you ever taken clothes out of a hot dryer? Perhaps they made a crackling noise when you pulled them apart. ● What do these observations—the shock, the spark, the crackling—mean?

When you scuff your feet on a rug, you rub electrons off the rug. You collect extra electrons on your body. You are *charged* with static electricity. Then you touch another person who doesn't have extra electrons. Some of your extra electrons rush to that person and leave you. Then you are *discharged*. You lose your static electricity. When this occurs, both of you feel a shock. You may even see a tiny spark as you are discharged.

Electrons often move to objects that do not have extra electrons. Electrons can move from one object to another very quickly. Rapid movement of electrons causes the shock, spark, and crackling noise that you sometimes feel, see, and hear. You feel a small shock because a small stream of electrons passes through your finger.

A cloud also can become charged with static electricity. In fact, it can become charged with a huge amount of static electricity. In time the static electricity will leave the cloud. The stored-up electrons in the cloud move with great speed to another cloud, or to the ground. Then the cloud becomes discharged. When the cloud discharges its electricity, you see a huge "spark." This is a flash of lightning. ■ Lightning displays in the night sky can be quite spectacular. So can the loud clap of thunder caused by the discharge of electricity passing through the air.

Many homes and buildings have lightning rods on their roofs. Lightning rods protect these homes from lightning damage. When lightning strikes one of these rods, electric charges pass safely through the rod into the ground. ●

Current Electricity

Both the cloud and your finger became charged with static electricity. In each case the static electricity was discharged as a stream of electrons. The moving electron stream is called **current electricity.** The word current means *moving*. A movement of electrons from one place to another is an electric current.

On a separate sheet of paper, write each statement with the best ending.

1. A part of the atom that has no charge is
   a. a proton   b. a neutron
   c. an electron

2. When you rub a balloon with a wool cloth, the balloon
   a. gains electrons
   b. loses electrons
   c. remains neutral

3. A charge that builds up on an object is
   a. static electricity
   b. current electricity   c. a spark

4. Two objects will be attracted if they
   a. are both positively charged
   b. are both negatively charged
   c. have opposite charges

5. The statement that fits the *main* concept of this section is:
   a. Electrons collected on an object cannot be removed.
   b. A transfer of electrons from one object to another gives one object a charge of extra electrons.

YOU CAN DISCOVER

Harry the clown has blown up many balloons and rubbed them with wool cloths. The balloons stick to his clown outfit. Harry says it's magic, but you know that it is due to a build-up of static electricity. Later, all the balloons have fallen to the floor. ▲ What happened to the static electricity on the balloons?

Hint: You should use the concept of moving electrons to explain the loss of static electricity.

▲

Static electricity can be discharged and become a spark of current electricity. In lightning, the spark can be very powerful, even dangerous. However, it is not very useful. It can't light a lamp or run a motor. For appliances in your home, you need a steady flow of electric energy. You need a way to move electrons from one place to another in an orderly way.

The Path of Electric Current

First you need a source of electrons. Inside this dry cell are chemicals. ■ The chemicals will provide the electrons you need. How do you get the electrons from the dry cell? On top of the dry cell are two terminals. One terminal is marked negative (−) and the other positive (+).

A chemical reaction in the dry cell causes electrons to pile up at the negative terminal. When you attach a wire from the negative terminal to the positive terminal, electrons are pushed out of the dry cell. They move from the negative terminal through the wire and back to the positive terminal of the dry cell. ● This path the electrons take is the **electric circuit.**

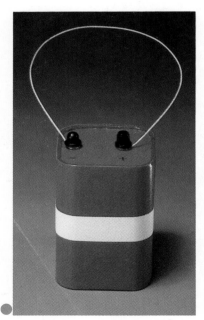

Let's see how we can use the electricity from the dry cell to light a small light bulb. First we can attach a wire from the negative terminal to the bulb. We might expect electrons to flow through the wire to the bulb. Yet this does not happen. The bulb does not light. ▲ However, when we attach another wire from the bulb to the positive terminal of the dry cell, the bulb lights up immediately. ◆ If we remove either wire, the bulb goes out again.

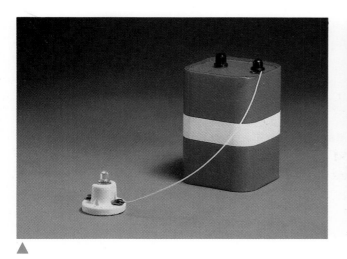

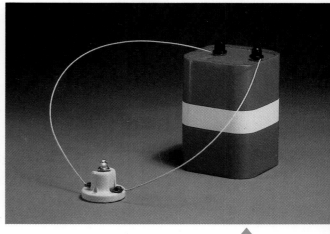

Electric current from the dry cell flows through one wire to the bulb. It flows from the bulb back to the cell through the other wire. Electric current must have a "round trip" or it can't flow. The electrons on a round trip travel through a *closed* circuit. If we remove one of the wires, the circuit is *open*. The electrons cannot flow.

Types of Circuits

There are two different ways to make an electric circuit. In a **series circuit,** the current follows a single path all through the circuit. ★ Trace the flow of electricity in this series circuit. You can draw a line from the dry cell through each part of the circuit and then back to the dry cell. You can even add more bulbs if you like. You can also add more dry cells as well. The electricity still has only one path to follow.

Now study this circuit. ☐ Again two bulbs are connected to a dry cell. This time the electricity has more than one path to follow. In a **parallel circuit,** the electricity has two or more paths to follow. Of course, it does not have a choice of paths. Some of the electricity must flow through every possible path.

Does it make a difference if we connect the bulbs to a parallel or series circuit? *ACTIVITY*

series circuit ★

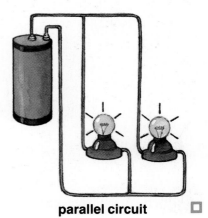

parallel circuit ☐

135

Series and Parallel Circuits

You can use: 1½-volt dry cell, scissors, 6 pieces of insulated wire about 15 centimeters long, 6 pieces of insulated wire about 8 centimeters long, 3 flashlight bulbs, 3 bulb holders

1 First use the scissors to strip away one centimeter of rubber from the ends of all the wires. Then screw the bulbs into each of the bulb holders.

2 Now set up a series circuit. ■ Do all the lights go on? If not, check to make sure all your wires are connected properly. What will happen if one of the bulbs is removed? Try it. Then put the bulb back in. What happens?

3 Reconnect your bulbs in a parallel circuit. ● Again, check all your connections if any of your bulbs do not light. Now remove one of the bulbs. What happens? Remove a second. Predict what will happen if you remove the third bulb. Try it. Explain your results.

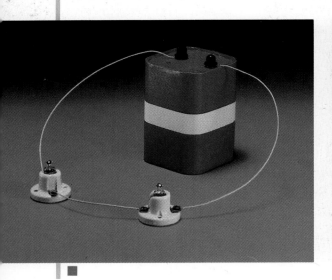

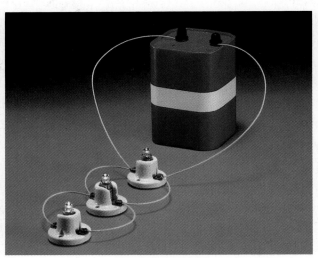

■   ●

Circuits in Your Home

If you remove any bulb in a series circuit, you cut off the current through the entire circuit. When you take out one bulb, the other bulb goes out, too. By removing one bulb you are opening the circuit. As you know, electricity cannot flow in an open circuit. Many older holiday ornaments were arranged in a series circuit. If one light went out, they all went out.

In a parallel circuit, you can remove one bulb without the others going out. Even when you remove two bulbs, the circuit stays closed. The last bulb stays lit. Today, for example, most holiday lights are arranged in parallel circuits. ■ Even if one bulb burns out, the rest stay on.

The electric wiring in homes is also in parallel circuits. You can turn off a light without worrying about the television or radio going off as well. If homes were wired in series, what would happen if you turned off one appliance?

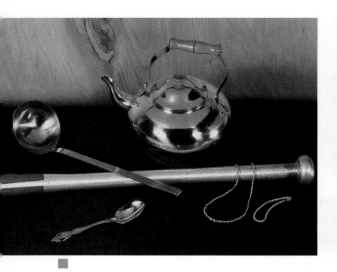

Conductors and Insulators

Some materials allow electricity to pass through them easily. In homes, wires and circuits may be made of copper. Copper and other metals such as silver and gold let electricity flow through them. ■ These materials are called **conductors.** Ordinary conductors lose energy in the form of heat. That is why you can feel heat near an air conditioner. Scientists have found that electricity flows through supercold materials without losing energy. These supercold materials are called *superconductors*. In the future, superconductors may change how electricity is used.

Some materials such as wood, plastics, and rubber do not allow electricity to flow easily. They are **insulators.** ● Insulators are important even though they do not carry electricity. Wires attached to appliances are covered by plastic or rubber insulators. Wires that carry electricity are also covered with insulation.

Rubber or plastic insulation protects you. It keeps electricity from coming in contact with you or an object that touches the wire. If the wire insulation becomes cracked or frayed, it should be replaced.

You can test different materials to learn which make better insulators or conductors. *ACTIVITY*

Electricity Through Different Materials

You can use: 1½-volt dry cell, flashlight bulb, flashlight bulb holder, 3 insulated wires, pieces of metal, rubber eraser and other materials, scissors

1 Strip about one centimeter of rubber from each end of the wires. Connect the dry cell, bulb and bulb holder, and wires as shown. ■ With the wires not touching, does the bulb light? What happens when you touch the wires together?

2 Touch a piece of metal with the wires. ● Does the metal allow electricity to pass through easily? What is your reasoning? Now try other kinds and sizes of metal.

3 Put a piece of rubber eraser in the path of the electric current. ▲ Do electrons flow easily through the rubber? What is your reasoning?

4 Now try other materials. Try wood, rock, plastic, aluminum foil, paper, a piece of glass, and perhaps even a strand of hair. Which allow electricity to pass through? Which do not?

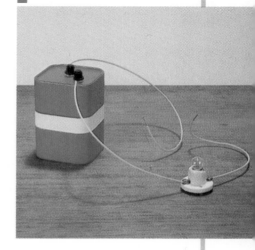

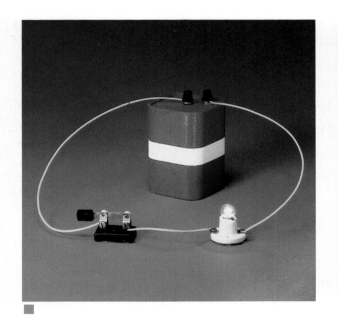

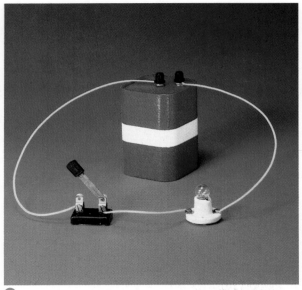

Turning Power On and Off

You are in your room watching television. Your father calls you to dinner. Naturally, you turn off the television before you leave the room. How do you do it? One way would be to pull the television cord out of the wall socket. That would certainly cut off the flow of electricity to the television. It would also be the hard way. Instead, of course, you turn the switch on the television to *off*. Immediately, the picture goes blank. The power is gone. As you leave the room, you turn off the lights as well. Again, you might pull the lamp cord out of the wall socket, but you don't. You simply flick the switch and the lights go out. What are you really doing when you turn a switch to the on or off position?

As you know, electricity can flow only in a closed circuit. A switch, then, can do two things. It can open or close a circuit through which electricity flows. When a switch closes the circuit, electricity passes through the switch and continues through the circuit. ■ When the switch opens the circuit, the flow of electricity stops. ●

Do you recognize this push button switch? ▲ You often use it when you ring a doorbell. Pushing the button makes a contact between two pieces of metal. The path is complete. Electrons flow. What happens when you take your finger off the button?

There are many switches in your home. For example, electrical appliances usually have switches. Here are a few. ◆ What will the flick of the switch do in each case?

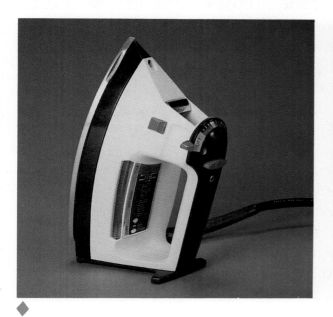

On a separate sheet of paper, write each statement with the best ending.

1. When you attach a wire to both terminals of a dry cell, the electrons flow from
   a. negative terminal to positive
   b. positive terminal to negative
   c. in both directions

2. For electrons to flow in a circuit, the circuit must be
   a. open   b. closed   c. broken

3. You remove one bulb from a three-bulb circuit and the others go out. The circuit is wired in
   a. parallel   b. series

4. Electrons flow most readily through
   a. a wooden spoon
   b. a plastic spoon
   c. a metal spoon

5. The statement that fits the *main* concept of this section is:
   a. We can use either static or current electricity to do useful work.
   b. To run appliances, we need the steady flow of electrons in an electric current.

YOU CAN DISCOVER

This person is using electricity to weld, or melt, two pieces of metal together. ■ The visible electric flow is called an electric arc. See if you can find out what material, if any, is the conductor for the arc of electricity.

3 ▶ Electricity from Magnets

Long ago people's muscles had to supply whatever force they wanted. Later, the muscle power of donkeys, camels, oxen, and horses was added to human muscle power.

In time, people learned how to harness the force of the wind. Perhaps sails for rafts and boats came first. ● Then came windmills. With the steam engine and the gasoline engine, we began to use the energy in fuels. ▲

Today you flick a switch and an electric current flows. Current provides us with the power to cook our food and wash our clothes. It provides power to keep our refrigerator cold or to type a letter. ◆ How many other ways do you use electricity?

Perhaps the most amazing thing of all is that at the same time, in other houses in your community, other people are using electricity as well. Unless there is an accident or temporary shortage, there is usually more than enough electricity for all of us. Where does all this energy come from? How is it produced? *ACTIVITY*

Generating an Electric Current

You can use: galvanometer, about 15 meters of insulated wire, cardboard tube, strong magnet, weak magnet, scissors

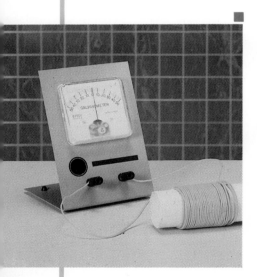

1 Strip about one centimeter of insulation from each end of the wire. Wind the wire around the cardboard tube to make a coil. Connect the bare ends of the wire to the galvanometer. ■ Any electric charge that flows through the coil of wire must also pass through the galvanometer. The needle on the galvanometer shows the amount and direction of the flow of electricity.

2 Place one end of the strong magnet in the coil. Does the galvanometer show any current? Move the magnet back and forth in the coil quickly. How far does the galvanometer needle go? ●

3 Now move the magnet slowly. Which produces more current—fast or slow movement?

4 What happens if you hold the magnet still and move the coil back and forth? Try it.

5 Put one end of the weak magnet in the coil. Move the magnet back and forth quickly. Which makes a greater current, the weak or strong magnet?

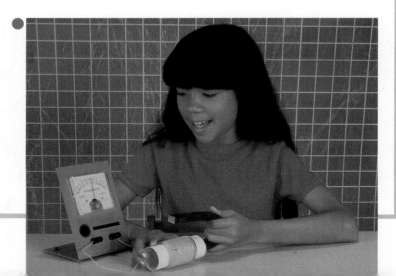

Currents from Magnets

With a simple magnet and coil of wire you can generate an electric current. That is amazing, isn't it? You can control the amount of current in several different ways. You can, for example, increase or decrease the current by using a weak or strong magnet. Or you can change the current by moving the magnet faster or slower. Finally, changing the number of loops of wire on the coil also changes the current. More loops on the coil produce more current.

It doesn't really matter whether you move the magnet or the coil. As long as you move one of them, you can generate an electric current. Why is movement necessary?

Lines of Force

Take a piece of glass and place it over a strong magnet. Then sprinkle iron filings on top of the glass. Shake the glass gently so that the filings can spread out over the entire magnet. The filings don't spread out evenly, do they? They arrange themselves in a pattern. ■

The iron filings line up this way because of the force of the magnet. The filings show where the force of the magnet acts. We call this pattern the magnet's **lines of force.** ●

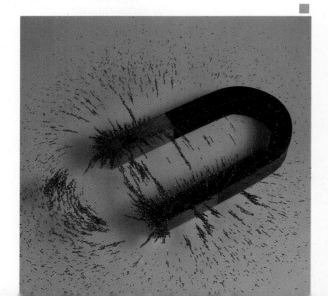

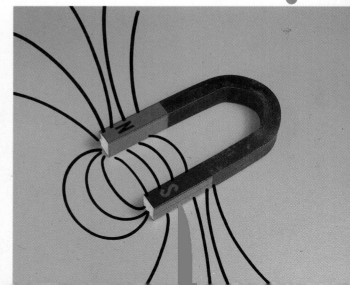

If you look at the magnet carefully, you will notice that one end is marked with an N and the other with an S. These are the north and south poles of the magnet. The lines of force are strongest between these poles.

Scientists discovered, quite by accident, that moving a wire through these lines of force causes electrons to be pushed along the wire. The electrons flow along the path of the wire and an electric current is produced. ■ That is exactly what you did in the activity. When the wire in the coil cuts across the lines of force of the magnet, the galvanometer shows a current being generated. It doesn't matter whether you move the coil or the magnet. In either case, the wire is cutting across the lines of force. However, if you do not move either the magnet or the coil, nothing happens.

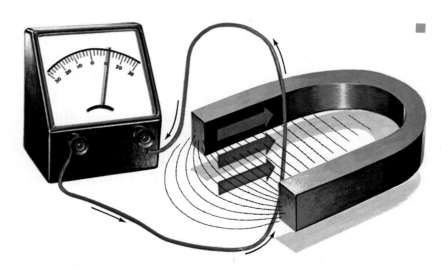

Generating a Weak Current

Susan is riding home from her friend's house on her bicycle. She stayed later than she meant to, and it is getting dark. Susan is not worried. She stops her

bike for a moment and reaches down to move a tiny **generator** near her front wheel. ● When she pedals away, the light on her bike flashes on. ▲

The generator on Susan's bike provides the electric current to power her light. Inside the generator is a magnet and a coil of wire. When the generator wheel touches the moving wheel of the bike, a coil of wire spins inside the generator. As the coil spins, it cuts through the magnet's lines of force, and a current is produced. The light goes on.

Simple generators like Susan's can supply a weak current. Suppose we wish to generate more electricity? We could, as you know, move the coil or magnet faster. That is not always easy. For example, there is certainly a limit to how fast Susan can pedal. We could also increase the number of loops in the wire. However, if we make the coil too large it will be very difficult to move. A third way is to make the magnet stronger.

How can we get a stronger magnet than the kind you used in the activity? We can use electricity to make an **electromagnet.** *ACTIVITY*

Making an Electromagnet

You can use: 1 meter of insulated wire 3 meters of insulated wire, large iron nail, two 1½-volt dry cells, box of paper clips, scissors

1 Strip one centimeter of insulation from the ends of each wire. Coil most of the 1-meter wire around the nail. Connect the ends of the wire to one of the dry cells. ■ Your electromagnet is ready.

2 Use the electromagnet to pick up the paper clips. See how many paper clips you can pick up with the end of your nail electromagnet. ● Then try other parts of the nail. Where is the best place on the electromagnet to pick up the paper clips? What other materials can you pick up with your electromagnet? Can it pick up any objects an ordinary magnet cannot?

3 Now add a second dry cell to your circuit. Does this increase the strength of the electromagnet? How can you tell?

4 Repeat the activity, but this time use the 3-meter wire. Does adding more turns increase the strength of the electromagnet? What is your reasoning?

Powerful Magnets

An electric current in a coil can make a nail become an electromagnet. When you increase the current by adding a second dry cell, the magnetism of the nail grows stronger. Also, if you increase the number of loops in the coil, the magnet becomes stronger. So if you want a very strong magnet, you should use an electromagnet. This powerful electromagnet, for example, can lift heavy scrap metal. ■

You saw how a magnet and a coil of wire can be used to generate an electric current. Electromagnets in generators produce far more electric power than an ordinary magnet. For example, you probably know that the battery in a car provides the electric power to start the car and help keep it running. (A battery is made up of several dry cells.) However, a battery can only provide so much energy before it needs to be recharged. To keep a battery charged, a car also needs a generator. A coil in the car's generator spins when the car's wheels are turning, much like the simple generator on Susan's bike. The generator produces an electric current which charges the battery. Why does a battery go dead if the car has not been driven for a long time?

Power Plants

Hoover Dam, over 200 meters high, blocks the flow of water from the Colorado River. ■ The dam can help prevent floods during heavy rains. Also, the reservoir of water formed behind the dam can be very useful when water is in demand. The reservoir behind Hoover Dam is called Lake Mead. Lake Mead is one of the largest and most widely used recreation areas in the entire Southwest.

Hoover Dam has yet another job. Near the dam is a giant power plant. ● Inside the power plant are electric generators. ▲ When water from Lake Mead is allowed to fall through a pipe into the power

150

plant, it turns a wheel called a *turbine.* ◆ The spinning turbine causes a ring of electromagnets to spin. Surrounding the electromagnets are huge coils of wire. When the electromagnets spin, an electric current flows through the wire. The generators at Hoover Dam provide enough electricity to supply much of the electric power for the states of Arizona, Nevada, and California.

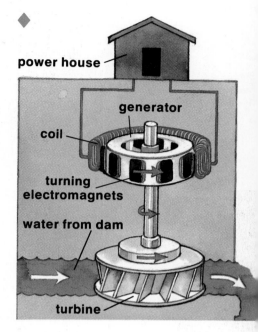

Almost all the electric energy we use in this country comes from power plants. Each year more and more generators are spinning all over the world, producing more and more electric energy. It is energy we can use in a great many ways. All of this can occur because moving a wire through the magnet's lines of force causes a current to flow.

From the power plants, electricity is carried by power lines throughout the country. ★ These lines can carry tremendous amounts of electric power, far more than the wires in your home can carry. So

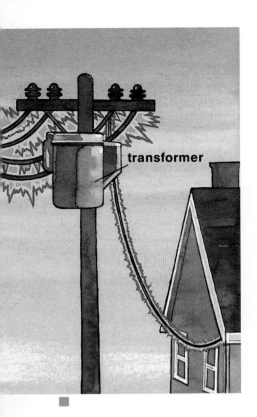

transformer

before the electricity gets to your home, a transformer box on the power line "steps down" the electricity to a safe level that your home can use. ■ When you turn on a light or a radio, you can be sure that your appliances are getting just the right levels of electricity.

Electricity: Energy from Energy

You have seen a number of ways to produce an electric current. In fact, by now it may very well seem as if we can make electricity out of thin air. Don't be fooled. You cannot get something from nothing. To produce electric energy, we must first have some other form of energy.

Think about when you scuffed your feet on the rug and made a spark of current electricity. Although you probably didn't realize it at the time, by rubbing your feet on the floor you were providing a form of energy—mechanical energy. If you didn't first rub your feet, there would be no spark. A similar thing happened when you moved a magnet through a coil of wire. You provided the mechanical energy by moving the magnet with your muscles. Without this mechanical energy, the magnet would not move and there would be no current.

The dry cell you used in your activities also produced an electric current. Again, the current did not simply appear. The energy from chemicals in the dry cell was converted into electric energy.

The same is true for the generators that produce most of our electric energy. At Hoover Dam, for example, the energy provided by moving water turned the turbine. The mechanical energy from the spinning turbine turned the electromagnets. Only then did an electric current flow. In each and every case, the only way you could obtain electric energy was to start with another form of energy.

Superconductors—Changing the World

Imagine going to work in the future. You board a train that has no wheels. Instead the train travels upon a magnetic cushion, carrying you across several states to your job. ■ You pass the time by running a data search on your wristwatch computer or talking on your pocket telephone. When you arrive at the station, you unplug your electric car and drive to the office. ▲

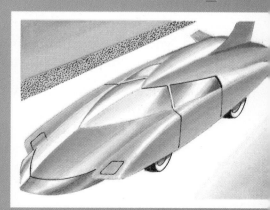

All these things may become part of your life because of superconductors. *Superconductors* are materials that transmit electricity without wasting energy. Ordinary electric wires lose power every time they are used. Superconductors hold the energy and do not produce heat.

Scientists have known for many years that some metals become superconductors when they are kept so cold that they are almost at absolute zero (−273°C). Keeping the metals that cold is expensive and impractical. Until recently, many people believed that superconductors would never be used in everyday life.

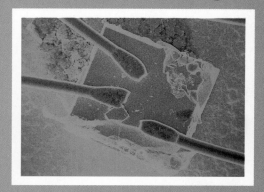

In 1987, scientists made a major discovery. They created some new materials, which are not metal, that become superconductors at −175°C. ● The scientists immediately realized they now had a more practical superconductor. These new materials could be kept at −175°C in a bath of liquid nitrogen, a relatively inexpensive process. Continuing their search, scientists are now on the track of finding even warmer superconductors, some even at room temperature. ◆ When that happens, magnetic-cushioned trains, practical electric cars, and miniature computers will become commonplace.

On a separate sheet of paper, write each statement with the best ending.

1. To generate electricity in a coil of wire, a magnet
   a. must be curved   b. must move
   c. must remain stationary

2. To generate even more current in a coil of wire, you can
   a. use fewer turns
   b. move the magnet slower
   c. move the magnet faster

3. To give electrons in a wire a push, move the wire
   a. along magnetic lines of force
   b. beside magnetic lines of force
   c. across magnetic lines of force

4. In the generators at Hoover Dam, moving water spins
   a. an electromagnet
   b. a coil of wire   c. a turbine

5. The statement that fits the *main* concept of this section is:
   a. Magnetism is always electrical in nature.
   b. We can get electricity from other forms of energy.

YOU CAN DISCOVER

The *High Speed Surface Transport* (HSST), a Japanese magnetic train, set the world maglev speed record at over 512 kilometers an hour. *Transrapid,* a German maglev, can travel over 400 kilometers an hour. What makes these two maglev trains so remarkable is that they never touch the tracks. They just seem to float above them.

Find out more about these trains and about the maglev already being used in Great Britain. ■ Discover how each maglev works. What are some of the good points and bad points about this form of high speed travel?

4 ▶ Electricity at Work

Moving water in a power plant helps convert mechanical energy to electric energy. However, to put electric energy to work we must often convert it back to mechanical energy. Using an electric motor is often the easiest way to do this.

To understand how a motor works, first take another look at the magnet. Or look, in this case, at two magnets.

Magnetic Poles

Take two magnets and hold them close to each other near their poles. When the north and south poles of each magnet are held next to each other, the magnets attract each other. ● *Opposite poles attract.* However, when you hold the south pole of one magnet beside the south pole of the other and the north beside the north, the magnets repel each other. ▲ *Similar, or like, poles repel.* Recall that the same was true for electric charges.

Earlier you made an electromagnet with an iron nail. That electromagnet also has poles. The poles of the electromagnet will attract or repel the poles of an ordinary magnet in exactly the same way. Now let's see how the poles of magnets help run a motor.

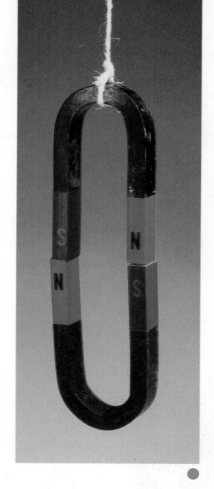

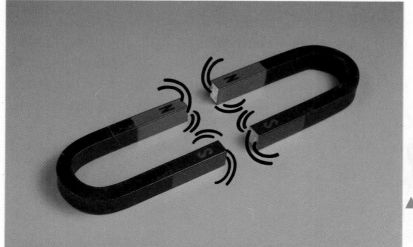

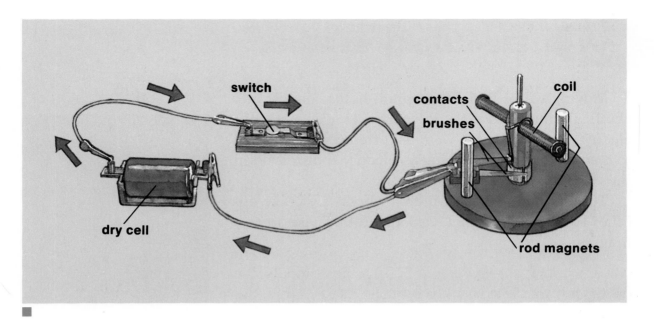

The Electric Motor

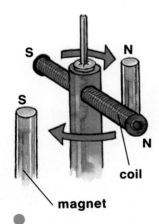

Here is a simple electric motor. ■ When you close the switch, the circuit is complete. The current flows from the dry cell to one of the metal *brushes*. Notice that there is a coil of wire in the center of the motor. The current passes through the metal brush and flows through a *contact* into the coil of wire. The contact, then, is the place where current passes from the brush to the coil.

You know what happens when the current goes into the coil. The coil becomes an electromagnet. One end becomes a south pole and the other a north pole. Now let's look a bit closer at the motor. ● Attached to the base are two rod magnets. One magnet has its north pole on top and the other magnet has its south pole on top. As soon as the coil of wire becomes an electromagnet, the north pole of the magnet attracts the south pole of the coil. Of course, the south pole of the other rod magnet attracts the north pole of the coil. Remember, opposite poles attract. Because of this attraction, the coil spins around toward the magnets.

Just as the poles of the coil reach the poles of the rod magnets, the contacts change from one brush to the other. Then the electric current in the coil changes direction. When this happens, the poles of the coil change, too. The south pole becomes a north pole, and the north pole becomes a south pole. However, the poles of the rod magnets do not change. So the south pole of the coil is now over the south pole of a rod magnet. The north pole of the coil is over the north pole of a rod magnet. What do you think happens next?

If you said that the coil turns some more, you are correct. It turns because its north pole repels the north pole of the rod magnet. At the same time, the south pole of the coil repels the south pole of the other rod magnet. Remember, like poles repel.

So the coil keeps on turning until its south pole is again over the north pole of a rod magnet, and its north pole over the south pole of a rod magnet. Now the same thing happens as before. The contacts change from one brush to the other. The poles in the coil are again reversed. So the coil keeps spinning.

In most motors, the spinning coil turns a shaft attached to the motor. The spinning shaft in a small motor turns the blades of this fan. ▲ This giant industrial motor is much more powerful. ◆ Large or small, however, most motors work in the same way.

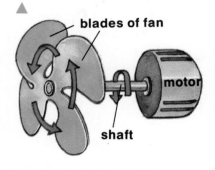

blades of fan
motor
shaft

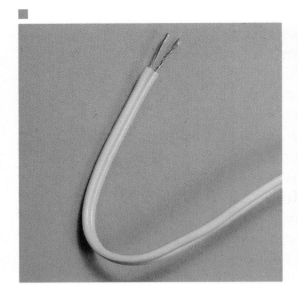

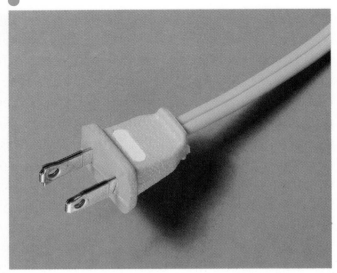

Electricity at Work in the Home

Hair dryers, irons, air conditioners, refrigerators, vacuum cleaners, electric blankets, electric razors, and dishwashers are among the machines that use electricity. The list may seem endless.

To work, these appliances need a steady flow of electric current, and that requires a closed circuit. However, you plug these appliances into the wall socket with a single cord. How can there be a complete circuit with only one cord?

Let's cut the insulation on a typical cord and look inside. ■ When we do, the answer seems clear. There are actually two copper wires in the cord. Each is attached to one prong of the plug. ● Electric current can flow from the plug to the appliance and then back to the plug. It makes a complete, closed circuit.

Fuses and Circuit Breakers

The wiring in your home is covered by rubber or plastic insulation. One reason, as you know, is to prevent electric shock. Yet another reason is heat.

Whenever current runs through a wire, heat is produced. The rubber or plastic around the wire keeps the outside of the insulation from getting too hot.

The wires in your home can usually carry a great deal of current without becoming too hot. Sometimes people plug too many appliances into a socket. ▲ If the wires are old or damaged, the heat may burn through the insulation. There is an **overload** of current in the wire. The walls may begin to heat up from the hot wires. The results can be deadly. ◆

If an electric cord becomes damaged, the two wires in the cord may touch each other. ★ A **short circuit** is produced. Much more heat than normal builds up in the wires. A short circuit can cause a serious fire very quickly. Since the short circuit could be inside the walls, you may not be able to tell if the wires are heating up until its too late.

▲

★

◆

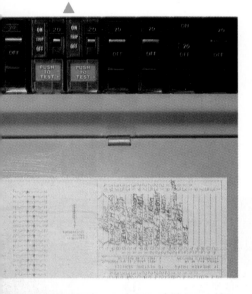

How can we protect ourselves from fires due to short circuits or overloads? Many homes are protected by **fuses.** The current that enters a home goes through the fuses first. Look at this new fuse. ■ Can you see a thin strip of metal? When there is a short circuit or overload, the thin strip of metal quickly melts. ● The connection between the current and the wires in the house is then broken. The current stops flowing. The fuse protects you before any damage can occur.

Many homes have **circuit-breaker** switches instead of fuses. ▲ Each circuit breaker is connected to some of the wires in the house. If there is a short circuit or overload, the circuit-breaker switch turns to the off position immediately. Again, the electric current is stopped. When the overload is corrected, you can flick the switch back on and the current flows again. Circuit breakers are more convenient than fuses, since they do not have to be replaced.

Measuring Electricity

Have you ever seen a meter like this? ◆ It measures how much electricity a home is using. Electric energy is measured in units called *kilowatt-hours.* Each month or so a meter reader from the electric company comes to check the meter to see how much energy was used. Then the company knows how much to charge.

Electricity at Work All Around Us

Since the discovery of electricity, people have found more and more ways to put electricity to work. Electric power is used to transport millions of people each day. This railroad, for example, gets its power from the electrical lines above it. ★   Perhaps in the future we will be driving electric cars. ▫

Most industry in this country would come grinding to a halt without electricity. Electric motors run powerful machines such as the presses that print our newspapers. ○   On an assembly line, auto parts are carried along conveyor belts with electric power. Giant electric cranes carry huge girders skyward to help build tall buildings. ◇

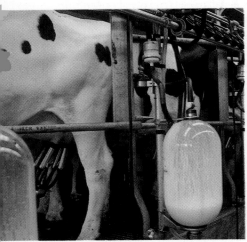

Business, too, would be helpless without electric power. Elevators and escalators need electricity to carry people and supplies. ■ Typewriters, adding machines, and computers need electricity as well.

Even on the farm, electric power has brought a new age. For example, electric heaters keep baby chickens warm when they are first born. ● Very often cows are milked by electric machines. ▲ An electric pump also sends water to fields to help keep crops growing well. ◆

How many other ways can you think of that we put electricity to work?

On a separate sheet of paper, write each statement with the best ending.

1. Two magnets are attracted when we place the
   a. south pole of one beside the south pole of the other
   b. north pole of one beside the north pole of the other
   c. south pole of one beside the north pole of the other

2. In an electric motor, the place where the current flows from the brush to the coil is the
   a. rod magnet   b. contact
   c. switch

3. When we turn a switch to the off position, the circuit is
   a. open
   b. insulated
   c. closed

4. The insulation around the wiring in your home is probably made of
   a. wood   b. rubber   c. metal

5. The statement that fits the *main* concept of this section is:
   a. In a motor, one form of electric current is changed to another.
   b. In an electric motor, electric energy is changed to mechanical energy.

YOU CAN DISCOVER

Scientists have discovered that the Earth is like a giant magnet with both a North and South Pole. Lines of force from the Earth's magnetic field surround us. When you use a compass, the needle on the compass lines up along the magnetic lines of force from the Earth. The needle points toward the north. ★

Suppose we place a coil of wire with a current flowing through it near the compass. ☐ Will the compass still point to the north, or will something else happen? See if you can find out.

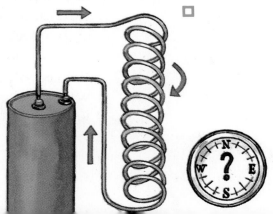

The rider and his horse seemed like one as they sped through the countryside. Night and day they continued. Rain and snow did not stop them. Attacks from bandits would not slow them down. They were the mail carriers of the pony express. ■

Pony express riders carried the mail from Missouri to California. The trip took about ten days. That may seem like a long time, but it was more than twice as fast as a stagecoach. Along the way, each rider would stop for fresh horses at relay stations. Only once was the mail lost by the pony express.

The pony express began in 1860. It was a complete success. Yet by 1861 it had ended. People found a way to send messages from coast to coast through a wire.

The Telegraph

Here is a simple **telegraph.** ● You can see that it has three main parts:
(1) a *key* to send the message
(2) a *dry cell* for electricity
(3) a *sounder* to receive the message

●

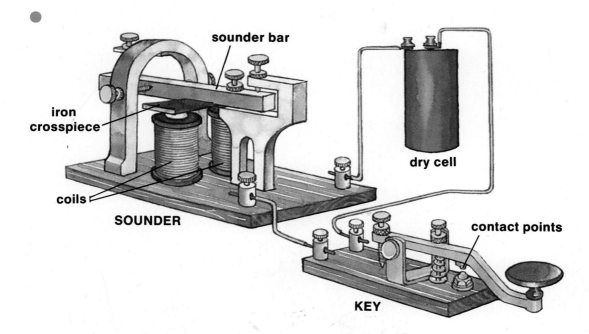

Notice that all parts of the telegraph are connected by wires. However, the circuit is usually open. When you push down on the key and touch the contact, you close the circuit. At that moment, a current flows from the dry cell to the key and then to the sounder. The key is really nothing more than a simple switch that opens and closes the circuit.

When current flows through the coils in the sounder, the coils become an electromagnet. The electromagnet attracts the iron crosspiece. Notice that the crosspiece is attached to the sounder bar. The sounder bar is pulled down quickly. The near end of the bar hits the frame below it with a loud "click." Let up the key and the sounder goes "clack."

With a simple code, this "click-clack" sound could be used to send messages. Different combinations of the sounds stood for different letters. Telegraph wires were strung throughout the country. ■ Soon it became possible to tap on a key on one coast and send a message through wires all the way to the other coast. It was this development that ended the need for the pony express. Later, telegraph wires were laid down under the Atlantic Ocean. ● Then it was possible to send messages as far as Europe faster than the mail once traveled from town to town.

The telegraph was just the beginning. Some people dreamed of sending more than a code through a wire. They wanted to send spoken messages. Many people doubted that such a thing was possible. However, a young inventor named Alexander Graham Bell had an answer.

The Telephone

Alexander Graham Bell was trying to invent a way of sending several telegraph messages at once. One day he heard a musical tone over the telegraph line! Could speech be sent, he wondered. Bell looked for a way, and found one.

This tall instrument is the **transmitter** of one of Bell's early telephones. It is the part you speak into. ▲ Bell's old transmitter didn't work very well, by the way. You had to shout. The smaller instrument is the **receiver** of one of Bell's first telephones. The receiver is the part of the phone you put to your ear. As you can see, Bell's transmitter and receiver were both rather large.

▲

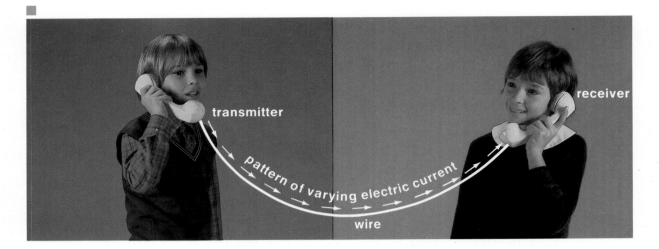

transmitter

receiver

pattern of varying electric current

wire

In a modern telephone, of course, the receiver and transmitter are contained in one small piece. However, both your modern phone and Alexander Graham Bell's early phone make use of electricity to send messages through a wire.

When you use the phone, an electric current flows from the phone company through your phone and back to the company. Inside the transmitter of the phone is a thin, metal disk. When you speak, the sound of your voice causes the disk to vibrate. The vibrations change according to the sounds you make. As the disk vibrates, it changes the amount and pattern of electricity that flows through the phone. In this way the transmitter converts the sound of your voice to a changing electric current. ■

The person you are speaking to listens through the receiver. Inside the receiver is another disk. When the current passes through the wire into the receiver, the disk vibrates. The vibrating disk makes the exact sound you made when speaking into the transmitter. The receiver changes the electric current back into sound.

Soon after the invention of the phone, cables carrying many phone lines were put up. ● Today there are many millions of phones all connected in one enormous phone system. When you make a call, you

168

dial the person's phone number. A current is carried by the phone line to a switching station. ▲ At the station, the wires from your phone are connected to the wires leading to the phone you are calling. Seconds later you hear the familiar "Hello" of your friend.

▲

microphone

amplifier   speaker

On Stage

You've been waiting all week and now Talent Day has finally come. You are excited because your best friend is the first singer. However, you are worried, too. You know she has a soft voice. Will everyone be able to hear her?

When she steps up on stage and sings, you realize that you were worried for nothing. Her voice fills the auditorium. How can such a soft voice sound so loud? Once again, the answer is electricity.

Your friend is using a **microphone.** ■ The microphone is a lot like the transmitter in the telephone. The sound of her voice causes an electric current in the microphone. The current then flows to a machine called an **amplifier.** In the amplifier, the electrical signal from the microphone is "boosted," or increased. That boost is what gave your friend's soft voice its loudness.

The amplifier cannot change the current into sound. So it sends the current through a wire to a speaker. The speaker causes the current to make a sound, much like the receiver in the telephone. Then your friend's voice is carried to the audience.

The Phonograph

Once people knew they could send sounds through a wire, they began to wonder if they could record and store sounds, too. Then the sounds could be played back at another time. It was not long after that the phonograph was invented.

A phonograph is a machine that plays back sounds that have been recorded on a phonograph record. This early phonograph was built by Thomas Alva Edison. ● The record it played was a metal tube wrapped in tin foil. Now records are flat disks made of plastic. Sound vibrations are recorded on the record as tiny grooves. A needle on the phonograph fits into the groove. ▲ When the record turns, the needle vibrates. In the phonograph, these vibrations cause an electric current.

Most phonographs today consist of a record player, an amplifier, and speakers. The current from the record player is sent to the amplifier, where it is boosted. Then it flows to the speaker and is changed back into sound. So what you hear is an exact copy of the sounds which made the record originally.

▲

●

171

The Tape Recorder

A tape recorder plays back sounds that are recorded on a plastic tape instead of a record. You can buy tapes of recorded music. With the tape recorder you can do more than with a record player. You can record sounds yourself. There are many different kinds of tape recorders and tapes. However, they all work in the same basic way.

Sound enters a microphone in the tape recorder and causes an electric current. ■ The current then passes through an electromagnet. At the very same time, the plastic tape passes by the electromagnet. The tape is coated with particles of a special material. When the tape passes through the electromagnet, the changing current in the magnet causes the particles on the tape to line up in a pattern. In this way the sound from the microphone can be stored on the tape.

172

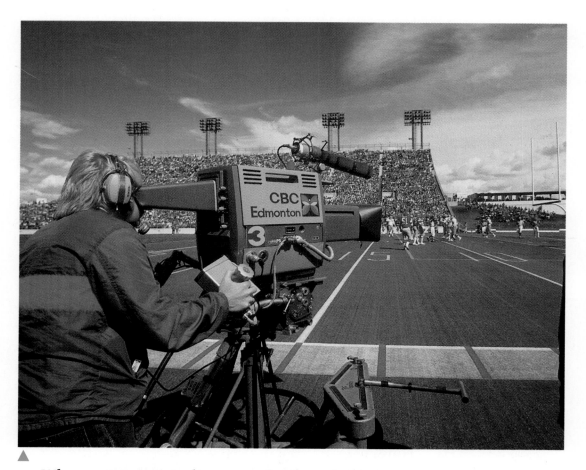

When you want to listen to the sounds, you run the tape through another electromagnet in the machine. The pattern of particles on the tape causes the current in this electromagnet to change as the tape passes through. The current flows through an amplifier, where it is boosted. Then it is sent to a speaker and is changed into sound once again.

In recent years scientists have found a way to record both sound and pictures on a wide tape called *videotape*. ● With videotape, a camera changes pictures into an electric current. The videotape machine uses the current to record the pictures on tape. Sounds can be recorded on the tape as well. Most television programs you watch today are recorded on videotape and stored. ▲ Then they can be played back the next week or years later.

Radio

Guglielmo Marconi was an Italian scientist. In 1894 he experimented with "wireless telegraph." Marconi wanted to send messages through the air itself, and he succeeded. Today, Marconi's idea has grown into what we call radio.

At the radio station, music and voices are changed into an electric current. ■ The current is carried to a large transmitter. The transmitter then changes the current into *radio waves*. Radio waves are a kind of energy. They can be sent through the air. (You will learn more about radio waves in Unit 5.)

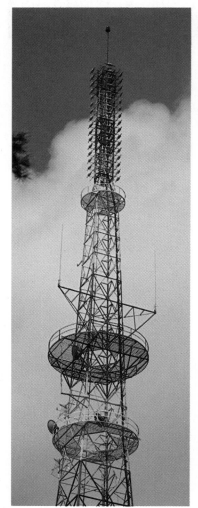

From a tall antenna at the station, radio waves are sent out in all directions. ● Some of the radio waves may be picked up by the small antenna on your radio. Your radio is a kind of receiver. The receiver then changes the radio waves back into an electric current. This current is sent into the speaker in the radio, where it is changed into sound. Then you hear the announcer's voice or perhaps your favorite song.

In a way, this person is carrying a radio station around with her. It's a *walkie-talkie*. ▲ The walkie-talkie changes her voice into radio waves. When the radio waves arrive at her friend's walkie-talkie, they are changed back into sound. So two friends are talking to each other by sending messages through the air, just as Marconi and others dreamed about almost 100 years ago.

Radio Waves and the Phone

Have you ever seen anyone making a phone call from a car? ◆ There are no long wires. You don't see the antenna, either. It's in the trunk. The antenna picks up radio waves from the air. Then the phone changes the radio waves into sound. To make a call to this phone, your call must first be changed to radio waves.

Not many people have radio phones in their cars. However, most of us have had our phone messages changed into radio waves when we dial long distance. Many long distance calls today are changed into radio waves. An antenna sends these radio waves to another antenna. If the call is very far away, there may be many antennas involved. Finally the radio waves are sent to an antenna near the person you are calling. There they are changed back into an electric current and carried to the person's house by cables. It has been estimated that over 36,000 calls can be sent with radio waves from one antenna to another at one time.

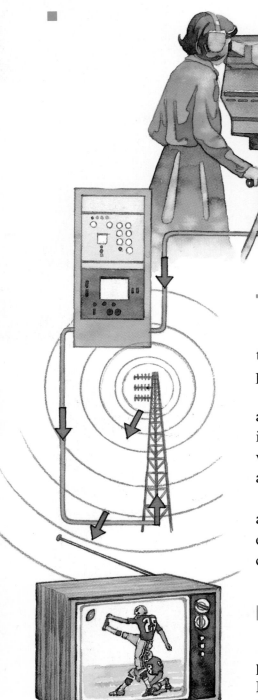

Television

Turn on a radio. Take a look at it. You can't see the radio waves, can you? But there is a way to send pictures with radio waves. We call it television.

At the television studio, pictures from the camera are changed into an electric current. ■ The current is sent to a transmitter where it is changed into radio waves. They are sent out in all directions from an antenna.

In your home, the radio waves are picked up by a television antenna. Then they are changed back into electric current. In your television the current is changed back into pictures on your television screen.

Relay Stations in Space

Not so long ago, if we wanted to watch a television program from another part of the world, such as Europe, we had to wait until the show was put on film or videotape. Then it would be flown to this country and sent out by a local television station.

Naturally, this took a lot of time and money. Live television from Europe or Asia was not possible.

Today, of course, you can turn on television and in an instant see a volcano erupting in Iceland as it is happening. ● Or perhaps you see a ski jump from Austria. ▲ How? Radio waves from a broadcast in Europe are sent into space. ◆ The radio waves are picked up by a satellite relay station. The station sends the waves back to Earth.

Relay stations in space have brought the peoples of the world closer together. They allow us to see our neighbors in other lands, just as they get a chance to see our way of life. Not only do they bring us closer in pictures, we now use such satellites to talk to each other. Phone messages from Europe, for example, are sent by radio waves to satellites. Then they are sent back to this country. So we can now talk to people in Europe almost as easily as we once shouted across the street to our neighbor.

●

▲

◆

EXPLORING SCIENCE AND TECHNOLOGY

Living with Computers

Computers! You've probably heard that word a lot lately. Your school may have computers, and you may have one at home. If you have a home video game, that's a kind of computer. If your family has a new car, it has a computer to help run the motor. Someone in your family may own a personal computer.

What exactly is a computer? A computer is an electrical machine that stores information and uses that information to solve problems. However, before it can do anything, a computer needs a set of instructions called the *computer program.* Think of the computer program as a kind of recipe that tells the computer how to use the stored information.

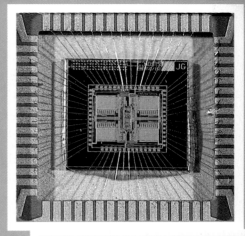

Inside the computer are many tiny electric switches. By turning each switch on or off, the computer does whatever task the program tells it to do. It can solve a simple math problem, figure out the correct path a rocket must take to reach a planet, or play your favorite video game.

Early computers filled an entire room. ■ The many millions of wires in their circuits took a lot of space. To change their program, the operators had to re-wire them. Although very simple compared to those used today, even an early computer could do more calculations in 4 hours than a person could do in about 1,500 years.

The modern computer works so fast that people measure its speed in hundred-millionths of a second. What's more, it's only about the size of a typewriter. ● Where has much of the wiring gone? Right here on this tiny computer chip. ▲ Modern chips are made of a mineral, either silicon or gallium. The computer chip may have nearly a million tiny switches on it. ◆

The computer has already changed the world in many ways. In science, computers help people solve problems that might otherwise take hundreds of years. In industry, computers direct and control factory robots. ★ In transportation, computers help run trains and automobiles and direct airplanes. Many bills, such as the telephone bill, are printed by a computer. Banks use computers to keep track of peoples' money. Someday we may have repair robot computers to fix appliances or to walk the dog. □

This is the age of computers. Some people may feel threatened by computers because they don't understand them. Remember, however, that a computer is just a tool built by people. It helps people solve problems and use information.

On a separate sheet of paper, write each statement with the best ending.

1. To close the circuit in a telegraph, you must push down on the
   a. sounder b. key
   c. rod magnets

2. Your voice is changed into an electric current in the telephone's
   a. receiver b. wire
   c. transmitter

3. To boost an electric signal, you can use
   a. a microphone b. an amplifier
   c. a speaker

4. A television signal is sent from the station to your antenna in the form of
   a. sound waves b. radio waves
   c. light waves

5. The statement that fits the *main* concept of this section is:
   a. We can send sound vibrations directly through a wire.
   b. We can change sound vibrations into an electric current in a wire.

YOU CAN DISCOVER

This device with beads is called an *abacus.* ■ An abacus is a kind of computer. It can help a person do complicated mathematical problems. The abacus uses no electricity. How does it work? Who invented it? See if you can find out.

■

Electrician

Before a house is built, electricians are on call. The electricians must read blueprints and install all the wiring. ■ The job must be done carefully. Improperly placed wires can cause a fire. Electricians also install the circuit breakers or fuse boxes. They set up the sockets for lamps and other appliances. If something should go wrong, they are the ones you call. However, electricians do even more.

Electricians install lighting systems and electric signs. They have to understand motors and generators. ● They also have to know how the many different electrical devices in our homes, offices, and industries work. If there is a power failure, electricians may be called to solve this dangerous problem. ▲

Do you have an interest in electricity? Do you like to work with your hands? Perhaps becoming an electrician is the career for you. Where could you find out more about such a career?

SCIENCE AND YOUR CAREER

✓ The build-up of charge on an object is called static electricity. Static means "not moving." An object, such as a cloud, may discharge its static electricity in a spark of current electricity. ■

✓ Electric current is the movement of negatively charged electrons. To get an even, steady flow of current we need an electric circuit.

✓ A simple switch is used to open and close a circuit. When a circuit is open, the current will not flow. When it is closed, the current will flow.

✓ If a current has only one path to follow, the circuit is called a series circuit. If there is more than one path to follow, the circuit is called a parallel circuit. Your home is wired in parallel.

✓ Electrons flow through a wire when the wire passes through a magnet's lines of force. ●

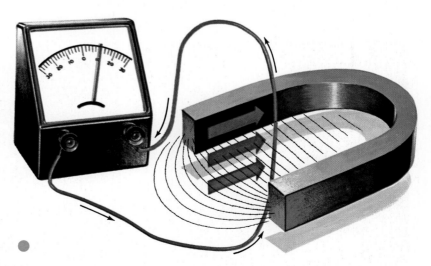

✓ In a power plant, strong electromagnets spun by a turbine generate electricity. This provides energy for our towns and cities.

✓ We have come then to another important concept: **We can use the energy of movement to generate another kind of energy—electric energy.**

✓ Electricity in an electric motor runs the large machines in our factories, as well as the appliances in your home.

✓ We use electricity to send messages through a wire, from a simple telegraph to the modern telephone. ▲

✓ We can send messages through the air by using electricity to generate radio waves. That is the way radio and television works.

✓ Today modern computers use electricity to store information and solve complex problems.

A. CHOOSE THE BEST ANSWER.

1. When you plug in a table lamp, you connect it to a source of
   a. static electricity   b. current electricity
   c. light waves

2. Both current electricity and the discharge of static electricity consist of a flow of
   a. magnetism   b. protons   c. electrons

3. To build an electromagnet, first coil some wire around
   a. a plastic rod   b. an iron nail
   c. a rubber rod

4. In a power plant, the spinning turbine turns a
   a. ring of electromagnets   b. coil of wire
   c. motor shaft

5. Current electricity moves only in a
   a. straight line   b. nucleus   c. closed circuit

6. When the direction of current changes in the coil of a motor,
   a. the north pole becomes the south pole
   b. the motor stops spinning
   c. the north pole remains the north pole

7. The part of the atom with a positive charge is the
   a. electron   b. proton   c. neutron

8. Homes are wired in
   a. parallel   b. series   c. both

9. A device that changes mechanical energy to electric energy is a
   a. transformer box   b. generator   c. motor

10. The statement that fits the *main* concept of this unit is:

    a. Energy can change from one form to another, and can be transferred from one place to another.

    b. When energy is changed in form and transferred from one place to another, some energy is lost.

B. ANSWER THESE QUESTIONS.

1. Imagine for a moment that there is no electricity. In how many ways would your life be changed?

2. Discuss the different kinds of codes we use to send messages.

3. What are the main differences between parallel and series circuits?

4. How do circuit breakers and fuses help protect your home and family?

Find Out More

This person has a broken arm. ■ The break would not heal properly. Then doctors used electric energy to help the bone heal. Find out how electricity can be used by doctors for the healing of broken bones.

Challenge Your Thinking

This tape is used to store information. ● However, it is not from a tape recorder or videotape machine. What kind of tape is it?

Light – Radiant Energy

In ancient Alaska, an Eskimo stared at green lights in the night sky. He knew that the strange lights were ghosts doing their dance of fire.

In ancient Norway, a young woman walking through the woods noticed a red light hanging overhead like a curtain. She was not afraid. She knew that the red light was caused by the shields of warriors as they battled in the sky.

While John and his sister Susan were driving north with their parents, they saw green lights in the distant sky. They thought the air had turned green and was glowing.

The *northern lights* have confused both ancient and modern people. How are they formed? Where do they come from?

As you read on, you will learn not only about the northern lights, but also about light.

187

Sharon and Doreen are taking their first airplane flight. From the window, they see many farms. ■ While Sharon is asleep, the plane begins to fly over water. Sharon awakens and can't believe her eyes. Instead of land below, she sees the Sun and clouds. "Is the plane flying upside down?" she asks.

Doreen knows that the lake they are flying over is acting like a giant mirror. Light is being **reflected** off the surface of the water. ● Some of the reflected light bounces toward the people in the plane. They see the reflected light as an *image*. Doreen explains that Sharon is seeing an image of the sky reflected by the water.

"I can understand that," answers Sharon. "But why didn't I also see an image of the sky reflected by the ground? What makes the difference?"

Why do some things reflect images while others do not? *ACTIVITY*

Reflecting Images

You can use: slide projector, slide, mirror, chalk erasers, aluminum foil

1 Put a slide into a slide projector. Hold the mirror in front of the projector. Darken the room. Then turn on the projector. Adjust the angle of the mirror until the beam of light from the projector is reflected onto the ceiling. Use the focus knob to make the image of the slide clear.

2 Take the chalk erasers and clap them in front of the mirror. The chalk dust will help you see the path of light. ■

3 Crinkle the aluminum foil into a ball. Flatten the foil and cover the mirror with it. Smooth out the foil just enough to cover the mirror. Use the erasers again to see the path of the light. What happens to the path? What happens to the image on the ceiling?

4 Repeat the activity using different materials. Try clear plastic wrap, wax paper, black construction paper. Will you see clear images with these materials? What is your prediction?

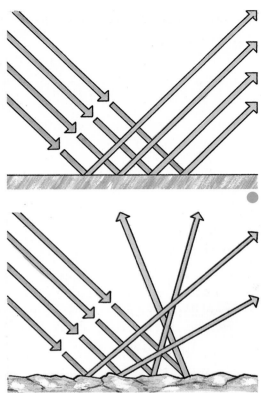

Images in a Mirror

Light is reflected by a mirror. ■ The mirror has a flat, smooth surface. So the light bounces off the mirror in a very orderly way. You can see the image very clearly.

When light bounces off any smooth, flat object in an orderly way, an image is formed. ● Look into a calm pool or puddle of water, for example. You can see your image reflected by the water. What happens to your image if you stir the water?

Light is also reflected by a rough surface such as wrinkled aluminum foil. However, a rough surface does not reflect light in an orderly way. The light is scattered in all directions. ▲ Although they may look smooth, most objects have rough surfaces. Most objects scatter reflected light. That is why you cannot see your image in a desk, a wall, or a sheet of paper.

190

On a bicycle or in a car, a mirror lets you see images of traffic behind you. A mirror lets you see people next to you, or even around the corner. Such mirrors are flat and the reflected images are clear. What happens to an image if the mirror is curved?

Curved Mirrors

These people are cooking—not with a gas flame or electricity, but with light and a mirror. ◆ A **concave mirror** is curved inward. Light rays from the Sun that strike the concave mirror are brought together, or *focused*, through a point. ★ This is the **focal point** of the mirror. When their dinner is placed at the focal point of the solar cooker, all the light energy strikes it. The light energy causes the food to become hotter. This solar furnace in France is a giant concave mirror. ◻ It can heat an object to over 3,000°C!

◆

★

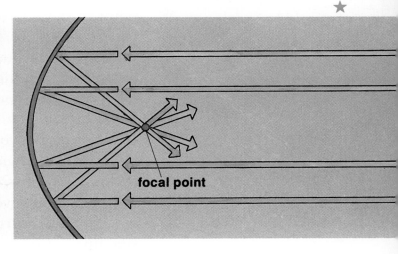

focal point

◻

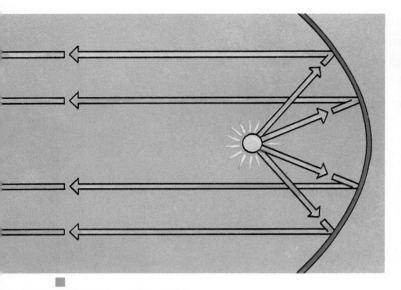

If we place a light source at the focal point of the concave mirror, something interesting happens. All the light is reflected back in one direction. ■ The concave mirror, then, can be used to form a beam of light. If you open a flashlight, you will see a concave mirror behind the bulb. ● The bulb is at the focal point of the mirror. The beam of light is sent out of the flashlight in one direction. There is a concave mirror behind the powerful lights in a spotlight and behind the headlights in a car.

We can use concave mirrors to form images, too. Look into a concave mirror formed by the bowl of a spoon. Do you see your image? Is it right side up or upside down? If you are outside the focal point of a concave mirror, your image will appear upside down. ▲ However, if you are inside the focal point of a concave mirror, your image will appear right side up.

Some mirrors are curved outward, such as the other side of a spoon. They are **convex mirrors.** A convex mirror produces a small, right-side-up image. You may have seen convex mirrors in some stores. In a small convex mirror, you can see images from a large part of the store.

Refraction

Have you ever reached into the water to grab something, only to discover that the object wasn't exactly where you saw it? Or have you ever wondered why a spoon in a glass of water looks broken? ◆ How can your eyes be fooled?

Suppose we shine a light into an aquarium. ★ The light passes through the air and then through the water. Does the path change? The light is still traveling in a straight path. However, when the light strikes the water, the light is bent. It is bent *away* from the surface of the water. Light is also bent when it travels from water to air. This time, the light is bent *toward* the surface of the water.

The bending of light is called **refraction** (ri-FRAK-shun). Light is refracted as it passes from air to water. It is refracted again when passing from water back to air. It is also refracted by glass, or ice, or a diamond. In fact, any material that light goes through can cause refraction.

Refraction can play tricks with your eyes. Can you see why? The spoon in the glass of water is certainly not broken. It *appears* broken because the light is bent as it travels from water to air. Where will this person see the shell underwater? □

Now let's see how we can use refraction to form images.

193

Magnifying Images

Look at some newspaper print with a magnifying glass. The words are *magnified*. They appear larger than the real ones. ■ Slowly move the magnifying glass away from the paper. Now the words become smaller, and they are upside down. ●

A magnifying glass is a kind of **lens.** Most lenses are made of glass or plastic. A lens has at least one curved side. Many, like the magnifying glass, have two curved sides. The magnifying glass is curved outward. It is thicker in the middle than near the edges. It is a **convex lens.**

Watch what happens when we shine light through a convex lens. ▲ Light passes directly through the center of the lens. But light striking the edges of the lens is bent, or refracted. The farther away from the middle, the more the light is refracted. The convex lens refracts the light through a point—the focal point. The distance from the lens to the focal point is the **focal length.**

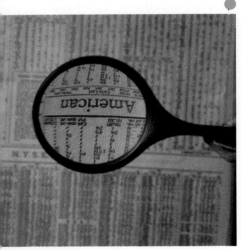

A convex lens refracts light in a very orderly way. When light is refracted in an orderly way, it forms an image. Think back to the magnifying glass. If you hold the newspaper outside the focal point of the convex lens, the image is upside down and smaller than the actual object. However, when you hold the newspaper closer so that it is inside the focal point, the image is right side up and magnified.

Microscopes, telescopes, and binoculars use convex lenses to magnify objects. ◆ Often two or more convex lenses are used together.

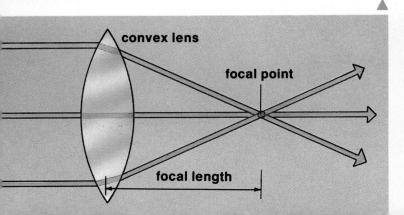

convex lens

focal point

focal length

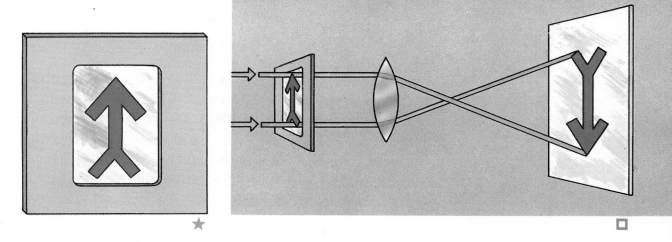

Projecting Images

You are at a drive-in movie. On the screen, warriors over 10 meters high are battling an enormous monster. Yet you know that the film in the movie projector is not big at all. How can we project giant figures onto the drive-in screen?

We can build a simple projector with a slide and convex lens. This slide has a small arrow on it. ★ We can shine light through the slide and a convex lens in front of the slide. The convex lens refracts the light in an orderly way. When we place a screen along the path of the refracted light, an image forms on the screen. ☐ However, the image is upside down.

Slide projectors and movie projectors use convex lenses to project an image onto a screen. The image from the slide projector is upside down. So we put a slide into the projector upside down. Then the image of the slide is right side up. A movie film is like a series of slides placed end to end. Again the film is placed upside down in front of the projector lens. The image produced is then right side up.

Whenever we project an image onto a screen, the farther away the screen, the larger the image. Because the drive-in screen is so far away, the images on the screen are very large. However, the drive-in screen is about as far as we can get and still project a clear, bright image.

195

Photographing Images

A simple camera also uses a convex lens. Behind the lens is an opening. Normally, light is blocked by the *shutter* before it can get through the opening. When you take a picture, the shutter opens for an instant. The lens refracts light from the outside world onto a piece of film. ■ The film, like your eyes, is sensitive to light. An image forms on the film.

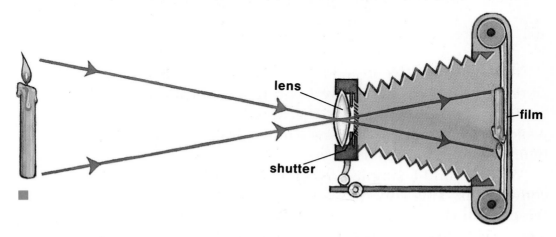

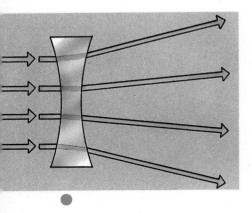

Not all lenses are curved outward like the convex lens. Some lenses are curved inward. They are **concave lenses.** When we shine light through a concave lens, it is not refracted through a point. ● It spreads outward, but in an orderly way. So we can use concave lenses to help us form images, too. In fact, modern cameras often use a series of convex lenses and concave lenses. ▲ They produce far better images than people once believed possible.

Images in Your Eye

A camera may seem complicated to you, but did you know your eye is a kind of camera? Well, your eye has a lens—a convex lens. ◆ The lens in your eye focuses light onto the lining of your eyeball. This lining is called the *retina* (RET-un-uh).

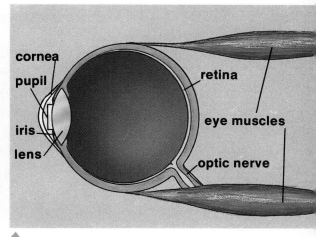

cornea
pupil
iris
lens
retina
eye muscles
optic nerve

The shutter in a camera only lets light in when you are taking a picture. However, unless you close your eye, light is always entering your eye. So a camera can take only one picture at a time. But your eye forms a continuous image on your retina.

Your eye can control the amount of light that enters. In front of the lens is the colored part of the eye, called the *iris*. The hole in the iris is called the *pupil*. It is through the pupil that light enters the eye. In dim light, the pupil will open wide to allow as much light as possible to enter. In bright light, the pupil will close to keep out some of the light.

Muscles in your eye can change the curve in the lens. By changing the curve, your eye can focus an image of faraway objects onto the retina. It can also focus an image of objects close by. The muscles change the shape of the lens all the time without you ever thinking about it.

Because the lens in the eye is convex, the image projected onto the retina is upside down. In the lining of the retina are special nerve cells. They carry a message about the image on the retina through the large *optic nerve* that leads to your brain. Even though the image on the retina is upside down, you do not see things upside down. In the brain, the image is turned right side up again.

197

Improving Eyesight

Some people have trouble seeing objects that are far away. Yet they can see clearly things that are close by. We say they are *nearsighted*. When people are nearsighted, light from objects far away is not focused properly onto the retina. Instead, the image forms in front of the retina. ■ The image the person sees is blurred. People who are nearsighted can wear glasses with concave lenses. The concave lens spreads out the light so that it is not focused until it reaches the retina. ●

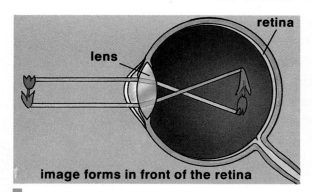

image forms in front of the retina ■

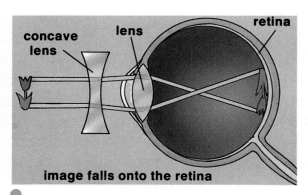

image falls onto the retina ●

Other people have trouble seeing objects that are close up. Yet they can see objects that are far away. We say they are *farsighted*. In this case, the lens in the eye focuses the light behind the retina. ▲ Again, the image the person sees is blurred. People who are farsighted can wear glasses with convex lenses. The lenses focus the light directly onto the retina. ◆

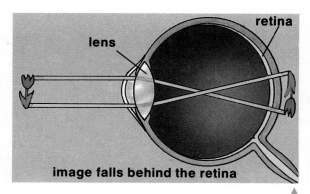

image falls behind the retina ▲

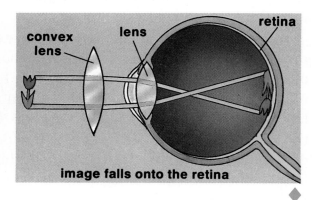

image falls onto the retina ◆

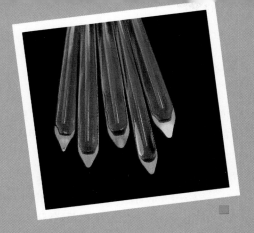

Using Fiber Optics

Optics is the science that deals with light, vision, and sight. Photography and astronomy use optics. The latest technology in medicine and telecommunications also uses optics.

Telecommunications refers to all the systems that communicate over distances such as telephones and radios. In recent years, the most important development in the field of telecommunications has been in fiber optics. In 1980, in Atlanta, Georgia, Southern Bell installed the first fiber optic telephone system in the United States. Engineers used glass, or optical, fibers instead of copper wire for telephone lines. Light energy replaced electricity in transmitting conversations through the optical fibers. Most new and repaired telephone installations today have fiber optics.

Optical fibers have 2,500 times more capacity than the old copper-wire system. Each pair of optical fibers can carry over 8,000 telephone conversations at the same time. Besides that, optical fibers are much smaller than copper wire. They are about one-tenth the diameter of human hair. And, optical fibers do not suffer from static and other interference common to copper wires and electricity.

Medicine is also using fiber optics. Doctors use small fiber optic instruments to look inside a patient's body. That way, they can discover causes for certain health problems without operating. The laryngoscope (luh-RIN-guh-skohp) is an example of a fiber optic medical instrument.

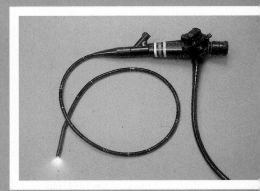

199

On a separate sheet of paper, write each statement with the best ending.

1. We do not see an image when light strikes a rough object because the light is
   a. reflected in an orderly way
   b. absorbed
   c. scattered in all directions

2. A mirror that is curved inward is
   a. concave   b. convex   c. flat

3. The bending of light passing from air to water is called
   a. projection   b. reflection
   c. refraction

4. Magnifying glasses use a
   a. convex lens   b. concave lens
   c. convex mirror

5. The statement that fits the *main* concept of this section is:
   a. The path of light can never be changed.
   b. The path of light is changed when it reflects off an object, or when it is refracted as it passes through an object.

YOU CAN DISCOVER

In a movie projector a shutter allows light to pass through the frames of the movie film. ■ Then the shutter closes until the next frame is in place. While the shutter is closed, no light can be projected onto the screen. So after each frame the screen becomes dark for a moment. Yet we do not see the dark areas. See if you can discover why.

These people are sailing through the sky in hot air balloons. ● Why are they called hot air balloons? That's simple. A burner beneath the base of each balloon causes heated air to rise and fill the balloon. Soon the balloon is flying overhead, carried gently by the wind.

On this day the Sun is shining brightly. Light from the Sun reflects off each balloon. The light from the Sun is white light. Yet we see some balloons are red, others green, and still others come in many different colors. Is white light really white? Or are there other colors in white light? *ACTIVITY*

White Light Through a Prism

You can use: glass prism, book, sheet of white paper, pencil, sunlight

1 Stand the book on end in the sunlight so that it casts a shadow. Place the sheet of white paper in the shadow. Now hold the prism just above the book. ■

2 Turn the prism slowly until a patch of colored light appears on the paper. Here is what one student saw. ● Observe that the colors are in bands. Can you name the colors?

3 While you hold the prism steady, have a partner outline the bands of color. Label the colors. Are the bands all the same width? What color is the light entering the prism? What does the prism do to the sunlight?

4 Beginning with red, what is the order of the colors? Does the order change if you turn the prism? What is your prediction? Try it.

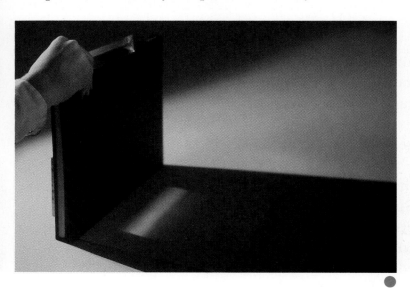

The Spectrum

White light from the Sun or from an ordinary flashlight enters a glass prism. When it comes out, the light is no longer white. It is light of different colors. It forms a series of colors in this order: red, orange, yellow, green, blue, and violet. The series of colors is called a **spectrum** (SPEK-trum). White light, then, is not really white at all. A combination of colors makes up what we call white light.

When light passes through a prism, it is refracted. 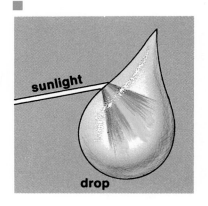 Some colors are refracted more than other colors. Violet is bent the most. Red is bent the least. Whenever white light passes through a prism, a spectrum is formed. The same colors always appear in the same order.

A drop of water can act like a prism. ■ A rainbow is a spectrum formed by sunlight shining onto many drops of water in the sky. ● Where else have you seen the spectrum of light?

sunlight

drop

Seeing Colors

Now let's think back to the colored balloons. When white light strikes the red balloon, the balloon looks red. The red part of the white light is reflected off the balloon and reaches our eyes. What happens to the other colors in white light? They are not reflected. They are absorbed by the red balloon. Whenever you see a red object, you know it is reflecting red light and absorbing the rest of the colors in light.

A similar thing is true for the green balloon. Green light is reflected off the green balloon. All the other colors in light are absorbed. So the green balloon looks green.

Suppose you shine white light through a piece of red cellophane. ■ Red light passes through the cellophane. What happens to the other colors?

Light We Cannot See

In the year 1800, a scientist named William Herschel looked at the colored bands in a spectrum of sunlight. He wondered if any band of color was hotter than another. He placed the bulb of a thermometer in each band of color and observed its temperature. The red band had the highest temperature.

He found something else besides—something he had not expected to find at all. He held the thermometer bulb just below the red end of the spectrum. There was no light he could see. Yet the temperature rose even higher than in the red band!

William Herschel reasoned that there must be a kind of light from the Sun that the eye could not see. He reasoned that this invisible light raised the temperature of the thermometer. More experiments showed that he was right.

We call this kind of invisible light **infrared** (in-fruh-RED) **light.** *Infra* means "below." This light is below the red band of the spectrum. ● At the other end of the spectrum is the violet band. Beyond the violet band is another kind of invisible light. It is called **ultraviolet** (ul-truh-VY-uh-lit) **light.** ● *Ultra* means "beyond." Both infrared and ultraviolet light are part of sunlight.

The prism, then, sorts out the colors that make up white light. Our eyes sense the light in the spectrum from red to violet. We call this part of the spectrum *visible light*. The prism also sorts out infrared and ultraviolet light. They cannot be seen by our eyes. They are *invisible light* but they are very real. In fact, there are some animals, such as bees, that can sense ultraviolet light.

ultraviolet light

infrared light

On a separate sheet of paper, write each statement with the best ending.

1. In the spectrum, the color red is next to
   a. orange   b. green
   c. ultraviolet

2. In the spectrum, the color violet is next to
   a. yellow   b. blue   c. infrared

3. In William Herschel's experiment, the part of the spectrum causing the highest temperature was
   a. red   b. green
   c. infrared

4. Blue light that strikes a blue balloon is
   a. reflected   b. absorbed
   c. refracted

5. The statement that fits the *main* concept of this section is:
   a. White light is made up of different colors that can be sorted out by a prism.
   b. White light is made up of different colors that can be sorted out by a mirror.

YOU CAN DISCOVER

We can pass white light through a red filter. The filter allows only the red part of white light to pass through. What will happen if we then pass that red light through a green filter? ■

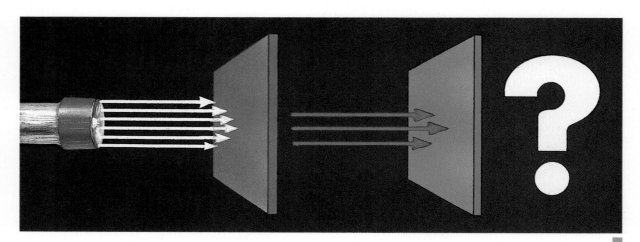

3 ▶ The Nature of Light

It was night and the cave people huddled together to keep warm. They heard wild animals outside. But there was no Moon this night and it was far too dark to see anything. Suddenly a lightning bolt struck a nearby tree, setting it on fire. The cave people learned a valuable lesson that night. Fire provides heat and light as well. In time, they made lamps from hollowed-out stones filled with animal fats. ● They used reeds for the wicks of their crude lamps.

We have come a long way since the first lamps of the cave people. We have found ways to light our homes, our towns, and even our big cities. ▲ Yet all light, whether it comes from burning animal fats or modern electric bulbs, has one source—the atom.

Photons of Light

As you know, all matter is made up of atoms. Each atom has a certain amount of energy. Sometimes an atom can absorb more energy. ■ In a short while, the *excited* atom may lose its extra energy. When it does so, it can give off, or radiate, the extra energy. ● The energy given off by the excited atom is **radiant energy.**

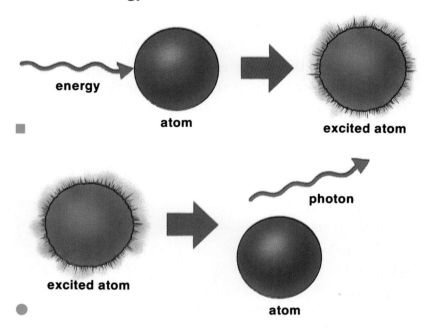

An atom releases radiant energy in a tiny bundle called a **photon** (FOH-tahn). You can think of a photon as a packet of energy. One atom may give off one photon at a time. A group of many atoms may give off a stream of photons, radiating in all directions.

Light is a stream of photons—a stream of tiny bundles of energy. You know that white light is really a spectrum of colors. So red light is made up of red-light photons. Blue light is made up of blue-light photons, and so on. Ultraviolet and infrared light are also streams of photons.

Each kind of photon has a different amount of energy. At one end of the light spectrum is ultraviolet light. The photons that carry ultraviolet light are the most energetic light photons. Next are the photons of violet light, then the photons of blue light. At the other end of the light spectrum is the infrared light. Photons of infrared light have the least energy.

Other Kinds of Photons

This chart shows the different kinds of radiant energy that may be given off by an excited atom. ▲ In the middle are the photons of light, ranging from the ultraviolet to the infrared, with all the other colors in between. Now look beyond the ultraviolet. Notice that **X rays** are on the chart. X rays are also a stream of photons. They are like light. But photons of X rays have more energy than light photons. Now look at the other end of the chart. You will find **radio waves.** Radio waves are also a stream of photons. However, radio wave photons have less energy than light photons.

An excited atom, then, can give off many kinds of radiant energy, from X rays to radio waves. The kind of radiant energy released depends on the amount of energy in the photons. Does it surprise you that X rays and radio waves are very much like light? Suppose our eyes had developed so that they were sensitive to X rays or radio waves instead of light. How different our world would appear!

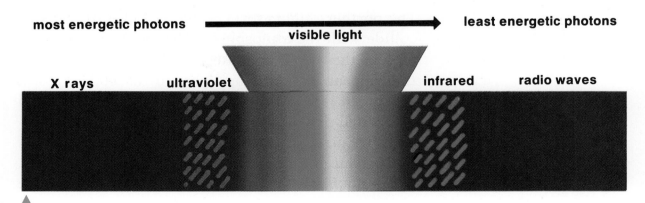

most energetic photons   ⟶   least energetic photons

visible light

X rays   ultraviolet   infrared   radio waves

Excited Atoms

There are many ways an atom may become excited and give off photons of radiant energy. Some occur naturally. On the Sun, atoms collide and become excited. Photons of light energy are released.

The tiny fireflies also make light naturally. ■ The energy from chemical reactions in a firefly's body excites atoms, releasing photons of light.

We began this unit with another kind of naturally occurring radiant energy—the northern lights. ● The northern lights form when particles from space collide with the atmosphere. The particles excite atoms in the air. The excited atoms give off photons that appear as flickering lights in the northern sky. The green lights John and Susan saw were released by excited oxygen atoms in the air.

A fire gives off light, doesn't it? ▲ The heat of a fire produces excited atoms. Heat is also used in a lightbulb. First, electricity is sent through a thin wire

in the bulb. ◆   The electricity causes the wire to
heat up. The atoms in the heated wire become excited
and give off photons of light. ★

On the Sun, in the firefly, or in a light bulb, one
kind of energy excites an atom. Then the atom releases photons of light. You have come, then, to an
important concept:

**Whenever light is given off, one form of energy has
been changed into another.**

This concept, of course, applies to all forms of
radiant energy, including X rays and radio waves.

◆

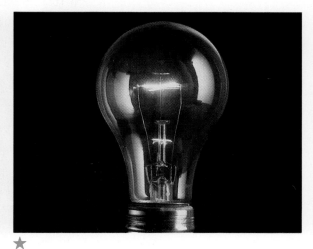

★

Waves and Particles

People have wondered—and argued—about light for many centuries. By the end of the 1600's there were two main theories about light. One group of scientists believed that light was made up of tiny particles. Another group believed that light was made up of waves, similar to the waves that move on water. Today, of course, we know that light is made up of a stream of photons. Do the photons in the stream act like particles of energy? Or do they combine to form a wave of energy? To answer that question, you must first look closer into the nature of waves and particles.

Imagine that particles are like balls in a game of pool. ■ The balls collide. They bounce off each other and scatter. ● Some of the energy of motion from one ball is transferred to the other balls. Particles, too, can collide. They scatter. Energy is transferred from one particle to another.

Do waves transfer energy and scatter when they collide as particles do? We can make a wave by moving one end of a spring up and down. Suppose we start a wave at each end of the spring at the same time. ▲ The waves do not crash when they reach each other. They pass through each other. ◆ When waves pass through each other, they do not collide. They keep on going. There is no transfer of energy from one wave to another.

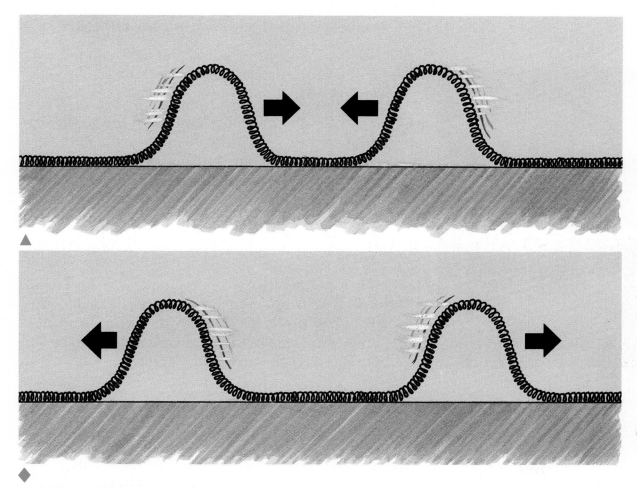

What will happen when two streams of light photons meet? Will they collide like particles of energy and spread out in all directions? Or will they pass through each other and keep on going in their original directions like waves of energy? *ACTIVITY*

Light as Waves or Particles

You can use: slide projector, slide, screen, flashlight

1 Set up the slide projector and screen. Put the slide into the projector. Darken the room. Turn on the projector. Turn the focus knob of the projector until the image on the screen is clear.

2 Pass your hand in front of the light coming out of the projector. ■ Does the light go through your hand?

3 Now take the flashlight and stand to the side of the projector. Turn on the flashlight. Pass the beam of light from the flashlight through the light from the projector. ● What happens to the image on the screen when the two beams of light pass through each other? Do the photons in the light beams act more like particles or like waves?

4 If you can, set up two screens and two projectors, each with a different slide. Pass the beam of light from one projector through the beam from the other projector. What happens to the images on the screens?

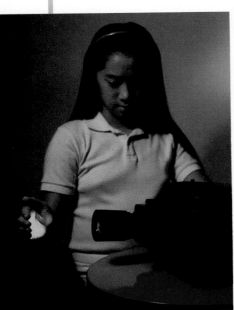

The Nature of Waves

Have you ever dropped a pebble into still water and watched the wave it made? ■ The wave spreads across the surface of the water in all directions at once in a growing circle. The wave travels at a certain speed until it fades away. Somehow, energy is being carried across the surface of the water.

What happens if you dip your hand in and out of the water? It makes a parade of waves. One wave follows another across the water, all at the same speed.

Notice that there is a top, or crest, to each wave. The distance from one crest to the next crest in a wave is called the **wavelength.** Suppose you move your hand with a steady rhythm. The waves follow one another at the same distance. They all have the same wavelength. ●

Move your hand quickly. You are adding energy of motion more often. Do the wavelengths move across the water more quickly? No, they move at the same speed as before. However, there is a difference. The waves are closer together. ▲ In other words, now the wavelength is shorter. Waves can have different wavelengths. You can see this for yourself by making waves in water.

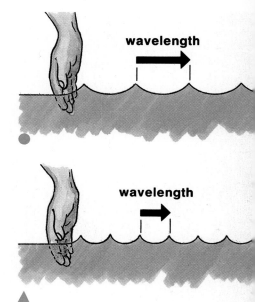

215

Light as Waves of Energy

We can pass the beams of light from two slide projectors through each other. ■ The beams do not collide. The images on both screens are clear. The stream of photons in each beam behaves like a wave. So we can draw a model of the stream of photons as a continuous wave. Since white light is made up of a spectrum of colors, we can draw white light as many continuous waves. ● Each wave is a stream of photons of a different energy, corresponding to a different color.

Of course, light is not exactly like the waves on water. Yet there are some likenesses. For example, each kind of photon of light has a different wavelength. Red light has the least energy of visible light.

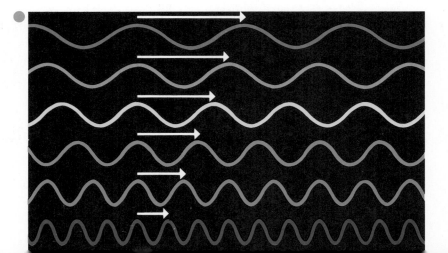

It also has the longest wavelength. Violet light has the most energy. Violet has the shortest wavelength of visible light. Scientists have measured the wavelengths of all the colors in light. They found that wavelengths get longer as you move from high-energy violet to low-energy red light.

We can use the wavelengths of light to help understand how the prism sorted white light into its colors. ▲ When light is refracted through the prism, the light with the shortest wavelength is bent the most. The light with the longest wavelength is bent the least.

Recall that visible light is only one part of the radiant energy spectrum. ◆ As we go beyond the violet light, we pass through ultraviolet and X rays. Since these photons increase in energy, their wavelengths decrease. Thus, X rays have the shortest wavelengths. On the other hand, as we move away from the red end of the spectrum we pass through infrared and radio waves. Since the energy levels of these photons decrease, their wavelengths get longer. Thus, radio waves have the longest wavelengths of radiant energy. Keep in mind that the speed of the stream of photons from X rays to radio waves is the same. Photons all travel at the same speed. Only the energy and the wavelengths change from one kind of radiant energy to another.

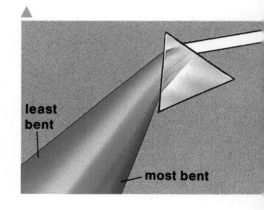

least
bent

most bent

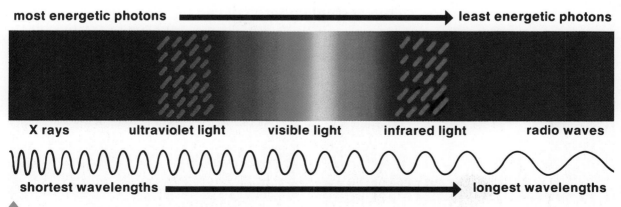

most energetic photons →→→ least energetic photons

X rays   ultraviolet light   visible light   infrared light   radio waves

shortest wavelengths →→→ longest wavelengths

Light as Particles of Energy

Our model of light as a continuous wave of photons helps explain why light often behaves like a wave. Light, then, must surely be made of waves. In fact, scientists have done many experiments that show light traveling as a wave. However, there is also evidence that points to a different explanation. Let's look at some of this evidence.

When light hits certain substances, their atoms give off electrons. For example, under some conditions a plate made of the metal *lithium* will give off electrons. As light collides with the electron in the lithium atom, the electron absorbs the light energy and is knocked right out of the atom. When scientists began to study this effect, they found some puzzling facts. Violet light easily knocked an electron from the lithium atom. ■ However, red light would never knock off an electron, no matter how bright the light was or how long it was left on. ● How can this be explained?

If light strikes an electron as a continuous wave, then eventually we would expect the electron to absorb enough energy to be knocked out of the atom. Suppose, however, that the stream of photons in light does not strike the electron as a continuous wave. Suppose one individual photon hits the electron like a particle. Since photons of red light are not energetic, a single photon of red light can never knock an electron out of the atom. No matter how long or how bright we shine the red light, each individual photon

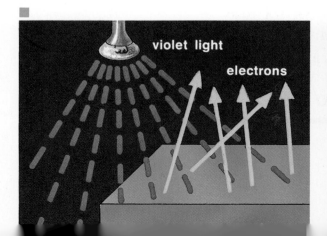

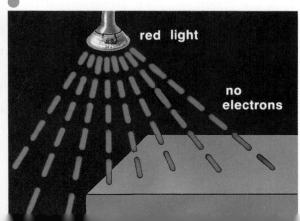

is still not energetic enough to do the job. You can think of a red-light photon as an energy weakling.

On the other hand, violet light is far more energetic. One photon of violet light does have enough energy to knock the electron out of the atom. So in this case, the stream of photons in light seems to act like individual particles of energy rather than a wave of energy.

What all this evidence means is this: *At times, a stream of photons in light acts as if it formed a continuous wave of energy. At other times, a stream of photons in light acts like individual particles of energy.* Thus we need two explanations to describe the behavior of light—the wave explanation and the particle explanation. ▲

Which explanation is better? Oddly enough, both explanations are correct. Part of the trouble is this: The particles we can see around us do not seem to behave like waves. The waves we see around us do not seem to behave like particles. We find it very hard to imagine, then, that light can be both particles and waves. This may be so, however. Photons of light are very, very tiny. The world of such tiny things is not like the world of things we know.

Predicting Weather

Tomorrow is the school carnival. Everyone is excited. However, rain would spoil the day. At home you watch the weather report on television. A satellite photo shows there are no clouds nearby. ■ The forecaster predicts a sunny day!

You would never see such a photo if light did not sometimes act like a stream of particles. Are you surprised? The photo is sent down to Earth by weather satellites. The satellites must have a source of energy to keep on working year after year. Almost all satellites orbiting Earth, including this Nimbus weather satellite, get their energy from large panels of solar cells. ● Light from the Sun strikes the solar cells. Photons of light knock electrons out of the atoms in the material of the cell. A stream of electrons forms an electric current. The current powers the satellite.

Not all solar cells are in space. You can find a simple solar cell in many electronic stores. ▲ You may be surprised at the number of experiments you can do with a solar cell kit.

On a separate sheet of paper, write each statement with the best ending.

1. Radiant energy is released by an atom in tiny bundles called
   a. light waves   b. photons
   c. light particles

2. The photons of radiant energy that have the most energy are
   a. visible light   b. X rays
   c. radio waves

3. When two light beams pass through each other, they act like
   a. waves   b. particles   c. lenses

4. The wavelength of visible light is shortest for
   a. red light   b. violet light
   c. green light

5. The statement that fits the *main* concept of this section is:
   a. Scientists use one explanation to understand how light behaves.
   b. Scientists use two explanations to understand how light behaves.

YOU CAN DISCOVER

The particle nature of light can be used to count these containers of yogurt as they pass along the conveyor belt. ■ How? There is a light on one side of the belt shining onto a photocell, also called an "electric eye." The electric eye converts the light into an electric current. Each time a container blocks the light, the current is stopped. Then a counter adds another number to its total.

Electric eyes can be used in a great many ways. See if you can discover some of the places in your community that use an electric eye. You may even find one in your home.

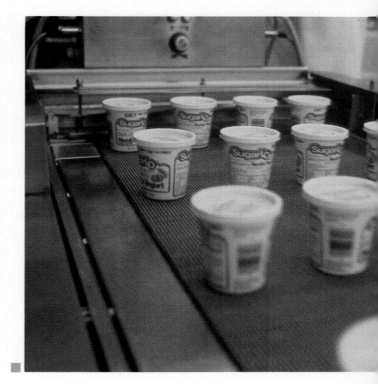

The night game is about to begin. Both teams are waiting in the locker rooms, anxious to play. The cheerleaders, umpires, and fans are ready, too. At home, millions of people surround their televisions waiting for the start. Suddenly, hundreds of lights above the stadium flash on at once. ■ The lights are so powerful that they seem to turn night into day.

Let's look at one of the uses of radiant energy that we are most familiar with—radiant energy used for lighting.

Incandescent Lighting

There are many ways to produce light. Early lamps burned animal fats or oils. By the nineteenth century, lamps that burned gas were common. ● Even now, you may use a gas lamp on a camping trip. ▲ Today, however, most lamps use electric energy.

The most common electric lights in your home are probably **incandescent** (in-kun-DES-unt). Incandescent means "glowing with heat." Earlier you read how an incandescent lamp works. Within the light-bulb is a thin wire, or *filament*. Electricity causes the filament to heat up. In most incandescent bulbs, the filament is made of the substance *tungsten*. Tungsten can be heated to over 2,000°C without melting. When the tungsten filament is heated, it gives off photons of light of all colors. So incandescent bulbs with tungsten filaments generally give off white light. White light is considered best for most home uses, such as reading and lighting rooms and stairways. ●

A clear lightbulb gives off a bright, direct light. If the light shines or is reflected into your eyes it can cause *glare*. Glare can make it difficult to read. It can strain your eyes. A severe glare, such as from the headlight of a car, can make it difficult for a person to see for a short while. To avoid glare, many lightbulbs are coated or frosted. The coating scatters the light as it leaves the bulb. This "soft" light is less likely to cause glare.

Gas-Discharge Lighting

A second type of electric lamp does not use a wire filament. In these lamps electricity is passed through a gas. Such lamps are often called gas-discharge lamps. Gas-discharge lamps are more expensive than incandescent lamps. However, they give off far more light, and they usually last much longer.

Most gas-discharge lamps are too expensive for home use. One kind is used in homes, as well as schools and offices. It has a **fluorescent** (flohr-ES-unt) bulb. Fluorescent bulbs are tube-shaped. ■ They may be long tubes such as those you see in school. Or they may be round tubes such as those you may have at home. Fluorescent bulbs use about one-fifth

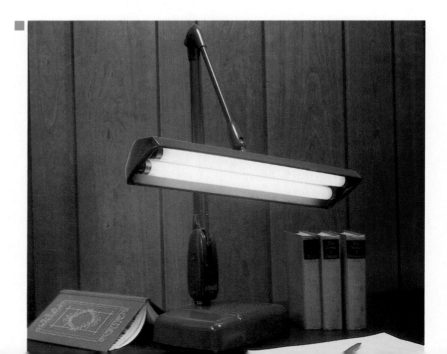

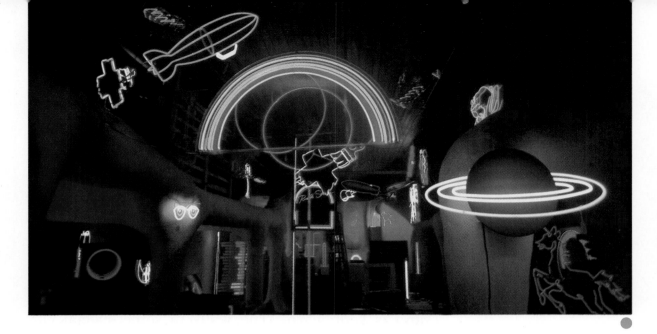

as much electricity as incandescent bulbs to produce the same amount of light. Also, they do not get as hot as incandescent bulbs. Fluorescent lamps are sometimes called "cool" lamps.

When a fluorescent bulb is turned on, an electric current flows through a gas in the bulb. Also in the tube is a very small amount of mercury vapor. The electric current flowing through the gas causes the mercury atoms to become excited. The excited mercury atoms then release photons of ultraviolet light. You know that the human eye cannot see ultraviolet light. So the fluorescent bulb is coated with a special substance called a **phosphor** (FAHS-fur). Phosphors absorb certain kinds of energy and then give off light. In this case, the phosphors absorb ultraviolet light and give off white light.

Neon bulbs are also filled with a gas—neon gas. When an electric current passes through the gas, the neon atoms become excited. Neon atoms do not give off photons of all colors. They give off red light only. However, by using other gases instead of neon, many different colors can be produced. Some people even use such lamps to make sculptures and other works of art. ●

Infrared Light

Think back for a moment to the experiment performed by William Herschel. He discovered infrared light when he saw that the temperature of invisible light from the Sun was higher than that of visible light. Today scientists know that it is mainly the infrared part of light that causes an object to become hotter. For example, it was infrared light that heated the food in the solar cooker.

We can build heat bulbs that produce mainly infrared light. You may have seen infrared bulbs in a restaurant. ■ The food absorbs the infrared light and is kept warm. The walls in some special car-painting rooms are lined with infrared bulbs. When the wet paint on the car absorbs the infrared light, the paint dries quickly.

All objects give off some infrared light. The hotter the object, the more infrared light it gives off. With a special camera and film that is sensitive to infrared light, we can actually "see" how much heat an object gives off. Since objects give off heat during day or night, an infrared camera can take pictures in the dark. It can take pictures through rain and fog as well.

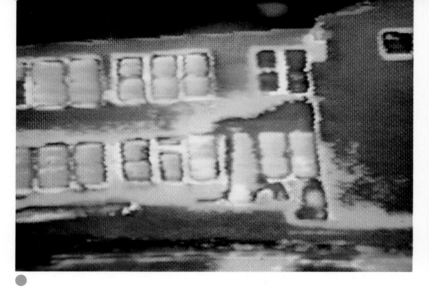

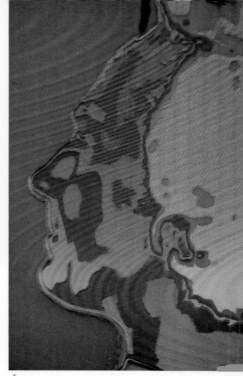

In an infrared photo, bright areas are the hottest and dark areas the coldest. This photo shows where heat is escaping from a house (light areas). ● The owner can then stop the heat loss and save a great deal of energy. Infrared photographs have medical uses, too. A doctor looking at this photo may discover possible diseases, including some kinds of cancer. ▲

Microwaves

Have you ever heard of a microwave oven? These ovens cook much faster than gas or electric ovens. The **microwaves** produced in these ovens are a kind of radio wave.

Microwaves can pass through glass or paper easily. However, they are reflected by metal. So food in a microwave oven must have a glass or paper container. ◆ In this way, the microwaves pass through the container and enter the food. When the microwaves are absorbed by water molecules in the food, the food heats up. Microwaves go deep into the food, heating it equally throughout.

If people are exposed to too much microwave radiation, they can become sick. Microwave ovens are built with special shields to keep the microwaves from leaking out.

Ultraviolet Light

Ultraviolet light is another kind of radiant energy that has many important uses. Ultraviolet light from the Sun helps your skin produce vitamin D. Vitamin D is important for strong bones and teeth. The light from an ultraviolet lamp can increase the amount of vitamin D in milk. ■

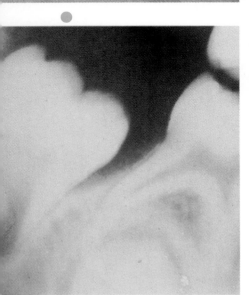

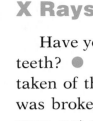

It is the ultraviolet light from the Sun that causes skin to become tanned. Ultraviolet lamps can also cause tanning. Ultraviolet light can damage the eyes, however. So people must always protect their eyes when using a sunlamp. Also, overexposure to ultraviolet light may cause skin cancer. For this reason, many doctors recommend that most people not use sunlamps. They also advise not staying out in the Sun too long at any one time. This is especially true for people with fair skin.

Ultraviolet light can harm other living things. Bacteria, for example, can be killed by ultraviolet light. In many food and drug factories, ultraviolet light is used to keep the product free of bacteria. Ultraviolet light is used to help keep some operating rooms free from bacteria as well.

X Rays

Have you ever had a dentist take a picture of your teeth? ● Perhaps someone you know had pictures taken of the inside of an arm or leg to see if a bone was broken. You probably know that these pictures were not taken with visible light. They were taken with X rays. Remember that X rays have much shorter wavelengths than visible light. They are more energetic as well. X rays can pass through things that visible light cannot pass through. Therefore, X rays have many valuable uses.

An X-ray picture is taken by shooting a beam of X rays through a part of the body. After passing through the body, the X rays strike a piece of film. Some parts of the body such as bones and teeth absorb more X rays than other parts. Bones, then, form a strong shadow on the film. Softer parts of the body form lighter areas on the film. This X ray was taken of a person who complained of stomach pains. ▲ The doctor found that the person had swallowed a coin. Can you find the coin in the photo?

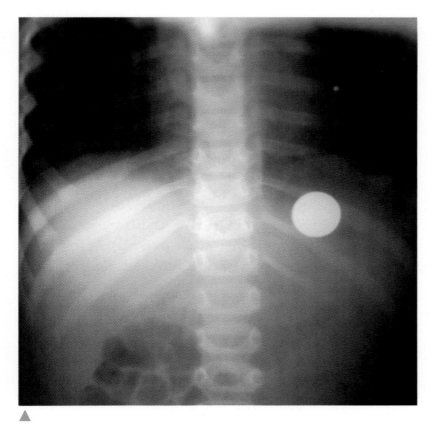

▲

It is dangerous for a person to be exposed to too many X rays in a short time. X rays can cause cancer. Always tell a doctor or dentist about any X rays you have received recently. Anyone who works with X rays a great deal must stand behind a lead shield while the X-ray machine is on. X rays cannot pass through the lead shield.

Lasers

The year is 1969. The place is the Moon. United States astronauts position a curved, reflecting mirror on the ground. ■ Back on Earth, scientists hope the mirror will help them measure the distance from the Earth to the Moon more accurately than ever before. They plan to use a special beam of light called a **laser** beam.

Laser beams are different from other kinds of light. When you turn on a lamp, white light travels in all directions. A laser beam is only one color. If we could look at the laser light, we would see something interesting. In a laser beam of red light, for example, the crests of each light wave are directly in line with the crests of the other waves. ● All the waves in the laser beam, then, are perfectly lined up. The laser beam does not spread out in all directions. It travels in one direction in a narrow beam.

Scientists were able to bounce a narrow laser beam off the mirror on the Moon. They knew the speed of light. So by measuring the time it took for the light to reflect off the mirror and return to Earth, they were able to find the exact distance from the Moon to the Earth.

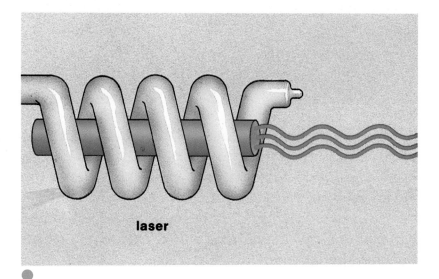

laser

Since the laser beam is so narrow, the light energy from the laser can be aimed at a very tiny spot. A laser beam can cut a precise figure out of this thick steel plate, for example. ▲ Another type of laser beam is so accurate that it is used in the operating room. The laser beam cuts through unhealthy tissue without damaging nearby cells.

Communicating with Light

"One if by land. Two if by sea." Have you heard these words before? They are a part of American history and the tale of the *Midnight Ride of Paul Revere*. By placing lanterns in the steeple of a church, a friend was able to signal which way the British soldiers were coming. Paul Revere then rode off on his horse to warn others.

People have always looked for new and better ways to communicate. Light has long been an important tool of communication. In ancient times, for example, shiny flat objects were used to reflect sunlight. Simple messages, such as "someone is coming," could be sent from place to place. Perhaps you have used mirrors to communicate with your friends. In a similar way, messages are often sent from boat to boat by using lights. ◆

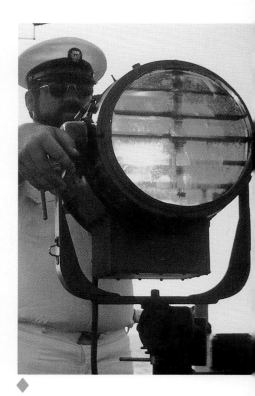

In ancient Africa, in the city of Alexandria, a stone tower over 130 meters high was built. On top of the tower a fire burned to warn sailors that they were approaching the coast. The lighthouse of Alexandria came to be called one of the Seven Wonders of the World. ■ Of course, there are no fires in modern lighthouses. However, the light they send out still carries an important message to sailors on dark, stormy nights. ●

Today, many communication systems use radio waves. Radio waves carry sound messages to your radio. They carry picture and sound messages to your television. However, scientists have now found a way to use laser light to carry messages. Since laser light does not spread out, it can send messages over long distances, even from Earth to space. Laser light may soon replace electricity. This tiny cable contains several fibers that can carry laser light. ▲ Each fiber can send many more phone calls than a large telephone cable.

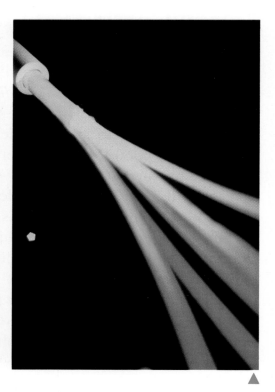

Radar

In the control tower the air traffic controller is watching the screen carefully. ◆ Each tiny blip of light is a plane approaching the airport. Suddenly he sees that two planes are flying too close to each other. He quickly sends a message and the planes change course. Both land safely.

The controller was able to tell the direction of the planes on his screen through the use of **radar.** Although radar equipment can be very complex, the basic idea is not. With radar, radio waves are sent out by a large, dish-shaped antenna. ★ When the radio waves strike a moving object, such as a plane, they are reflected. The waves that bounce back toward the antenna are collected and displayed on the radar screen as blips of light. By measuring the time it takes for the radio waves to reach an object and return, we can find how far away the object is. Also, by measuring the angle of the radio waves when they return, the location of the object can be found.

Boats also have radar. At night, in fog, or in stormy weather, the captain uses radar to steer around other boats, hidden reefs, and even icebergs. Many police cars have small radar sets to check for speeding cars. Weather forecasters use radar to check weather conditions in their area, especially the location of clouds. Radar is important for space travel, too. Radar on Earth tracks satellites in orbit around our planet, as well as satellites sent to other planets.

233

On a separate sheet of paper, write each statement with the best ending.

1. To avoid glare, many incandescent bulbs
   a. use little electricity
   b. are frosted
   c. are filled with gas

2. In a restaurant, food is kept warm by
   a. red light   b. infrared light
   c. X rays

3. Microwaves are a form of
   a. invisible light   b. X rays
   c. radio waves

4. The amount of vitamin D in milk is increased if the milk is exposed to
   a. infrared light
   b. ultraviolet light   c. X rays

5. The statement that fits the *main* concept of this section is:
   a. Every form of radiant energy has important uses.
   b. Visible light is the only really important type of radiant energy.

YOU CAN DISCOVER

The light from the Sun is white light. However, at sunset we may see different colors in the sky. ■   See if you can discover how white sunlight can form such beautiful sunsets.

Special Effects

Sometimes images are deceiving. Think of a movie where cartoon characters walk hand in hand with live actors. You know that what you are seeing isn't real. Yet you probably don't know how your eyes were fooled. It is the job of the special-effects person to make the unreal seem real on the screen.

Some special-effects people work in carpentry, building tables that collapse and doors that break easily. Some are artists. This person is painting a scene on a pane of glass. ■ Later, film with live actors will be placed over the glass. When you see the shot it will look like the actors are actually in the painting.

Special-effects people may be asked to build a monster attacking a miniature city or alien rocketships. Some models are large and others can fit into the palm of a hand. ● Although the ship looks like it is speeding through space in the movies, it never even moves. Instead, a special camera moves around the model.

Special-effects people can create laser beams shooting through the air, boats sinking in icy waters, or a gorilla atop a skyscraper. ▲ Special-effects people work behind the scenes. Their rewards are the cheers and shouts from people caught up in the imaginary world they create.

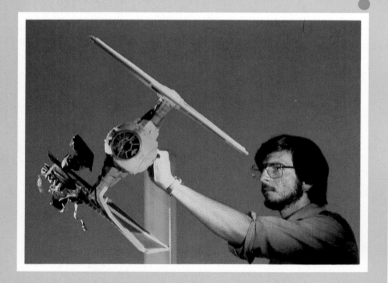

✓ Light reflected off a smooth, shiny surface is reflected in an orderly way. ■ An image forms.

✓ Light reflected off a rough object is scattered.

✓ When light passes through an object, it may be bent or refracted.

✓ Lenses refract light in an orderly way. A convex lens focuses light through a point. Convex lenses are used in cameras, microscopes, movie projectors, and the eye.

✓ A prism refracts light into a band of colors. Sometimes a drop of water, or many drops of water, can do the same. ●

✓ An atom can absorb energy and become excited. It may then release the energy as radiant energy. Radiant energy is made up of photons. Photons are tiny bundles of energy.

✓ Visible light is a form of radiant energy. It is made up of a spectrum of colors. ▲

✓ Ultraviolet and infrared light are invisible. X rays and radio waves are also radiant energy. Wherever we find any form of radiant energy, we know that an excited atom has given off photons.

✓ This leads us to yet another important concept: **When radiant energy is given off, one form of energy has been changed into another.**

✓ Photons of different kinds of radiant energy have different amounts of energy. X rays have the most energetic photons. The photons of radio waves have the least energy.

✓ Sometimes a stream of photons may act as a wave. We can measure the wavelength of radiant energy. X rays have the shortest wavelengths and radio waves the longest.

✓ You have come then to a second important concept:

X rays, visible light, and all other forms of radiant energy are basically alike and travel at the same speed. They differ only in the size of their wavelengths and the energy of their photons.

✓ Scientists have found many ways to use radiant energy as a tool—from X rays to laser beams. In the future we can expect new and better ways of using radiant energy.

A. CHOOSE THE BEST ANSWER.

1. When light bounces off an object, we say it is
   a. refracted   b. reflected   c. absorbed

2. A mirror that is curved outward is
   a. concave   b. convex   c. flat

3. The lining of the eye onto which light is focused is the
   a. iris   b. retina   c. pupil

4. All of the following are forms of radiant energy *except*
   a. sound waves   b. light waves   c. X rays

5. The top of a wave is called the
   a. wavelength   b. valley   c. crest

6. In an electric eye, light acts as a
   a. wave   b. particle   c. mirror

7. The wavelength of visible light is longest for
   a. red light   b. violet light   c. orange light

8. At an airport, radar equipment tracks the paths of planes with
   a. radio waves   b. light waves   c. X rays

9. The photons of radiant energy that have the least energy are
   a. ultraviolet light   b. X rays   c. radio waves

10. The statement that fits the *main* concept of this unit is:
    a. Whenever radiant energy is released, one form of energy has been changed to another.
    b. Visible light, X rays, and radio waves are very different kinds of energy.

B. ANSWER THESE QUESTIONS.

1. Why can you see your reflection in still water but not in choppy water?

2. A mirage is an image of an object that is not really there. Yet we can still photograph the mirage. Explain why.

3. How is your eye like a camera?

4. In a way, a red balloon is really every color except red. Explain what that statement means.

5. Discuss evidence for both the wave and particle nature of light.

Find Out More

Drawings like this are part of a test for colorblindness. 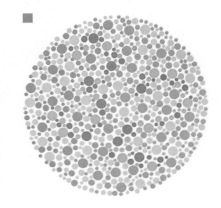 Most colorblind people have trouble seeing the difference between certain colors, such as red and green. They would not see the number in the drawing.

You know that light is focused through the lens in your eye onto the retina. Find out what part of the retina helps us see colors. What part helps us see black and white?

Challenge Your Thinking

Look carefully at the shadows formed by two wood poles. 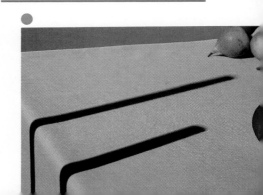 You might think that one pole is much bigger than the other. They are actually the same size. How can that be?

Energy from the Stars

Joyce and her friends are camping in her backyard. They like sleeping under the stars. Joyce begins to tell a story. She has just finished reading *The Time Machine* by H. G. Wells. She tells her friends how the hero has many adventures in a time machine.

The others are excited by the story. Mary says she would like to travel into the future. Laura says she would rather go back in time and visit the past, maybe even to the time when the dinosaurs lived. Joyce announces that they can't go back in time, but she does know a way they can *look* back in time.

"What!" shouts Mary.

"How?" asks Laura.

"Easy," answers Joyce. "Just open your eyes and look up."

What did Joyce mean? Can you really look back in time by looking at the stars? What else can the light from the stars teach us? Read on and find out.

241

Your home is a medium-sized planet. It's name, of course, is planet Earth. The Earth and the other eight planets in our solar system revolve around the Sun.

Our Sun is but one of countless stars in the sky. A great many stars have been discovered and recorded throughout history. Astronomers assume that some of these stars also have planets, but they are not sure. How can we count so many stars and not be able to find any more planets?

Stars produce and give off radiant energy. Our Sun, for example, produces tremendous amounts of radiant energy every second. The energy from the Sun lights the Earth. It heats the Earth as well. The Earth, however, does not produce radiant energy. Neither do any of the other planets. We can detect stars, even stars great distances away, because of the energy they give off. Since planets do not produce radiant energy, we cannot see planets outside our own solar system.

Studying the Stars

Since they first looked up at the night sky, people have wondered about the stars. When people wonder about something, they usually try to find an explanation for it. Ancient people didn't have tools to study the sky. They used only their eyes. Yet they built *observatories*—places where they could observe the stars. This observatory was built by the Mayans in Mexico over a thousand years ago. ■ Stonehenge, in England, may have been an ancient observatory, too. ●

After years of observing, people could identify stars and predict when they would appear. They learned a great deal from the stars. Farmers planted their crops when certain stars appeared. Travelers used the stars to guide them on their journeys. In time, people gave names to stars and groups of stars that appeared together. Some groups of stars were given the names of figures from mythology. These groups of stars are called **constellations.**

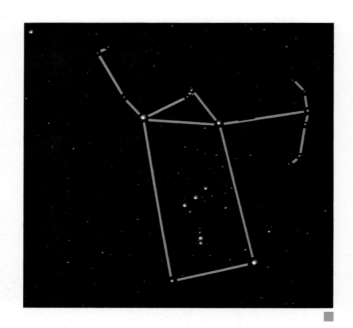

Here is the constellation *Orion*. ■ Orion was a mighty hunter who was said to be able to walk on land or water. This is what Orion looked like to ancient civilizations. ● Notice the three bright stars that form Orion's belt. Orion is holding a club and uses a lion's skin as a shield. Orion, according to legend, used the club and shield to fight the bull in the constellation *Taurus*. Here we see Taurus, just as it was observed thousands of years ago. ▲ Can you see why it was named the Bull? ◆

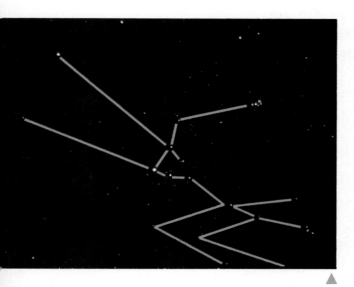

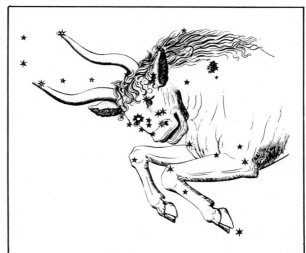

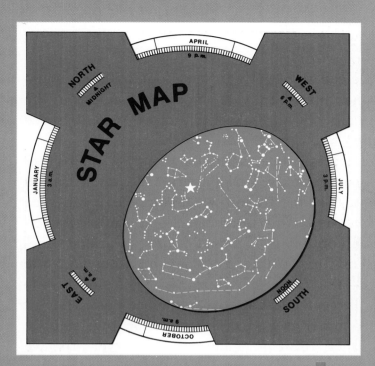

STAR MAP

Finding Your Way with the Stars

To find your way on land, you might use a street map. To find your way on water, you could use a star map. This map shows the stars you can see in the Northern Hemisphere. ■ In the center is the North Star. The North Star is at the end of the handle of a constellation called the Little Dipper. The position of the stars changes from hour to hour, and month to month as the Earth moves. Can you figure out how to work the star map?

Since ancient times, navigators have used the stars to find their way at sea. Early sailors learned that if they could figure out the angle of known stars above the horizon, they could pinpoint exactly where they were. Sailors first used an *astrolabe* (AS-truh-labe) to figure out the approximate angle of the stars. ● Later, the astrolabe was replaced by the *sextant* (SEK-stunt), an instrument that accurately measures the angle of stars. Today, ships still have star maps and sextants. They also have radios and computers to help sailors find their way.

245

Telescopes on Earth

On a clear night you can see about 2,500 stars just by looking up at the sky. ■   Suppose you look at the sky with a powerful tool—a telescope. You might see something like this. ●

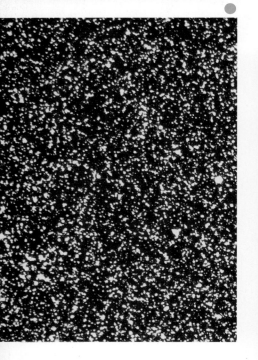

The telescope reveals many more stars, doesn't it? It has been estimated that there are over a billion billion stars in the Universe. Of course, we can't see all those stars with a telescope. Even the largest telescope can only look at a part of the sky at one time.

High on top of Mount Palomar in California is the Big Eye—the Hale telescope. ▲   It is one of the world's largest telescopes of its type. Let's visit it. The astronomer greets us. The telescope towers above us. To reach the cage where the observer sits, we enter an elevator and go up eight stories. We are near the top of the telescope and inside it.

In the Hale telescope, a huge mirror almost four times your height collects light from the stars. Such a mirror collects far more light from a distant star than your eye can. The Hale telescope can "see" the fainter stars that your eye cannot.

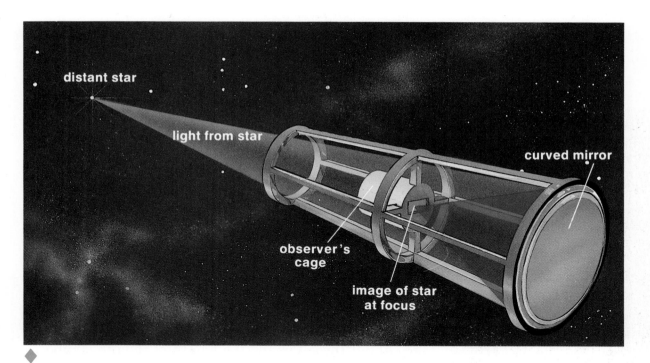

distant star

light from star

curved mirror

observer's cage

image of star at focus

◆ The giant mirror in the Hale telescope is concave. As you know, a concave mirror reflects light to a focal point. Find the focal point in the diagram of the Hale telescope. ◆ Suppose you were to hold a piece of paper at the focus. You would see an image of the star on the paper. However, the image would be very small indeed. The eyepiece inside the observer's cage magnifies the image of the star. By placing film at the focus, the stars can be photographed.

Telescopes that use concave mirrors to reflect light are called **reflecting telescopes.** The larger the mirror, the more powerful the reflecting telescope. Yet large mirrors are very difficult and expensive to make. A new kind of reflecting telescope uses many small mirrors. A telescope of this kind sits on top of Mount Hopkins in Arizona. ★

Telescopes that use lenses instead of mirrors are called **refracting telescopes.** Recall that light is re-fracted as it passes through a lens. You can build a simple refracting telescope with two convex lenses.

ACTIVITY

★

Making a Refracting Telescope

You can use: 2 convex lenses (magnifying lenses will do), 2 cardboard tubes (one should fit tightly inside the other), clear tape, scissors

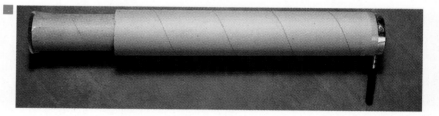

1 First cut the smaller cardboard tube so that it is about three-fourths the length of the other tube. The smaller tube should fit tightly inside the larger tube, but not so tightly that it cannot move in and out.

2 Carefully pick up one convex lens. (*Note:* If one of your lenses is thicker than the other, use the thicker lens.) Make sure the lens does not have any smudges of dirt on it. Then fit the lens into one end of the larger cardboard tube. Try not to touch the curved part of the lens with your fingers. Use the tape to attach the lens securely. Make sure the tape does not cover the lens.

3 Now attach the second lens to the smaller tube. Fit the smaller tube into the large one so that each end of the telescope contains a lens. ■

4 Look through the smaller end of your telescope at an object that is far away. ● Can you see it clearly? If not, twist the smaller tube in or out until the object is in focus. **Caution:** Never look at the Sun or any bright object with a telescope. You could burn your eyes, even if you look for a very short time.

The Space Telescope

Before light from the stars reaches an observer on Earth, it passes through the Earth's atmosphere. The atmosphere reflects much of the light back into space. It also scatters some of the light. So most of the large telescopes on Earth are built near the tops of tall mountains, above as much of the atmosphere as possible. In this way, scientists can collect more light from space. Also, the light from cities and towns does not enter the telescope.

This is NASA's space telescope. ■ It will be carried outside the Earth's atmosphere by the Space Shuttle. ● It will allow astronomers to see dim and distant objects. The space telescope will be able to see stars that the most powerful telescopes on Earth cannot see. Some scientists believe that with the space telescope we will even see out to the very edge of the Universe.

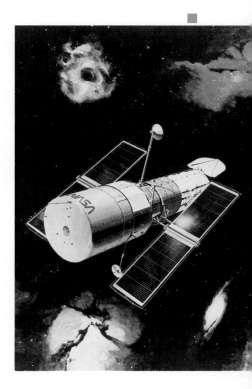

Telescopes are powerful tools. They magnify objects. They also show faint objects. Now let's look at a few of the objects in the sky we have found since telescopes were first invented.

Algol

dark companion

Binary Stars

Long ago Arab shepherds noticed that about every three days one bright star became faint. The Arabs were fearful of this winking star. So they called it *Algol,* the demon. Why does Algol shine steadily for almost three days, become fainter, then brighten again? It took many years to solve this mystery.

Algol has a companion. Algol and its companion star circle around a common center. The companion is much dimmer than Algol. Compared to Algol it is dark. How does this dark star make Algol seem to grow dark? Here's a clue. ■

Two stars circling around a common center are called **binary stars.** (Binary means having two parts.) Sometimes, such as with Algol, the companion appears dim. In other binary stars, both are bright stars. With the aid of telescopes, we have discovered a great many binary stars.

The star closest to Earth, after our Sun, is *Alpha Centauri.* Alpha Centauri was seen by ancient peoples. You can see it today as well. If you could somehow travel to Alpha Centauri, you would see that it is not one star at all. In fact, it is not even a binary star. Alpha Centauri is really three stars. Two are bright, one is dim. Scientists know that many stars, like Alpha Centauri, are multiple stars.

Galaxies

Peter and his classmates are on a class trip to a nearby observatory. Inside, the astronomer asks who would like to look first. Peter quickly raises his hand. He thinks he knows what to expect—a few stars in more detail than he can see with his eyes alone. Peter is in for a shock. When he looks through the telescope, his eye is flooded with light from a giant cluster of stars. ● In the center there are so many stars he cannot tell one from another. Swirling from the center are thin fingers reaching out into the dark of space.

The astronomer explains that stars are not spread evenly in space. They are grouped into clusters called galaxies. A **galaxy** is a large group of stars, as well as the planets, gases, and other objects around those stars. A large galaxy may contain trillions of stars. Even a small galaxy may have several billion.

Our Sun and almost all the stars you can see without a telescope are in the Milky Way Galaxy. ■ If you could somehow travel far into space and look at the Milky Way, you would see that it is shaped something like a pancake with a bulge in the middle. Spreading out from the bulge are long, spiral arms like the spokes in a pinwheel. The Milky Way is a *spiral galaxy*. Our Sun lies near the edge of the spiral. Astronomers have found and photographed many other spiral galaxies much like the Milky Way. They have also found other galaxies that have a variety of shapes, such as ellipses. ●

All the stars in galaxies are on the move. They revolve around the center of the galaxy. Even our Sun is revolving around the center bulge in the Milky Way. Does it surprise you that our Sun moves through space? Actually, all objects in space are in constant movement. Moons revolve around planets. Planets revolve around stars. Stars revolve around the centers of galaxies. Do galaxies also move through space? What is your prediction?

Galaxies are spread throughout the Universe. Between most galaxies there is mainly empty space. We do not know how many galaxies there are. Several million have been discovered. Scientists believe there may be many billions of galaxies, each with billions of stars. ▲ Are you beginning to get some idea of the enormous size of the Universe?

Nebulae

Between the stars and planets there may be a huge cloud. This cloud, made of dust and gas, is called a **nebula** (NEB-yuh-luh). Some nebulae are ring-shaped. ◆ Can you see why this nebula is called the Horsehead Nebula? ★

You may think of the Universe as being very old. Yet new stars are forming and old stars are dying off all the time. The new stars may form from the gases of a nebula. Some nebulae are so large they contain enough gas to form over 100,000 new stars.

▲

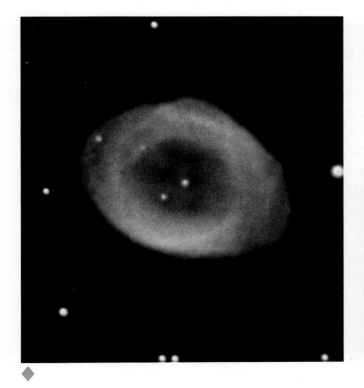

◆

★

On a separate sheet of paper, write each statement with the best ending.

1. On a clear night, the unaided eye can see about
   a. 2,500 stars   b. a million stars
   c. many billions of stars

2. Groups of stars given the names of figures from mythology are called
   a. constellations   b. galaxies
   c. nebulae

3. Since the Hale telescope uses a mirror, it is a
   a. refracting telescope
   b. multiple mirror telescope
   c. reflecting telescope

4. The Milky Way is an example of
   a. a nebula
   b. an elliptical galaxy
   c. a spiral galaxy

5. The statement that fits the *main* concept of this section is:
   a. Stars are spread evenly throughout space.
   b. Stars are clustered into groups in space.

YOU CAN DISCOVER

Some constellations have come to be known as the signs of the zodiac. Every person, depending on the date he or she is born, falls under a sign of the zodiac. For example, people born between December 22 and January 19 are born under the sign of Capricorn, the goat. ■ Find out what sign you were born under and try to draw the stars in the constellation.

2 ▶ A New Way of Looking

In 1930 a young scientist was given an assignment. He was asked to find what caused the static in radio messages sent to ships at sea. The young scientist, Karl Jansky, built a special antenna. ● He listened to the static from nearby storms, and from far off storms. He heard something else, too. He heard sounds from beyond the Earth. In fact, the sounds he heard were coming from outside the solar system. What did he hear?

Light, as you know, is a kind of radiant energy made up of photons. Excited atoms can give off photons of light. They can also give off photons of another kind—radio waves. In space, some objects do give off both light and radio waves. It was these radio waves that Karl Jansky picked up.

Radio Telescopes

Doesn't it sound exciting to listen to radio waves from space? Strangely enough, few people were interested in what Jansky discovered. However, a young engineer, Grote Reber, wanted to learn more about the discovery. He built an antenna in his backyard. The antenna was shaped like a dish. ▲ It could collect and focus radio waves from space. A new science—*radio astronomy*—began.

Reber's antenna was the first **radio telescope.** Today, there are radio telescopes all over the world.

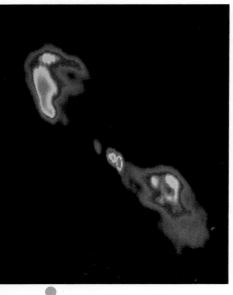

This giant one is in Puerto Rico. ■ It can be aimed at a large part of the sky. The radio waves from space are focused at the center of the radio telescope. They produce electrical signals that can be recorded and printed by a computer as wavy lines on paper. Often they are placed over a photograph of the same area taken through a light telescope. These "radio maps" of space can help astronomers learn more about the area they are studying. The computer can do even more. The computer can use the signals from the antenna to draw a picture of the place sending the radio waves. ●

Radio Waves from Stars

Many stars give off radio waves as well as visible light. Our Sun, for example, gives off radio waves. However, with the radio telescope, we discovered that some stars give off only radio waves. These *radio stars* are invisible to our eyes. They would never have been discovered with light telescopes alone. Thus, the radio telescope and the light telescope are both important tools of the astronomer. With these new tools, we can get a new picture of the universe.

In 1967 a very different kind of star was discovered. This star gave off radio waves in "beeps," or pulses, every few seconds. These **pulsars** (PUL-sahrs) send out beams of radio waves at regular intervals. Scientists are not exactly sure what causes a pulsar. One theory says that the pulsar is a small, spinning star. Like a rotating beacon, it sends out radio waves in much the same way a lighthouse sends out a beam of light. ▲ Every time a pulsar is aimed toward Earth, a pulse of radio waves is beamed in our direction.

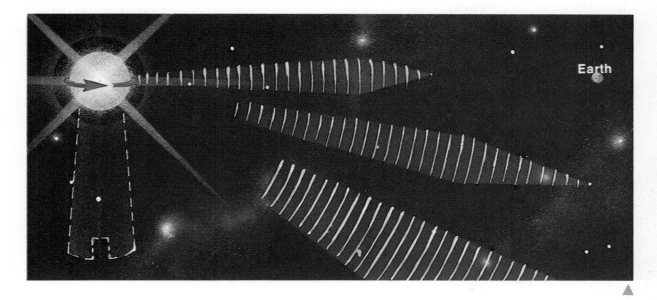

Radio Waves from Galaxies

Using the radio telescope, astronomers discovered that there are large galaxies that give off mainly radio waves. They named them *radio galaxies*. However, the discovery of radio galaxies did not prepare astronomers for another astonishing find. In the early 1960's the radio telescope was turned toward deep space.

Near the very edge of the Universe an unbelievably powerful source of radio waves was found. This same radio source, called a **quasar** (KWAY-zahr), could also give off tremendous amounts of light. ■ Could quasars be individual stars? Some quasars give off more energy than 10 trillion of our Suns combined. It did not seem likely that one star could give off so much energy.

Even today quasars are not well understood. Many scientists believe they are actually entire galaxies, perhaps the beginnings of new galaxies.

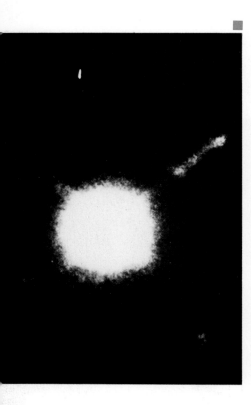

Radio Waves from Satellites

Stars are not the only objects that give off radio waves in space. This magnificent photograph of Saturn was sent to Earth through radio waves. ● The photograph was taken by the Voyager spacecraft as it passed by the planet. In 1986 Voyager passed the planet Uranus. From this far-off place, the spacecraft again sent back photographs and information through radio waves.

In the last unit you read how radio waves used in radar can track satellites as they pass through space. Now we see that radio waves are also the way satellites send information to Earth. Clearly, radio waves from space have helped us understand the nature of the Universe in a great many ways.

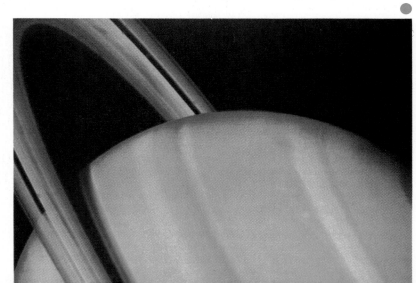

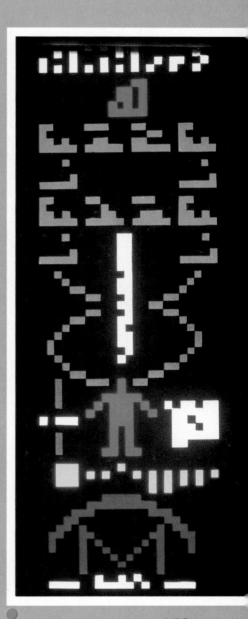

A Message to the Stars

In about 25,000 years, a radio message sent from Earth will reach this cluster of stars. ▪ Suppose there is life on a planet circling one of these stars. If they have a radio telescope pointed in our direction, then the message may be picked up and read.

The message uses a mathematical language. Decoded, it looks like this. ● On top is a simple lesson in mathematics. Then a code for hydrogen, carbon, nitrogen, oxygen, and phosphorus shows the basic elements needed by life as we know it. A stick figure of a human shows what we look like. Next is information about the location of our planet and our solar system. The message ends with a picture of the radio telescope from which the message was sent.

Since the message will take thousands of years to arrive, we can't expect an answer for at least that long. But one day, a radio message from space may reach Earth. The message could be from neighbors that are billions upon billions of kilometers away. If such a day comes, we will know that life exists on other planets.

259

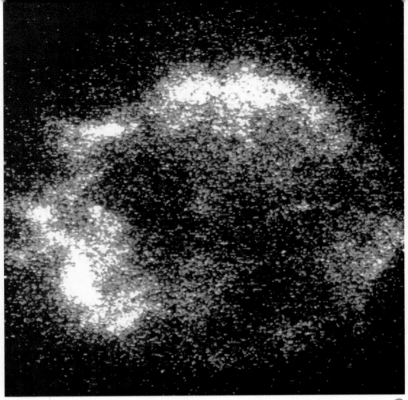

X Rays from Space

Since stars give off visible light and radio waves, many scientists believed for a long time that some stars might give off X rays as well. X rays, remember, are another kind of radiant energy made up of a stream of photons. How could X rays from space be detected since they cannot pass through our atmosphere?

In 1978 the Einstein Observatory satellite was launched into space. ■ This satellite contains a telescope that collects X rays. This photograph from an X-ray telescope shows bright, new stars in a gas cloud or nebula. ● The photograph adds new evidence for the theory that stars begin in a nebula. X rays from space have been discovered from a great many sources. Quasars, for example, are extremely powerful sources of X rays. Stars like our Sun also give off some X rays. The X-ray telescope is another important tool of the astronomer.

On a separate sheet of paper, write each statement with the best ending.

1. Grote Reber built the first
   a. refracting telescope
   b. X-ray telescope
   c. radio telescope

2. A source of tremendous amounts of energy near the edge of the universe is a
   a. pulsar   b. quasar   c. nebula

3. The Einstein Observatory satellite studies space by collecting
   a. radio waves   b. X rays
   c. visible light

4. A star that sends out beams of radio waves at regular intervals is a
   a. pulsar   b. binary star
   c. quasar

5. The statement that fits the *main* concept of this section is:
   a. Stars give off mainly visible light.
   b. Stars give off many kinds of radiant energy.

YOU CAN DISCOVER

In 1955 astronomers were surprised to discover that the planet Jupiter is a powerful source of radio waves from space. ▲ Jupiter is made up mainly of gases. It is often called a gas giant. Find out if there are any other gas giant planets in our solar system. Do any of them give off radio waves?

3 ▷ A Ruler to the Stars

If you wanted to measure the distance from the top of this page to the bottom, you would probably reach for a ruler. It is marked off in units, such as centimeters. You must have used one often.

Rulers Using Time

You use different kinds of rulers for measuring distance. Sometimes you measure distance in units of length, such as kilometers. Sometimes you measure distance in units of time, such as minutes, days, and years.

For example, you may say that a certain town is 50 kilometers away. You may also say that the same town is an hour away. Of course, you mean that a bus (or car) would reach it in about an hour. When you speak of distance in this way, you are using a ruler that measures a distance in units of time.

People often make use of this "time" ruler. "How far do you live from school?" asks one student. "Oh, about a 5-minute walk," says the other. In other words, the distance from school to home is about 5 walking-minutes. The distance from New York to London is about 6,000 kilometers, or 6½ jet-hours—the distance a jet plane can travel in 6½ hours. ■

The distance to the Sun is 150 million kilometers. We could also measure the distance to the Sun with the time ruler. Suppose you walk at a normal speed.

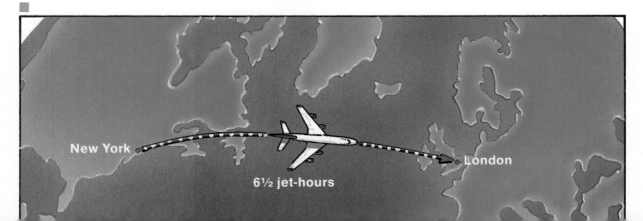

New York   6½ jet-hours   London

Then it would take about 23 million hours to walk from the Earth to the Sun! This is about 1 million days. Thus, it would be correct to say that the distance to the Sun, from where you are on the Earth, is about 1 million walking-days.

A walking-day is not a very good unit to use, is it? Distances in space are very great. Astronomers need a ruler for measuring distances in space that would give smaller numbers, if possible. In fact, astronomers have made such a ruler.

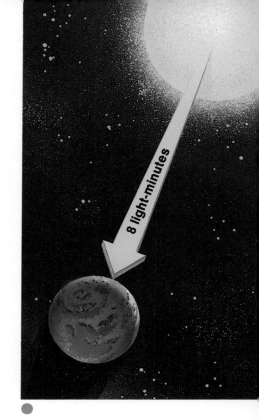

A Ruler Made of Light

You flip a light switch. Light reaches all parts of the room at once. You push the switch on a powerful flashlight. The beam of light hits its distant target at once.

Light seems to take no time at all to get somewhere. Yet light does take some time to travel. Light travels so fast, however, that we cannot notice the time. Light travels at the speed of about 300,000 kilometers in 1 second. In fact, all forms of radiant energy, including radio waves and X rays, travel at this same speed.

How fast is the speed of light? It is hard to imagine. Try this. Say "one hundred and one" slowly. It takes about one second to say it. In that time, light can travel more than seven times around the Earth!

Light from the Sun takes almost 8 minutes to reach the Earth. We can say, then, that the Earth is 8 light-minutes from the Sun. ● It takes about 4 minutes longer for sunlight to reach Mars. So Mars is about 12 light-minutes from the Sun. By the time sunlight has reached the ninth planet, Pluto, almost 300 minutes have passed. Pluto is about 300 light-minutes from the Sun. The numbers are getting bigger, but we can still work with them.

After we leave our solar system, we find that the next nearest star system is Alpha Centauri. Alpha Centauri is about 270,000 times as far away from us as the Sun. The distance from the Earth to Alpha Centauri is about 2,200,000 light-minutes. This is the distance that light travels in 2,200,000 minutes.

Now we are getting into even larger numbers. We can get around this, though, by using a larger unit of time than minutes. Astronomers have decided to use a *year* as the unit of time. As a ruler for measuring great distances in space, astronomers use the **light-year.** A light-year is the distance light travels in one year—about 9½ trillion kilometers.

A Trip to the Stars

What is the distance to Alpha Centauri in light-years? Alpha Centauri is 4⅓ light-years from the Earth. That is, it takes light 4⅓ years to travel the distance from Alpha Centauri to Earth. This is certainly an easier number to work with than the distance in light-minutes. Perhaps it is easier to imagine, too. If you could travel in a spaceship at the speed of light, it would take you about 4 years and 4 months to reach Alpha Centauri.

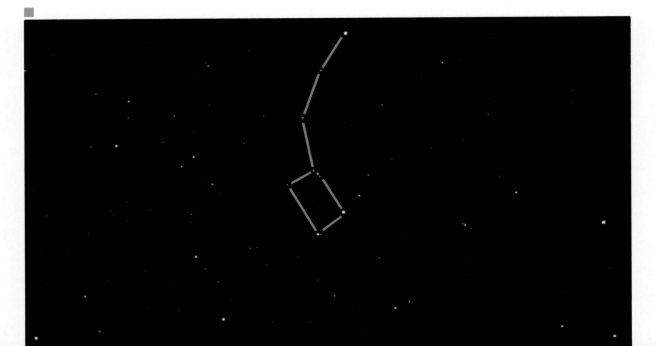

Such a trip seems incredibly long, and by Earth standards it is. But in space, 4 light-years is practically around the corner. The dog star, *Sirius*, for example, is over 8 light-years away from Earth. The next time you can look at the sky on a clear night, see if you can find the North Star. The North Star, remember, is part of the Little Dipper. ■ It takes light from the North Star over 680 years to reach Earth.

Our solar system is in the Milky Way Galaxy. We are about 30,000 light-years from the center of the galaxy and about 20,000 light-years from the outer edge. How large is the Milky Way itself? Traveling at the speed of light, it would take you over 100,000 years to cross our Milky Way Galaxy from end to end. In other words, the distance across the Milky Way Galaxy is 100,000 light-years. ● It doesn't seem like anything can be that big, does it? Yet you will find that in the vast Universe even those distances are not very large at all.

A Trip to Other Galaxies

Light from stars in the Milky Way must travel a long way before it reaches another galaxy. The closest galaxies to Earth are the *Magellanic Clouds*. ■ The Magellanic Clouds are about 200,000 light-years from Earth. The closest large galaxy is *Andromeda*. ● If you were to visit Andromeda in a spaceship traveling at the speed of light, it would take you over 2 million years to get there. It would take another 2 million years to return. It seems likely that the world you left, however, would be very different from the world to which you return.

Most of the galaxies in our part of the Universe are similar to the Milky Way. As we get farther away from the Milky Way we begin to find the large radio galaxies. If we go even farther, we finally reach the quasars. Recall that astronomers believe quasars may be on the very edge of the Universe. How far away are the quasars? Although it is difficult, if not impossible, to imagine such numbers, quasars seem to be about 10 billion light-years from Earth. After a journey across the entire Universe, taking 10 billion years, light and radio waves from quasars reach the Earth and are collected by telescopes.

4 ▶ Studying Starlight

To find out what a cake is made of, you take a bit of it and test it. How? It's easy. You simply put a piece in your mouth. To find out what the Earth is made of, you can follow a similar procedure. You can take bits of the Earth—the rocks and minerals that make up the Earth—and test them. You can learn about the different substances of Earth.

It is not quite as simple to test objects in space. Sometimes, of course, an object will fall to Earth as a meteorite. ● Then we can do tests to learn what the meteorite is made of. Also, with the help of spacecraft, we can travel to a neighbor in space. Astronauts have landed on the Moon and have brought back samples of the Moon to study. ▲

We have no spacecraft that can travel to our Sun or distant stars. Even if we did, we could not bring back bits of the Sun to study. However, even without the help of spacecraft we have discovered what the Sun and other stars are made of. To do so, we have studied starlight.

Colors in a Flame

Scientists have been able to predict what makes up the stars by observing how certain elements respond to a flame test. They know that different elements produce different colors when heated. So, they can use a flame test to help them learn about stars.

In a flame test, a scientist covers the wet tip of a spoon with the powder to be tested. The spoon is then held in a flame and the powder burns. Normally, the flame from a hot gas burner is a blue color. However, as some powders burn, the flame may be one of many colors such as red, yellow, and purple. The color of the flame can help the scientist determine the elements that make up the powder.

Table salt, the salt that is sometimes added to food, is made up of two elements—sodium and chloride. When salt is burned in a flame test, the flame appears yellow. ■

Another compound, potassium chloride, will produce a different color in a flame test. The element potassium causes the flame to burn a purple color. ● Lithium chloride is a compound that produces yet another color. A red flame is produced when this compound is burned. ▲

270

Fingerprints of the Elements

Sodium chloride heated in the blue flame of a burner produces a yellow flame. This yellow flame is one way of recognizing the element sodium.

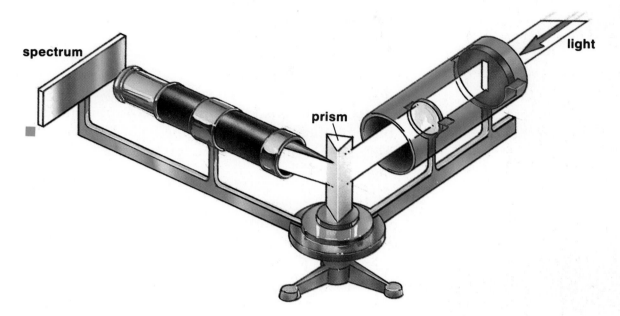

You can then send the yellow light from the flame through a **spectroscope** (SPEK-truh-skohp). ■ The main part of most spectroscopes is a prism. As you may recall, a prism separates white light into a band of colors, or a spectrum. When the yellow light goes through the spectroscope, you see two thin yellow lines. ● Sodium always produces these same two lines in a spectroscope. They are, in a way, the fingerprints of the element sodium.

● Not all spectroscopes have a prism. In a simple spectroscope, a piece of plastic called a diffraction grating can also be used to study light. *ACTIVITY*

Making a Simple Spectroscope

You can use: diffraction grating about 2½ cm square, shoe box, aluminum foil, single-edge razor blade, scissors

1 You can make your own simple spectroscope. In one end of the box, cut a small hole. Tape a small piece of aluminum foil over the hole. Then carefully slice a thin slit in the foil about 2½ centimeters long.

2 At the other end of the box, cut another hole about the size of your diffraction grating. Tape the grating over the hole. ■ Make sure the grating and the slit in the foil are opposite each other.

3 Put the lid on the box. To use the spectroscope, look through the diffraction grating and aim the slit at a light source. ● A light bulb that is not frosted is a good choice. Stand about 1 meter from the light.

4 What do you see when you aim your spectroscope at an unfrosted bulb? What other sources of light can you examine? **Caution:** Never aim the spectroscope directly at the Sun.

What Stars Are Made Of

Most substances can be turned into gases by heating them. When the gas is heated enough, it gives off light. If you examine that light through a spectroscope, you will find something astonishing. *Each element has its own spectrum.* Here is the spectrum of the element neon, for example. ■ This is the fingerprint of neon. The color and location of the lines in the spectrum of every element is unique.

What has this to do with the stars? Well, let's take our Sun, for example. The Sun is so hot that all the substances in it are hot, glowing gases. If a spectroscope is aimed at the Sun, many different lines appear in many different places. Among these lines, the astronomer can recognize the spectra of substances we know. In this spectrum of the Sun, the dark lines match the colored lines that are seen in the spectra of elements on Earth. ● By our study of the Sun's spectrum, then, we can tell what the Sun is made of.

Astronomers have found that our Sun and most of the other stars are made up mainly of the elements hydrogen and helium. The spectroscope also shows that there are small amounts of other elements such as aluminum, tin, and iron in our Sun. In fact, over 70 different elements found on Earth have been discovered in the Sun.

Star Colors

The stars in the night sky look like points of white light. Our Sun, of course, is a star, too. However, it often seems to have a yellow color. Is it possible that other stars have colors, too? If so, are they all yellow like our Sun?

Actually, people have known for a very long time that stars are not all yellow in color. With complex instruments like the telescope and spectroscope, today's astronomers have found stars in a wide variety of colors. ■

The star *Rigel*, for example, in the left leg of Orion shines with a blue light. Most of the other stars in Orion are blue-white stars. However, one star in Orion shines with a deep red color. Still other stars appear to be white, and orange stars, too, are not uncommon. Stars, it seems, are not all the same by any means.

The Temperature of Stars

The Sun is a great distance from the Earth—150 million kilometers away. Yet scientists know how hot it is on the Sun's surface. The temperature of the surface of the Sun is about 6,000 degrees Celsius. How can scientists on far-off Earth determine this temperature?

Scientists can determine the temperature of the surface of the Sun and other stars by observing materials on Earth. For example, a metal paperclip will change when it is held in a hot flame.

As the metal gets hot, its color changes. ● In a very hot flame, the metal may go from bright red to yellow and then to white-hot. As the temperature changes, so does the color of a hot object. This is true for all objects. The color of a heated object, then, can help reveal its temperature.

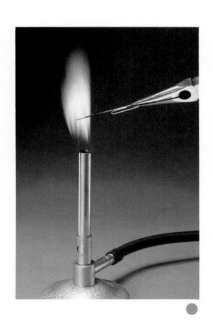

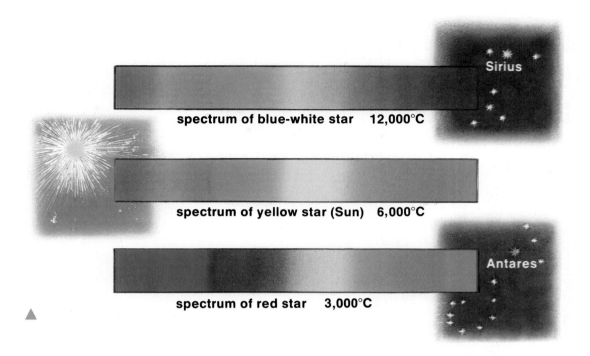

spectrum of blue-white star   12,000°C

spectrum of yellow star (Sun)   6,000°C

spectrum of red star   3,000°C

▲

Using the spectroscope, we can compare the spectra of stars. Look at the colors in the spectra of three stars of different colors. ▲ How are the spectra different? Scientists use information from these spectra to calculate the surface temperatures of stars.

As you see, the surface temperature of the blue-white Sirius is almost twice that of the yellow Sun. Blue stars are the hottest stars. Red stars are among the coolest stars. Thus the surface temperature of red Antares is about half that of our Sun. Clearly, a star's color and surface temperature are related.

Vast amounts of energy come out of a star. That energy must come from a very hot place at the center, or *core*, of a star. The core temperature of our Sun, for example, is about 15 million degrees Celsius. ◆ As we move away from the core, the temperature begins to drop. Since heat normally goes from a hot place to a cooler place, it is no surprise that the heat from the core of a star moves toward the surface and is radiated into space.

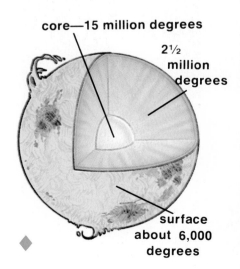

core—15 million degrees

2½ million degrees

surface about 6,000 degrees

◆

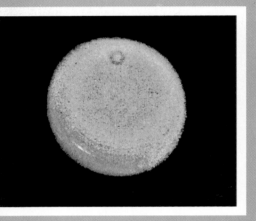

Exploring the Solar System and Beyond

Imagine sending a photographer on a 12 year mission through the solar system to visit Jupiter, Saturn, Uranus, and Neptune. Then imagine sending the photographer beyond the solar system into the galaxy for at least 25 years more of space exploration.

In fact, this is happening. NASA launched the unmanned spacecraft Voyager 2 in 1977. Voyager 2 reached Jupiter in 1979, Saturn in 1981, and Uranus in 1986. NASA expects Voyager 2 to reach Neptune in August, 1989, a distance of 4,486,100,000 km from Earth. Then Voyager 2 will travel beyond the solar system into the galaxy where it will orbit indefinitely. NASA expects to receive signals from Voyager 2 for at least 25 years.

Voyager 2 is equipped with cameras, computers, and scientific instruments. Photographs sent back to Earth of Uranus are considered even better than the pictures from Saturn and Jupiter. Thanks to Voyager 2, people now know that Uranus has 11 rings and 15 moons. In one day, Voyager 2 supplied more information about Uranus than astronomers had gathered since its discovery in 1781.

Voyager 2 passed within 81,000 km of the cloud tops of Uranus. The visit to Neptune will be much closer, within a few thousand kilometers. Neptune is a mysterious planet that astronomers know very little about. They do know that Neptune has two moons. Before leaving the solar system, Voyager 2 will photograph Triton, Neptune's largest moon.

medium-sized
star (Sun)

giant

dwarf

supergiant

The Size of Stars

Stars not only have a variety of colors and temperatures, but their sizes differ as well. Our Sun is considered a medium-sized star, but don't let that fool you. The distance through the center of the Sun, its diameter, is about 100 times greater than the Earth's diameter. We could line up over 100 Earths side by side through the Sun. If you were to draw the Sun as a 50-cent piece, the Earth would be no bigger than the period at the end of this sentence.

Many stars are much larger than the Sun, however. The diameter of the red star Antares is at least 320 times the diameter of the Sun. Red Antares is a *supergiant.* So is the blue star Rigel in the Orion constellation. ■ Supergiants have diameters up to 1,000 times the diameter of our Sun. If our Sun were a supergiant, the Earth would be inside it!

Next in size to the supergiants are the *giant* stars. Their diameter is about 100 times that of our Sun. Finally, there are much smaller stars than our Sun. *Dwarf* stars, for example, may be as small as the Earth—even smaller.

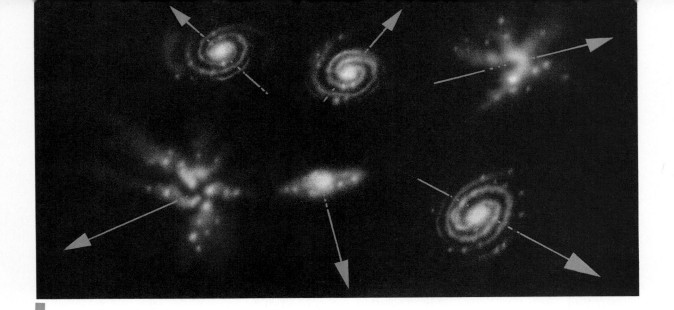

The Movement of Stars

You know that all stars move through space. Our Sun, for example, is revolving around the center of the Milky Way Galaxy. We can observe the movement of some stars by watching them change position over a long period of time. However, suppose a star is moving directly toward or away from Earth? It won't change position in the sky. Can we tell if there is any movement or not? Yes. We can use the light from the star.

Light from a star forms a spectrum when the starlight passes through a spectroscope. If a star is moving away from the Earth, its spectrum changes slightly from what we would expect. By measuring this change, we can tell if a star is moving away from us and how fast it is moving. By studying the spectra of many stars in different galaxies, we have found a very important fact about the Universe. All the galaxies seem to be moving away from each other at great speeds. ■ The quasars near the edge of the Universe are moving the fastest. If this is true, it means the Universe is getting bigger and bigger. The Universe is expanding. Change, it seems, is the one thing in the Universe we can count on.

On a separate sheet of paper, write each statement with the best ending.

1. Burning sodium produces a
   a. blue flame   b. orange flame
   c. yellow flame

2. The main part of the spectroscope is a
   a. thermometer   b. prism
   c. mirror

3. A yellow star is hotter than a
   a. blue-white star   b. blue star
   c. red star

4. The blue star Rigel is a
   a. giant   b. dwarf
   c. supergiant

5. The statement that fits the *main* concept of this section is:
   a. The heat, temperature, and size of a star can be determined by studying its light.
   b. The Sun is just like the other stars in the Universe.

YOU CAN DISCOVER

In the sky, the Sun and the Moon look about the same size. ● Yet the diameter of the Sun is over 400 times the diameter of the Moon. Why do they look the same size from Earth?

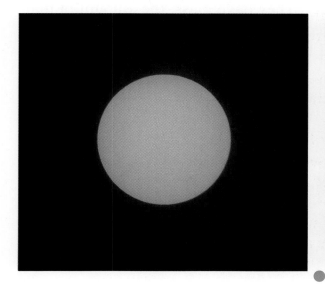
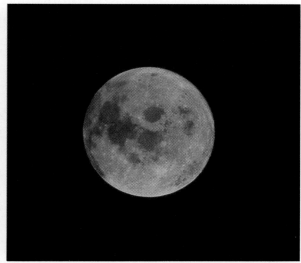

We plant a seed. A flower grows. It flourishes. In time, the flower's life comes to an end. However, even in its death it adds to the life of other living things. The matter in the flower is returned to the environment, to be used over and over by new flowers.

Most people think of the stars as being timeless, and why not. After all, we can look up and observe the very stars ancient people saw so many years ago. These same stars will be shining countless years from now as well. However, even the brightest stars must one day burn out. When a star dies, though, its matter is often used again and again in the creation of new stars.

There are many theories explaining the life and death of a star. Yet all scientific theories center around the concept of gravitation.

Gravitation

You know that all objects are made of matter. Since they are made of matter, all objects have certain properties. They have mass, the amount of matter in an object. They take up space. They also exert gravitational forces on each other.

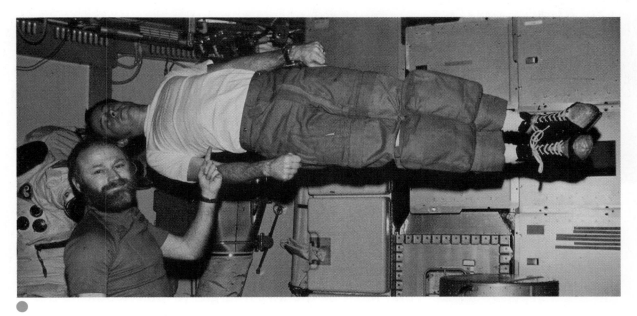

The gravitational force between objects is easy to see when at least one of the objects is fairly large. If you throw a ball, you can certainly predict that within a few seconds the ball will fall to the ground. Although these skydivers may take a bit longer, you know they too will soon be on the ground. ■ Why? Between the Earth and the objects on or around it there is a force—the force of gravity.

You live on the Earth. Your body has some mass. Because you have mass, you exert a tiny gravitational force on the Earth. Yet it has no real effect at all. The Earth, on the other hand, has a large mass. It exerts a large force on your body. Gravity is the force that holds you on the surface of our planet. What might happen if the Earth suddenly lost its force of gravity?

These astronauts are high above the Earth. ● What has happened to the pull of gravity on the astronauts? Now you know two things about gravitational force.

Gravitation depends on the masses of objects.

Gravitation between objects decreases as the objects get farther away from each other.

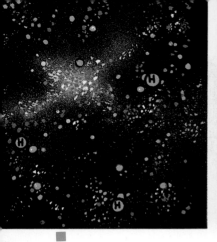
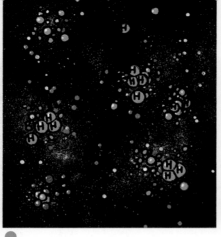
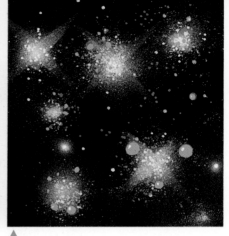

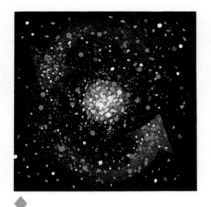

The Birth of a Star

As you know, stars are often born in the huge gas clouds called nebula. Let us imagine a visit to a nebula. Most of the swirling gas in this nebula is made of hydrogen atoms. Slowly, as the years pass by, gravitational forces pull the hydrogen atoms toward each other into a small clump. ■ As more gas is pulled in, the mass of the clump begins to get bigger and bigger. ● After millions of years the clump of atoms has become an enormous ball. ▲ Its mass and its gravitational pull are also enormous.

Within the ball, the atoms are not spread out evenly. The atoms near the core are packed together very tightly. ◆ As more and more atoms in the core are squeezed together, the temperature begins to rise. When the core reaches a temperature of about 15 million degrees Celsius, some of the hydrogen atoms join or *fuse* together. A star is about to be born.

Energy from Changing Atoms

When hydrogen atoms in a star's core are fused together, they form a new kind of atom—a helium atom. ★ If two or more atoms are joined together to form a new atom such as helium, the process is called **fusion** (FYOO-zhun). In fusion, then, new kinds of atoms are produced.

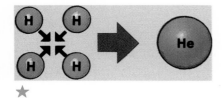

If we measure the mass of the hydrogen atoms we start with, and then measure the mass of the helium atom we end up with, we find something unusual has happened. The hydrogen atoms have more mass than the helium atom produced. Some of the matter, or mass, in the hydrogen atoms has somehow disappeared. Yet we find that energy appears. In fusion, then, some matter is changed into energy.

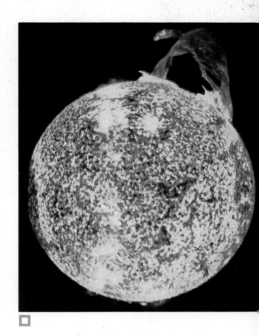

hydrogen atoms ⟶ fusion ⟶ one helium atom + energy

The energy of a star comes from the energy produced during fusion. The energy from our Sun is produced during the fusion of hydrogen atoms into a helium atom. We often say the Sun burns hydrogen as fuel. However, burning in this case is not like burning on Earth. In a star, burning means the release of energy when matter is changed into energy during fusion.

How much matter does the Sun turn into energy? Every second, the Sun changes about 4 million metric tons of matter into energy. ☐ On Earth, we receive only about one billionth of the energy the Sun pours out into space.

The Sun has been pouring out energy for billions of years, and will go on doing this for billions of years to come. Does that give you some idea of the amount of matter in the Sun?

Medium-Sized Stars

Let's follow the life of a medium-sized star such as our Sun. Like all stars, this star began its life by burning hydrogen fuel. Through the years, more and more of the hydrogen in the core is fused into helium. In time, most of the core is helium. However, the star continues to shine as it burns hydrogen in the shell surrounding the core.

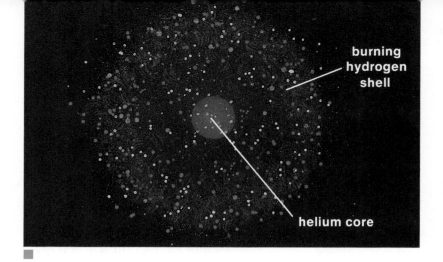

burning hydrogen shell

helium core

As the star continues to age, it begins to cool. At the same time, the last of the hydrogen gas in its shell expands greatly. The star gets bigger and bigger and glows with a red light. At this stage of its life it has become a **red giant.** ■

Almost all stars become red giants as they age. Our Sun will one day become a red giant. How big will it be at that time? Consider this: The Earth is about 150 million kilometers from the Sun. Yet when it expands and becomes a red giant, the Sun may fill most of the space to the Earth. Our planet will be turned to gas. There is no need to worry, however. Our Sun is not due to become a red giant for several billion years or more.

White Dwarf Stars

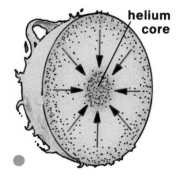

helium core

As the red giant star ages, its hydrogen fuel is used up. Yet even as the last of the cooling hydrogen shell is burning away, gravitational forces squeeze the helium atoms in the core tighter and tighter. ● The temperature of the core goes higher. At about 200 million degrees Celsius, helium atoms fuse and form carbon atoms. Since energy is released, the star continues to shine.

helium atoms $\xrightarrow{\text{fusion}}$ a carbon atom + energy

In time, of course, most of the helium fuel will be used up as well. Then the core will be mainly carbon atoms. Now the star's life is coming to an end. As the helium is used up, the star gets fainter. In time the star collapses and becomes a tiny **white dwarf.** Eventually, the very last of the energy given off by the white dwarf will be gone. It is a dead star.

How long does it take for a medium-sized star to become a white dwarf? ▲ It depends on the original mass of the star. A small medium-sized star may take up to 100 billion years to use its fuel. However, a medium-sized star the size of our Sun will take less time to die. In about 10 billion years, our Sun will go from birth to a white dwarf. A large medium-sized star gives off more light, grows old faster, and may only last a few billion years.

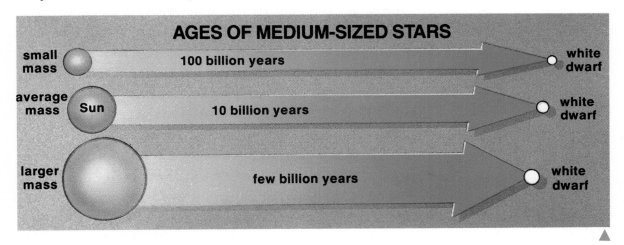

Massive Stars

There are stars with from 3 to as much as 50 times the mass of our Sun. For much of their life these massive stars hurry along the same path as medium-sized stars. When all the helium in the medium-sized star has been changed into carbon, the star becomes a white dwarf and dies. However, a massive star does not die at this point. It does not become a white dwarf.

Because of its tremendous mass, gravitation in the massive star continues to squeeze the carbon atoms in its core. The core may heat up to 600 million degrees Celsius. Then another kind of fusion can begin. The carbon atoms fuse, forming new, heavier kinds of atoms such as oxygen and nitrogen. Then these heavier atoms can also fuse to form even heavier atoms, and so on. The core of the massive star is a kind of factory. From the original hydrogen atoms that first formed the star, many kinds of elements are produced. Finally, the atoms fuse to produce iron atoms.

A Supernova

Not even the heat of a massive star can fuse iron atoms. So the fuel of the massive star begins to run out. Then at some point the massive star collapses in a tremendous explosion called a **supernova** (soo-pur-NOH-vuh). ■ In February, 1987, an astronomer saw the explosion of such a massive star. It was called Supernova 1987A. This supernova was brighter and closer than any one in our galaxy since 1604.

When the star blows up as a supernova, its temperature becomes unbelievably hot for a short time. Heavy elements such as uranium form by fusion. During the supernova explosion, much of the star's gases, including these heavy elements, are blasted out into

supernova explosion

nebula of spinning atoms

spin increases

bulge forms

bulge separates into rings

rings separate into planets

space. Slowly these gases may form a new nebula gas cloud. Yet unlike the original gas nebula we visited, this nebula gas cloud has atoms of hydrogen, helium, carbon, iron, as well as all the other heavy elements.

In a few million years, new stars may begin to form from this gas cloud. More importantly from our point of view, perhaps around this new star some planets may also form. Scientists think this may be the way our solar system was born. ● Scientists are continuing to study Supernova 1987A to discover the role the supernova plays in creating new stars and in forming parts of the solar system.

Neutron Stars and Black Holes

In the year 1054, Chinese astronomers observed a supernova explosion deep in space. The supernova produced so much energy that it could be seen both day and night for over a month. Today we

find the giant Crab Nebula at the place in the sky where they reported the supernova. ■ The Crab Nebula formed from the supernova explosion of a massive star. However, what happened to the core of the star that exploded?

After a supernova explosion, much of the star's core may be left behind. Gravitation may then pull the atoms in the core into what are called **neutron stars.** Scientists now believe that some neutron stars may become pulsars. Recall that pulsars give off energy in "beeps" or pulses. Today we know that there is a pulsar near the center of the Crab Nebula.

If a very large core is left behind after the supernova, it will not form a neutron star. Instead, gravitational forces will squeeze the atoms so hard they form a **black hole.** The large mass of the black hole is squeezed into a very small volume. Yet its gravitational pull is very, very strong. It is so strong, in fact, that nothing can escape the black hole. Light is trapped inside the black hole and cannot escape. Even light from other stars is pulled into the black hole when it passes by. Although we can't see a black hole, we can imagine what it looks like. ●

You read that a medium-sized star like our Sun will take about 10 billion years to die and become a white dwarf. Massive stars burn much brighter than our Sun, but they also burn out their fuel much faster. A massive star may take only about 10 million years to die and become a black hole or neutron star.

CHECK-UP TIME: Vocabulary . . . Facts . . . Concepts

On a separate sheet of paper, write each statement with the best ending.

1. Our Sun is made up mainly of the elements
   a. hydrogen and carbon
   b. helium and carbon
   c. hydrogen and helium

2. The amount of matter in an object is its
   a. weight   b. mass   c. gravity

3. As a star ages, it first expands. It has become a
   a. white dwarf   b. neutron star
   c. red giant

4. A supernova results when a star
   a. is born   b. explodes   c. cools

5. The statement that fits the *main* concept of this section is:
   a. All stars go through the same stages.
   b. Stars of different masses go through different stages.

YOU CAN DISCOVER

This photograph is of the Bay of Fundy. ▲ This is the same place several hours later. ◆ What has happened? See if you can discover how the force of gravitation affects the movements of water, or tides, on Earth.

▲

◆

Computer Artist

In an instant, a galaxy of stars appears before your eyes. With the push of a button, you can see the galaxy from any angle. Are you looking through the lens of a giant telescope? Not at all. You are viewing the screen of a computer. The galaxy is the work of a computer artist.

With a computer, the artist can form different shapes and patterns. ■ With a computer, the artist can create unusual landscapes. ● The artist can even produce scenes so lifelike that you can't tell them from the real thing.

Computer artists help bring exciting shapes and colors to television and movies. ▲ So the next time you see a rocket sailing through space, you will know that the computer artists were at work. ◆

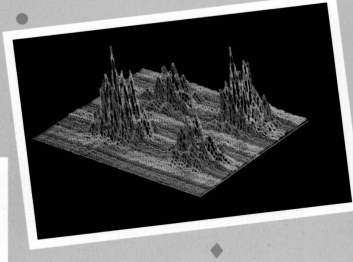

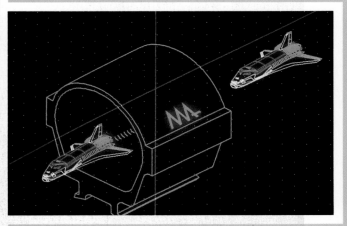

✓ Long ago people first looked up at the stars and began to chart their movement. They grouped stars into constellations and named them after figures in mythology.

✓ The discovery of the telescope opened more of the Universe. Binary star systems were discovered. Huge gas clouds called nebulae and giant star clusters called galaxies were found. ■

✓ Radio telescopes and X-ray telescopes gave us yet another view of stars. With them we found powerful sources of radio waves such as pulsars and quasars.

✓ Starlight can be a valuable tool. We use starlight to measure vast distances in space. Starlight tells us what a star is made of and how hot it is.

✓ Light from the stars has shown us that all the galaxies in the Universe are moving away from each other at high speeds. The Universe is rapidly expanding. ■

✓ Scientists once believed that mass could only be mass, and energy could only be energy. They also felt that the total mass or energy of an object would not change.

✓ Today we know that a star glows because a tiny part of its mass is changed into energy during fusion. ● A tiny mass disappears and a large amount of energy appears.

✓ This leads us to another important concept in science:

Radiant energy is produced when nuclear reactions in a star change mass to energy.

✓ All stars go through certain stages. A star with a very large mass will burn very hot because of its

tremendous gravitation. Yet it will not live very long before it explodes in a supernova.

✓ During a supernova, atoms of many heavy elements are produced and shot into space. In time, the once massive star will become a neutron star or black hole.

✓ A star that is not massive will burn much longer before it runs out of fuel. When it does run out of fuel, it will become a white dwarf.

✓ The gases given off by dying stars may form new stars, and perhaps even planets.

✓ You have now come to yet another important concept:

The Universe is in continuous change.

A. CHOOSE THE BEST ANSWER.

1. Telescopes that use lenses instead of mirrors are
   a. refracting telescopes b. radio telescopes
   c. reflecting telescopes

2. Vast clouds of dust and gas in space are called
   a. galaxies b. nebulae c. constellations

3. We can discover what a star is made of by studying its
   a. size b. temperature c. spectrum

4. An example of a yellow star is
   a. our Sun b. Antares c. Sirius

5. The temperature of a star is highest
   a. near the surface b. in a solar loop
   c. at the core

6. To study the spectrum of a star, we use a
   a. telescope b. spectroscope c. microscope

7. Light travels from the Sun to the Earth in about
   a. 8 minutes b. 16 minutes c. 8 seconds

8. New elements can be produced in
   a. comets b. stars c. planets

9. During fusion on the Sun,
   a. energy is changed to matter
   b. matter is changed to energy
   c. helium atoms unite to form hydrogen

10. The statement that fits the *main* concept of this unit is:
    a. Bodies in space are made of particles entirely unlike those on Earth.
    b. Bodies in space are always changing.

1. What are the advantages of the space telescope?

2. Why are meters and kilometers a poor way of measuring distances in space?

3. Looking at the stars is like looking back in time. Explain.

4. How can the death of a massive star cause the birth of new stars?

Find Out More

Find out how large telescopes can be. ■ What does their size refer to?

Challenge Your Thinking

A star does not give off any visible light. It does not give off radio waves or X rays. But it is not a dead star. What kind of radiation does it give off? *Hint:* Its radiation can make you very warm.

Energy—Yesterday, Today, Tomorrow

What was life like hundreds of years ago? Today you turn a faucet and water comes out— hot and cold water, at that. Long ago you had to pump water from a well. Then you had to carry it back to the house. Now you drop your clothes into a washing machine. Two centuries ago you may have washed your clothes in a stream.

Today people can travel thousands of kilometers in one day. In the past, riding a horse, you were lucky to go 30 kilometers before nightfall.

It seems that people's needs have not changed very much, but our standard of living certainly has. Today's modern kitchen may have an oven, a dishwasher, a refrigerator, a microwave, and much more. All these things need energy. In the past, the only thing in the kitchen that needed energy was the oven. Where does all the energy needed for today's standard of living come from?

Coal as a Fuel

Early people had few sources of energy. If a rock had to be moved, they used their strength. They gathered food by hand. Their muscle power propelled their weapons. ■ However, there was one source of energy early people did learn to harness.

Almost 500,000 years ago, people learned to use fire. Wood was their first fuel. **Fuels** are substances that release energy when they are burned. Burning wood helped provide heat and light. For thousands of years wood was the main source of energy.

Early Steam Engines

In about A.D. 60, a man named Hero used wood as the fuel to boil water. The steam from the boiling water powered the first steam engine. ● Many people enjoyed watching Hero's steam engine spin. You can, too. *ACTIVITY*

Making a Steam Engine

You can use: small spice can with press-on metal lid, nail, hammer, water, thread, candle, ring stand

1 Near the top of the can, carefully punch two holes with the nail and hammer. The holes should be in opposite corners. Pour about 10 ml of water into the can.

2 Place the thread under the lid and attach the lid to the can so that equal lengths of string come out of each side. ■

3 Hang the can from a ring stand. Be sure the can hangs without twisting. Place a candle under the can. Light the candle. ● **Caution:** Do not touch the can once you have lit the candle. Let the can cool before taking the setup apart.

4 What happens when you first light the candle? What happens after the water begins to boil and produce steam? How would you describe the motion of the can?

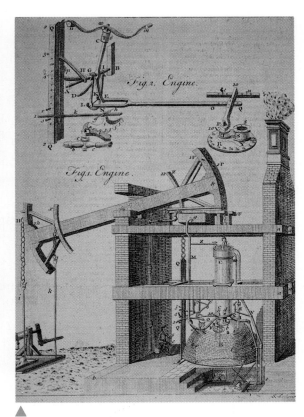

A simple steam engine like Hero's can make a can spin, but it is not very practical. However, by 1700 steam engines could do useful work. Machines driven by steam replaced muscle power in factories. Steam engines replaced the sails on ships. ■ The first vehicle that wasn't pulled by animals was powered by steam. It was a tractor for pulling a cannon. ●

The tractor's top speed was about 7 kilometers an hour. Even at that, it had to stop every block to build up steam. Its builder finally drove the vehicle into a stone wall. He was promptly thrown into jail—the first traffic offender.

The widespread use of the steam engine was the beginning of modern industry. The need for energy was increasing. Another fuel, **coal,** had already begun to replace wood. So it is really no surprise that the first working steam engines were built to pump water out of coal mines. ▲

How Coal Formed

You know that wood comes from plants. It is a product of living things. But how was coal formed? Perhaps this piece of coal can give you a clue. ◆ Do you see the imprint of a plant in the coal? This imprint is a **fossil.** Fossils are the imprints or remains of plants or animals. Could coal, then, come from living things?

Millions of years ago, there were many vast swamps on Earth. In the swamps grew tall ferns and other plants. ★　When the plants died they fell into the swamps. Layers of plant matter formed on the swamp bottom. After many years, some of this plant matter hardened and became **peat.** Peat is the first stage in the formation of coal. There are still large deposits of peat on the Earth today. Peat can be collected and burned as fuel. □

In time, much of the peat became buried under sand and mud. Year after year, more and more layers built up. Some of the layers turned to rocks such as shale and sandstone. The heavy rock layers greatly increased the pressure pushing down on the peat. The peat then changed to coal. When we burn coal today, we are burning what is left of plants that lived on Earth millions of years ago. Can you explain why coal is often called a *fossil fuel?*

The energy we get from coal was once the energy in sunlight. Once again we see that the Sun is the main source of energy on Earth. In some parts of the world, such as the Florida Everglades, plants still capture sunlight and fall to the bottom of swamps. Perhaps in a few million years a living plant of today will be burned as coal.

From Coal to Electricity

A great deal of coal was burned in early industrial steam engines. However, even more coal was used as a fuel to heat homes. Coal gave more heat than burning wood. It burned more slowly and with a steadier flame. It was also easier to store. In just about every way, coal was a better fuel than wood. In many parts of the world, coal is still the most important source of heat for homes. However, in this country most coal is used to produce electricity.

Many homes depend on the electricity produced by large generators. Inside the generator a turbine spins day and night. ■ What produces the motion? First a conveyor belt carries coal to large boilers. There the coal is burned to heat water and produce steam. The steam then spins the turbine.

Almost half the electricity generated in this country comes from burning coal. With this electricity we do a great many things, including powering the appliances in a modern kitchen.

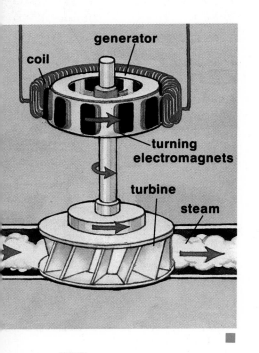

coil
generator
turning electromagnets
turbine
steam

Some Problems with Coal

There are vast deposits of coal in this country and throughout the world. You may wonder, then, why we don't burn even more coal than we do. Perhaps this photograph can give you part of the answer. ● When we burn coal, substances such as soot and ash are released into the air. The air pollution that results can damage our lungs and cause other serious health problems.

Some coal contains large amounts of sulfur. When the coal is burned, the sulfur combines with oxygen from the air and forms compounds with an unpleasant smell, much like rotten eggs. What is worse, the sulfur compounds can combine with water vapor in air, forming droplets of sulfuric acid. The acid can eat away at buildings. ▲ When it falls to the Earth as "acid rain," it can harm plant and animal life.

There are other dangers with coal as well. These miners are working several thousand meters below the surface. ■ To avoid accidents, they have to follow strict safety rules.

Even when the coal is near the surface, there are problems. Green, rolling hills once covered this area. ● The coal provided needed energy, but removing it damaged the ecosystem. In many places coal companies return the environment to nearly the same condition they found it. ▲

Coal All Around Us

When you see perfume or paint, you probably don't think of coal. Perhaps you should think again. In a special airtight oven, coal can be heated to over 1,000 degrees Celsius without burning. Some of the coal turns to gas. The rest becomes a substance called *coke.*

In a steel mill, the coke is added to iron ore inside a fiery blast furnace. The pure iron that is produced is the raw material we need to make steel. ■ The steel can be poured into molds to make products like these wrenches. ● With steel we build tall buildings and long bridges. We even make toy trains. ▲

The gas produced when coke is made is not wasted either. When it cools, it forms oily liquids as well as a sticky substance called *coal tar.* From these products of coal we manufacture perfumes and paints. We produce dyes for textiles. ◆ We make preservatives for wood. We make ammonia, medicines, and fertilizers as well.

Do you still think of coal as only a fuel? If you look carefully, you may find that products from coal are really all around us.

On a separate sheet of paper, write each statement with the best ending.

1. The main source of energy for early peoples was
   a. coal   b. steam
   c. muscle power

2. The first stage in the formation of coal is
   a. sulfur   b. peat   c. coke

3. Some coal contains large amounts of the mineral
   a. uranium   b. sulfur
   c. nitrogen

4. In this country, most coal is burned to
   a. heat homes
   b. heat office buildings
   c. produce electricity

5. The statement that fits the *main* concept of this section is:
   a. As society advances, our need for energy increases.
   b. Although our sources of energy have changed through the years, our need for energy has remained the same.

YOU CAN DISCOVER

Do you know anyone who cooks with *charcoal?* ■ Don't be confused by its name. Charcoal is not made from coal. See if you can find out what charcoal is and how it is made.

2 ▶ Oil and Gas

In ancient Egypt, oil from pools on the ground was used to grease the axles on chariots. The grease made them ride faster and smoother. ● Also, history tells us that George Washington was once amazed by a "burning spring" of water. The spring was probably caused by gas leaking to the surface and catching fire. What George Washington and the Egyptians found were two other fossil fuels. Usually these fuels, oil and gas, are found underground. To find out how they may have formed, we must once again travel back in time.

How Oil and Gas Formed

Ancient oceans covered much of the Earth millions of years ago. These oceans were teeming with tiny plant and animal life. Perhaps they were like these organisms living in our ocean today. ▲ When the plants and animals died, they sank to the ocean floor. Over the years they were covered by mud and sand.

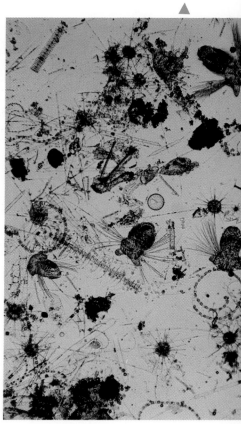

In time, the layers of mud and sand changed into rocks of sandstone or limestone. The pressure on the remains of the plants and animals increased. Heat built up as well. Perhaps aided by bacteria and other natural forces, the remains of the plants and animals changed to droplets of oil and bubbles of gas.

Drop some oil on a piece of sandstone. ■ Does the oil stay on top? No, it seeps into the rock. ● Sandstone and limestone have tiny holes or pores. So the oil and gas that formed beneath them could seep through these rocks. Later, when harder rock layers formed over the porous rocks, the oil and gas could become trapped under the ocean floor. When much of the ancient oceans drained away, the oil and gas was trapped under dry land.

Drilling for Oil and Gas

Most of the oil and gas on Earth is still underground. To locate it, we first must find a place that has the right layers of porous and nonporous rock. Then a tall derrick is built. The derrick holds up a long drill pipe. ▲ At the end of the drill is a sharp bit. ◆   With the drill bit we bore a deep hole into the ground. ★   It may take several months of drilling before oil or gas is reached. It is only when the oil or gas comes flowing out of the well that the workers know for sure if the area contains any fuel. Since much of the oil and gas on Earth is under the oceans, we also build offshore derricks in our search for fuel. ▢

Once oil and gas are found in a well, they must be removed by special pumps. From that point on they often travel different paths. Let's first follow oil on its journey from well to consumer.

The thick, dark liquid pumped from the ground is called **petroleum** (puh-TROH-lee-um), or crude oil. Petroleum is actually a mixture of many different substances. From the oil well the petroleum is transported to a processing plant, or refinery. Often the petroleum is carried through a vast network of pipelines. ■ It may be shipped in large tankers. ● At the refinery the different useful substances in petroleum are separated. ▲

Kerosene

One substance removed from petroleum is *kerosene*. In the 1800's kerosene lamps were the most common source of lighting. ◆ Today, of course, we use electric lights in their place. However, kerosene is still burned as a fuel for some farm equipment and for heaters. Most importantly, kerosene is the main fuel for jet engines. ★

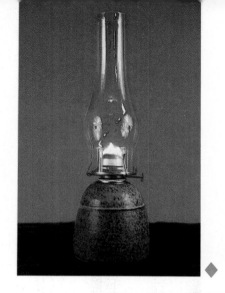

Gasoline

Kerosene was the first important fuel removed from petroleum by oil refineries. During the process, *gasoline* was removed, too. Unlike kerosene, gasoline explodes easily when lit. So it was of little use in lamps. In fact, most of the gasoline from refineries was thrown away, often dumped into nearby rivers. Then something happened to change the entire industry. In 1885 an engine that burned gasoline was invented. By the early 1900's cars that used gasoline were being mass produced. ☐ The need for gasoline increased year after year.

Today, with over 270 million cars in the world, it is easy to see that gasoline is one of our most important fuels. Many trucks and boats are also powered by gasoline. Small appliances such as lawnmowers, also use gasoline. In fact, sometimes our need for gasoline is greater than the available supply. ■

Many buses, trains, large ships, and road building equipment often burn *diesel oil* as fuel. ● Diesel oil does not require as much refining as gasoline and is cheaper. Today some cars burn diesel oil. They can usually go farther on one liter of diesel oil than on the same amount of gasoline.

Heating Oil

Have you ever seen a large storage tank being buried beside a new house? It will hold oil for the furnace that heats the house. The oil will also heat the hot water for washing. Heating oil is used in houses, factories, and office buildings.

We can also use heating oil to generate electricity. At the power plant, oil heats water and produces steam. As you know, steam can turn a turbine. So now we have seen three different ways to generate electricity: moving water from a dam, steam from water heated by burning coal, and steam from water heated by burning oil.

Some Problems with Oil

By now it may seem as if petroleum is the answer to all our energy needs. However, petroleum does give us some problems, too. Accidental spills from an oil well or a tanker can damage the ecosystem and destroy living things. ▲ Like coal, petroleum products cause air pollution. One car, of course, is not a problem. But add the exhausts of many cars, day after day, and air can become so polluted that it hurts the eyes and makes people cough. ◆ For some people, air pollution results in serious illness as well. Even with special equipment to make exhausts cleaner, cars are still a major cause of air pollution. Trucks and heavy equipment that burn diesel oil also cause dangerous air pollution.

Natural Gas

This gas stove is familiar, isn't it? ■ Gas is a popular fuel for cooking. Many people also use gas to heat their homes. We can burn gas to heat water, produce steam, and then generate electricity. There is an important advantage in using gas. It produces little or no dangerous pollution.

Remember, both gas and petroleum are found under the Earth. Because this gas was produced from the remains of plants and animals through natural processes, it is called **natural gas.** Gas pumped from wells is sent to a processing plant. At the plant the gas is cleaned, and unwanted substances are removed. Then it can be transported through pipelines wherever it is needed. You might think this is a modern idea, but the ancient Chinese discovered gas while digging for salt. They used hollow bamboo tubes to bring gas to the surface. ●

Other Products from Oil and Gas

These workers are paving a highway with petroleum. ▲ Confused? Don't be. Another material in petroleum, *asphalt*, is a black, cementlike substance.

314

In 600 B.C., asphalt was used to pave the roads in Babylon. Ancient Persians wiped sticky asphalt on reeds to help build and waterproof small boats. Today we combine asphalt with gravel and sand to make the pavement of streets, highways, and airport runways.

Industries use petroleum and gas to produce a wide variety of products. Many of them are very different from the thick liquid that comes out of the ground. Detergents, bug killers, medicines, soap, paints, wax paper, and rubber are some of these products. ◆ Nylon also comes from petroleum. ★ So does the cleaning fluid that makes your clothes clean. Plastics, too, are made from petroleum once trapped under the Earth. Just think of all the different plastics we use.

315

On a separate sheet of paper, write each statement with the best ending.

1. Sandstone and limestone
   a. contain coal   b. have pores
   c. are made from fossils

2. The different substances in petroleum are removed at the
   a. derrick   b. pumping station
   c. refinery

3. The main fuel in jet engines is
   a. gasoline   b. kerosene
   c. natural gas

4. Burning natural gas produces
   a. refined products
   b. dangerous pollution
   c. little pollution

5. The statement that fits the *main* concept of this section is:
   a. Burning oil does not produce pollution.
   b. Oil and gas are useful fuels. They formed from the remains of ancient plants and animals.

YOU CAN DISCOVER

1. How is gasoline burned in a car engine? ■   What are spark plugs for? What do the moving pistons do?

2. This camping stove burns *butane,* or bottled gas. ●   What other kinds of bottled gas do people use? *Hint:* Another kind is burned for heat and cooking in mobile homes.

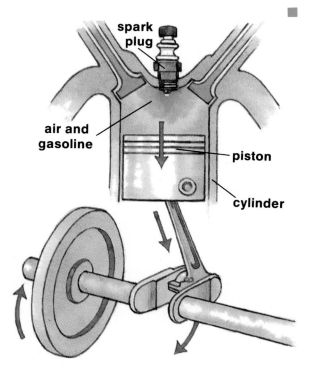

3 ▶ Nuclear Energy

Inside this large power plant, electricity is being generated. ▲ Yet this plant does not use coal or oil or gas. The energy in this plant comes from the atom. How can the atom generate electricity? To find out, let's take another look at the atom.

Inside the Atom

All atoms, remember, have a central nucleus. Particles called *protons* and *neutrons* make up the nucleus. Whirling around the nucleus are the *electrons*. Here are models of three different atoms: hydrogen, oxygen, and carbon. ◆ These substances are only three of the elements found naturally on Earth. There are actually over 92 basic elements—and more than that can be made in the laboratory. Yet they are all made up of protons, neutrons, and electrons. What, then, makes one element different from another?

You can see that the hydrogen atom has 1 proton and 1 electron. The carbon atom has 6 protons, 6 neutrons, and 6 electrons. How many particles does the oxygen atom have?

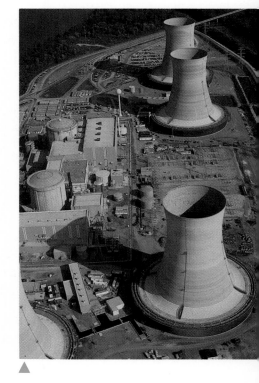

▲

- ● proton
- ● neutron
- ○ electron

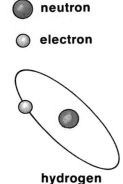

hydrogen

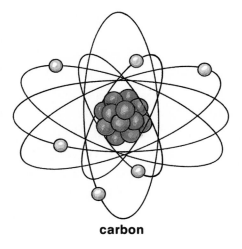

carbon

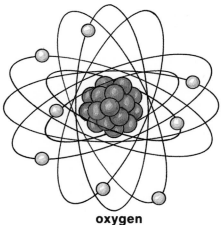

oxygen

◆

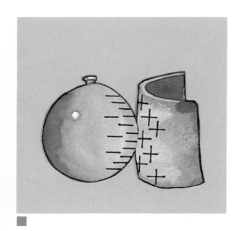

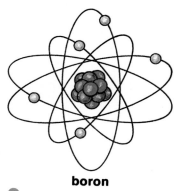

boron

The atom of each element has a different number of protons, neutrons, and electrons. When you studied electricity, you saw that you could rub some electrons off a wool cloth and onto a balloon. ■ However, even after the wool cloth lost some electrons, it was still a wool cloth. Losing electrons did not change the kind of atoms in the cloth. Gaining electrons did not change the kind of atoms in the balloon either. Even if an atom gains or loses electrons, it remains the same kind of atom.

Now let's compare this model of the boron atom with the carbon atom. ● Count the neutrons in each. Boron has 6 neutrons, but so does carbon. The number of neutrons in the atom does not seem to determine what kind of atom it is either. Now count the protons. Boron has 5 protons. Carbon has 6. Is the number of protons the important difference?

If you add or subtract a proton from an atom, you get a new atom—a new element. If we add, for example, a proton to the boron nucleus, we get a carbon atom. The number of protons in an atom is its **atomic number.** Hydrogen has one proton. Its atomic number is 1. Carbon has 6 protons. Its atomic number is 6. What is the atomic number of oxygen?

Splitting the Atom

Now that we have looked at the atom, let's go back to our first question. How can an atom help generate electricity? Can the energy we need come from inside the atom? Locked within the nucleus of every atom is a great deal of energy. If we could somehow break open or split the nucleus, we might release some of that **nuclear energy.**

Suppose we shoot a special "bullet"—a neutron bullet—at the nucleus of a uranium atom. The atomic number of uranium is 92. So uranium has 92 protons in its nucleus. However, when the neutron bullet strikes the uranium nucleus, the nucleus splits. ▲ Two new nuclei are formed. The splitting of a nucleus is called **fission.**

The nuclei that form from the fission of the uranium nucleus have different numbers of protons. One nucleus has 56 protons. This is the nucleus of an atom of the element barium. The other nucleus has 36 protons. It is the nucleus of the element krypton. Have any protons been lost? Let's count.

56 protons + **36 protons** = **92 protons**
(barium)   (krypton)   (uranium)

No protons have been lost. They have been arranged differently to form two nuclei of two new elements. Yet that is not all that happens. During the fission of the uranium nucleus, nuclear energy is given off. What's more, although only 1 neutron bullet was shot into the uranium nucleus, 2 or 3 neutrons are given off during fission. Can we use those neutrons to split other atoms of uranium? *ACTIVITY*

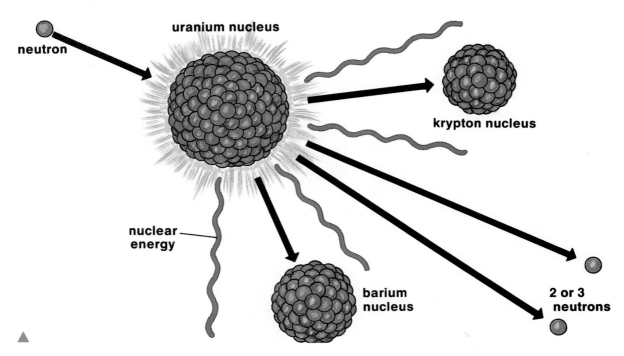

319

Chain Reactions

You can use: marbles and dominoes

1 Spread out the marbles. Leave plenty of room between each marble. From about 1 meter away, roll a marble towards the others. ■ Did the marble hit any of the others? How many? Were any of the marbles you hit knocked into other marbles as well? Try this a few times.

2 Again spread out the marbles on the floor. This time make sure the marbles are close to each other. Roll one marble at the others. How are your results different?

3 Line up dominoes in rows so that the first row has one domino, the second two, and so on. ● Make sure the rows are about half the length of one domino apart. Knock the first domino over. What happens. ▲

4 Line up your dominoes again, but this time remove the second row. What happens this time when you knock over the first domino?

Energy from a Chain Reaction

If you roll one marble into a group of marbles that are spread far apart, the marble will probably only hit one or two other marbles. However, if you roll a marble into a group of marbles that are close together, many marbles will be struck. The first marble hits one, which hits another, and so on.

When we shoot a neutron bullet into uranium, the uranium nucleus splits and releases 2 or 3 neutrons. Often the neutrons escape into the atmosphere. Now suppose there are other uranium atoms nearby. The neutrons may strike 2 more uranium atoms. They each split during fission, releasing at least 4 more neutrons. ■ They may, in turn, strike 4 more atoms of uranium. After fission, 8 more neutrons are now released. So you see, the fission of one nucleus can cause a **chain reaction.**

You might try carrying this chain reaction 10 steps further. First make a guess. How many neutrons will be set free at the tenth step? You may be surprised! Remember, at every step in the chain reaction, energy is released. In fact, an immense amount

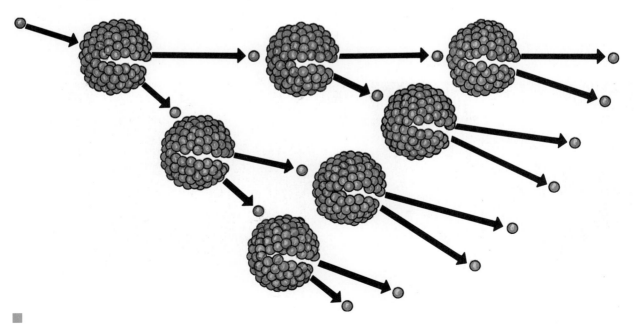

■

of energy can come from the chain reaction begun by only *one* nucleus. Thus, from only a small piece of matter, a great amount of energy is released. The fission of 1 kilogram of uranium, for example, can produce more energy than the burning of over 2,300,000 kilograms of coal. That's enough coal to fill 44 freight train cars!

Nuclear Reactors

A chain reaction can take place with unbelievable speed. It can release nuclear energy so quickly that the result is an explosion. This is what happens in an atomic bomb.

To use the energy released during fission, we must be able to control the speed of the chain reaction. A new kind of furnace, a **nuclear reactor,** will do just that. To build a nuclear reactor we first need a fuel—a nuclear fuel. One common fuel is uranium. The uranium is placed in the reactor in long rods. Here we see workers lowering uranium rods into the center or core of the nuclear reactor. ■ When neutrons strike these rods, fission begins.

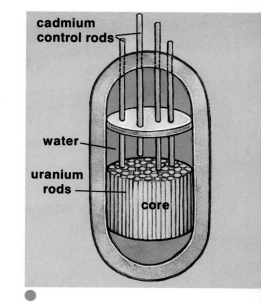

If the rods of uranium fuel are placed at the correct distances from each other, a chain reaction occurs. As more and more atoms undergo fission, large amounts of energy are given off. Some of this energy is in the form of heat.

Neutrons released during fission move very quickly. At such speeds they might miss the nearby uranium nuclei. So a material, like water, is added in the core to slow down the neutrons. Now the chances are greater that the neutrons will hit an atom of uranium.

Once the chain reaction has begun, it must be controlled. If too few atoms undergo fission, the chain reaction will slow down or even stop. If too many uranium atoms undergo fission, the chain reaction will go too fast. Too much heat will build up. The core of the reactor may even melt. When this happens there is a **meltdown.** This is very dangerous.

To control the rate of the chain reaction, rods of the metal cadmium are often placed in reactors. ● The cadmium can "soak up," or absorb, extra neutrons. When the chain reaction is going too slowly, the cadmium rods are pulled out slightly. Fewer neutrons are absorbed, and the chain reaction speeds up. If the chain reaction is going too fast, the control rods are placed deeper into the reactor. They absorb more neutrons, and the chain reaction slows down. In this way we control the rate of the chain reaction. We control nuclear energy!

Electricity from the Atom

Most nuclear reactors, of course, are in nuclear power plants. During fission in the reactor core, heat is produced. With this heat we can turn water to steam. Steam can then spin a turbine and generate electricity. Powerlines carry the electricity from the power plant to cities and towns, homes and factories.

Nuclear reactors provide the power to run some large ships and submarines. ■ The U.S.S. Enterprise, for example, is an aircraft carrier that is driven by nuclear power. ● Because its reactor uses very little uranium fuel, the ship has a great advantage over other ships. It can travel long distances on one supply of fuel. A ship that runs on ordinary fuel would have to stop several times for fuel to travel the same distance.

Some Problems with Nuclear Energy

This person is holding a *Geiger counter* near rocks containing the element radium. ▲ The Geiger counter begins to click. The clicking sound means that radium is giving off **radiation.** The nucleus of the radium atom naturally breaks down, or *decays*. It releases radiation in the form of particles and energy. This radation can be very dangerous.

▲

Many other elements also decay naturally. One is uranium. Since we use uranium in nuclear reactors, people in and around the power plant must be protected from the radiation. In March 1979, a meltdown occurred at Three Mile Island, Pennsylvania. A thick shield around the reactor kept the radiation from escaping into the air. On April 26, 1986, the Chernobyl reactor in the Soviet Union also had a meltdown. Because this reactor did not have a thick shield, radiation did escape into the air. Meltdowns like the one at Chernobyl are very dangerous.

Nuclear reactors are often built near bodies of water. The water is used to help cool the reactor core. This heated water is then returned to its source. If the temperature of a lake or river rises, fish and other living things may, in time, be destroyed.

When you burn coal or oil, waste products that cause air pollution are released into the air. Nuclear reactors do not release wastes into the air, but they do produce waste products. In fact, because the wastes are radioactive, they are probably the most serious problem of nuclear power. Some of the radioactive wastes remain dangerous for thousands, even millions, of years. They could outlast any container in which they are stored.

What can be done about the problems of nuclear wastes? There is no complete answer yet. However, if nuclear energy is to become a more important source of energy, an answer must be found.

Flowers That Detect Radiation

People who work near radioactive elements may wear a badge like this one.  If exposed to too much radiation over a period of time, the badge turns black. However, it cannot always detect low levels of radiation. Today we know that even low levels of radiation can damage living things. How can we help protect people who work near low-level radiation?

A tiny plant may provide the answer. The spiderwort has an attractive blue flower. The stamens of the flower are also blue. However, when the spiderwort is exposed to radiation, the stamens turn pink. Even in low levels of radiation they turn pink. The more radiation the plant receives, the more stamens turn pink. If we count the number of pink stamens under a microscope, we can measure how much low-level radiation the plant was exposed to.

Today many nuclear power plants all over the world are growing spiderworts. Nature, it seems, provided us with an excellent radiation detector long before people ever dreamed of nuclear power.

Fusion Power

Nuclear reactors use the energy released during fission. There is yet another kind of nuclear energy. Recall that atoms of hydrogen in the Sun join, or fuse, to form new elements. During fusion, energy is released. Can we produce this kind of energy on Earth? Can we build a tiny Sun?

The fusion of hydrogen atoms on the Sun starts at a temperature of about 15 million degrees Celsius. The first thing we must do, then, is create such high temperatures. One possible method is to shoot high energy laser beams at a tiny pellet of fuel. However, this process cannot yet come close to the temperatures we need to cause fusion.

Even if we could create such temperatures, we need a way to contain them. Of course, no normal container could hold a tiny Sun without melting. Perhaps the answer is a container made with magnets. If we place large magnets at the proper places, the magnetic field might hold the hot gases formed during fusion. Such giant magnets are now being tested in fusion experiments. ■

We are a long way from a working fusion reactor. Perhaps we will never be able to build one. Think of the things a fusion reactor could do, however. With seawater as the fuel, we could have an endless supply of energy. Little dangerous pollution would be produced. Fusion, it seems, could solve our energy problems for centuries to come.

On a separate sheet of paper, write each statement with the best ending.

1. An atom with one proton is
   a. carbon   b. hydrogen
   c. boron

2. To change an atom of one element to an atom of another element, we must add or remove
   a. an electron   b. a neutron
   c. a proton

3. To absorb extra neutrons in the nuclear reactor, scientists can use
   a. water   b. cadmium rods
   c. uranium fuel

4. Two hydrogen atoms combine and release energy in a process called
   a. fission   b. atomic explosion
   c. fusion

5. The statement that fits the *main* concept of this section is:
   a. Energy can be released by fission of atomic nuclei; the rate of fission can be controlled.
   b. Electrons, when traveling at the right speed, cause fission.

YOU CAN DISCOVER

Radiation can be very dangerous to living things. Yet sometimes it can be helpful. This machine, for example, uses radiation to kill cancer cells without harming healthy cells nearby. ■ See if you can find other ways we use radiation to help cure disease.

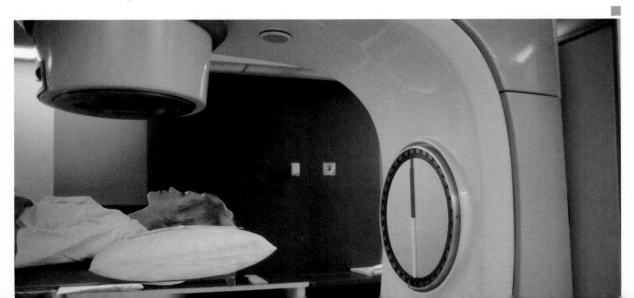

Other Sources of Energy

Since 1900, our use of energy has doubled every 20 years. Our supplies of fossil fuels are running low. Where will we find other sources of energy? Since 1900, pollution from energy use has also increased. Where will we find energy sources that will not damage our environment?

Many "new" energy sources are really based on old ideas. Others are very new. Let's look at some of these other sources of energy.

Water Power

For many years, people used the moving water in rivers to turn water wheels. ● Today the swift-moving water in a river spins blades like those in a windmill. The blades of a "watermill" are attached to a generator that produces electricity.

Off the coast of Florida are the swift moving currents of the Gulf Stream. Large generators anchored to the ocean floor could use the energy from these currents. ▲ When water passes through them, it will spin turbine blades and generate electricity. The electricity will then be sent to the surface through wires.

329

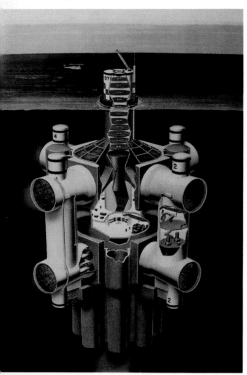

Would you think of glaciers as a source of energy? In the ice caps of Greenland, frozen glaciers contain almost 20 times more fresh water than all the Earth's rivers and streams combined. Each summer much of the ice melts and running water pours down into the lowlands of Greenland. With this running water we could generate electricity. ■ The electricity would then be carried by undersea cables to other parts of the world.

Much of the sunlight that reaches Earth strikes the oceans. It heats the water near the surface. The water deep below the surface remains cold. This difference in temperature is also being used as a source of ocean energy in places like Hawaii. ● In one method, the warm surface water heats liquid ammonia. The ammonia turns to a gas and passes through a turbine. Electricity is generated. The ammonia gas is cooled by deep ocean water into a liquid again. Then it can be reheated to spin the turbine once more.

These are only a few of the ways that water power could be used. Some may be too expensive or too difficult. Other ideas may take their place. There are certainly vast amounts of energy from water that we have not yet begun to use.

Wind Power

For many years windmills pumped water and ground grain into flour.  Today windmills generate electricity.  The windmill blades are attached to a generator. When the blades spin, electricity is produced. Few places have enough wind all the time for windmills to meet all their energy needs. However, they can help cut down on our use of other energy sources. A small farm, for example, could use small windmills to provide electricity for farm equipment. Like water power, the energy of wind power does not pollute.

Another kind of wind power is even older than windmills. For centuries sailboats were an important way of transporting people and materials.  Eventually, engines replaced sails. Today vessels like the research ship Westward are going back to sail power.  Such ships also have engines, but the sails can cut fuel costs up to 90 percent.

Winds are produced because the Sun heats the Earth unevenly. So, in a way, wind power comes from the Sun. How can we use this **solar energy** in other ways? *ACTIVITY*

Heating with Solar Energy

You can use: 2 plastic jars with plastic lids, white and black construction paper, tape, 2 thermometers, water

1 Tape two layers of black paper around one plastic jar. Cover the other jar with two layers of white paper. Fill each container with water at room temperature.

2 Seal each jar with its lid. Each lid should have a hole large enough to hold a thermometer. Place a thermometer through the hole in each lid. Make sure the bulb is below the surface of the water. ■ **Caution:** Handle the thermometer very carefully.

3 Put the jars in a sunny window. Record the temperature of each jar at five-minute intervals. After about an hour, make a bar graph of the time and the temperature change. Here is one student's graph. ●

4 Did the light energy from the Sun heat the water in the containers? Does the color of the container affect the way light energy heats water? Which reflected more light? Which absorbed more?

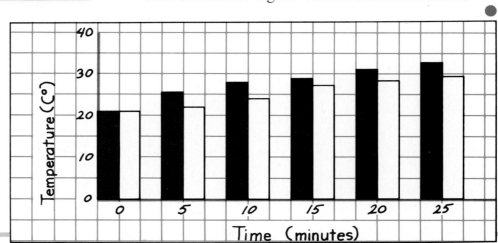

Solar Heating

This house is heated by the Sun. ■ On the roof are solar collecting panels. A black plate in each solar panel absorbs sunlight. (Why do you think a black plate is used?) The heated plate in turn heats a liquid inside the solar panel. The hot liquid flows to a storage tank. There the heat is transferred to water inside the tank. Then the cooled liquid is sent back to the solar panel to be heated once again. The hot water in the tank can be used for washing or to heat the house.

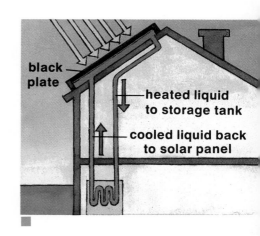

black plate

heated liquid to storage tank

cooled liquid back to solar panel

■

Solar Electricity

In July 1981, the Solar Challenger made its first flight over the English Channel. ● The Challenger was not an ordinary plane. It was powered by sunlight. On top of its wings were over 16,000 solar cells.

Most solar cells are made of a layer of the element silicon. The cells are about as thin as a human hair. When sunlight strikes the cells, electrons are knocked off the silicon. ▲ A current flows. The current can light a bulb, power a small appliance, and even provide electricity for satellites in space. Since the electrons flow back onto the silicon layer, the cells can last for many years. One day soon you may find panels of solar cells on the roofs of most houses.

●

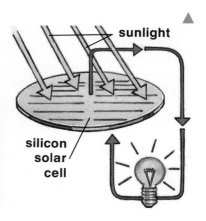

sunlight ▲

silicon solar cell

333

EXPLORING SCIENCE AND TECHNOLOGY

Solar-Powered Cars

From November 1 to November 6, 1987, 25 cars competed in a 2,000 mile race across Australia. What made this competition so special was that the cars were experimental solar-powered cars. ■

These cars provided a glimpse at the future—a car powered by the Sun that would be inexpensive to buy and operate. And, by using the Sun as their source of energy, these cars would help conserve oil and other precious fossil fuels. They would also help control air pollution.

This race was a major breakthrough for those people who had been experimenting with solar-powered cars for years. Several large automobile manufacturers from Japan, Great Britain, and the United States as well as car hobbyists entered the race. The winner was a car called the *Sunraycer*. It weighed 500 pounds and was built on an aluminum-tubing frame with a body, a covering, and a solar panel. It cost $2 million. The *Sunraycer* used solar cells and batteries and adapted space technology to help the car move quickly.

Geothermal Energy

The water in this outdoor swimming pool in the capital of Iceland is warmed by heat from deep within the Earth.  In fact, many places in Iceland get their heat and hot water in this way. Where does the heat come from?

Deep below the Earth the temperature is often much higher than at the surface. This heat is called **geothermal** (jee-oh-THUR-mul) **energy.** Cool water seeping down from the surface can be changed to steam by the high temperature. Or it may remain as hot water. At hot springs and geysers the water makes its way back to the surface.

Geothermal energy can be used to produce electricity. Wells are dug into the underground hot water and steam. ▲ The hot water rushes upward and is collected in storage tanks. The steam spins a turbine and generates electricity. This power plant in California is one of the first in this country to produce electricity with geothermal energy.  In the future we can expect to find geothermal power plants wherever conditions are right.

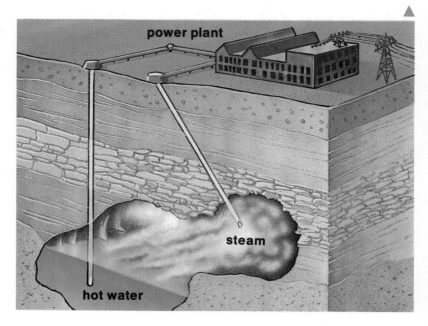

power plant

steam

hot water

Energy from Garbage

Garbage! What can we do with the enormous amounts of garbage we throw away each day? Dade County, Florida, may have an answer. It plans to burn more than half its garbage. The heat will boil water, making steam to spin a turbine and generate electricity. Dade County hopes that some day it can produce enough power from garbage to send electricity to over 40,000 homes. In this large plant in Switzerland, burning garbage is already an important source of electric power. ■

In Staten Island, New York, is Fresh Kills—the world's largest garbage dump. ● Deep in the pile, tiny bacteria use the garbage for food. In the process, they change some of the garbage to gas. Power companies drill into the garbage and collect the gas. They believe that the gas from Fresh Kills could one day provide fuel for over 16,000 homes.

On a separate sheet of paper, write each statement with the best ending.

1. Every 20 years since 1900, our use of energy has
   a. been reduced   b. doubled
   c. tripled

2. To produce electricity, blades of a "watermill" are attached to a
   a. refinery   b. waterwheel
   c. generator

3. Compared to the water near the surface, the deep water of the ocean is
   a. warmer   b. colder
   c. about the same temperature

4. We would not expect to find a house using solar energy
   a. on top of a mountain
   b. in the desert
   c. in a forest of tall trees

5. The statement that fits the *main* concept of this section is:
   a. Wind, water, and solar power will never be able to replace fossil fuels as our main source of energy.
   b. As we run short of fossil fuels, we may have to rely on other sources of energy, such as the Sun.

YOU CAN DISCOVER

1. Solar heating is not a new idea. Over 100 million years ago, the dinosaur Stegosaurus used solar heat to keep warm. ▲ Can you discover what parts of its body acted like solar panels?

2. Many people have found an interesting way to save energy in their homes. They live in homes that are partly or completely underground. ◆ Find out about the energy advantages of these "Earth Houses." Would you like to live in an Earth House?

Particle Physicist

You know what maps are, don't you? A road map, for example, shows different ways to get from one place to another. Here is another kind of map. ■ Its "roads" show the paths of different parts of the atom after it is split by an atomic bullet.

The person who can read this kind of map is a particle physicist. By measuring the length of the paths and their angle, the physicist can determine what kinds of particles were produced in the collision. In this way, the physicist can get a better understanding of the particles that make up atoms and what happens when atoms collide with particles.

Particle physicists work with many kinds of atomic bullets. They spin particles around and around in this accelerator. ● The particles pick up speed and energy each time around. The particles may have to go around several million times before they have the proper speed and energy to split the atom. Sometimes, instead of splitting the atom, the bullet attaches to the atom. A new kind of atom may be formed. In fact, by shooting protons into a nucleus of one atom, physicists can produce new atoms that do not exist naturally on Earth!

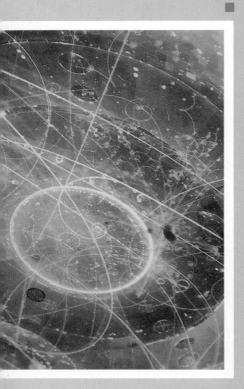

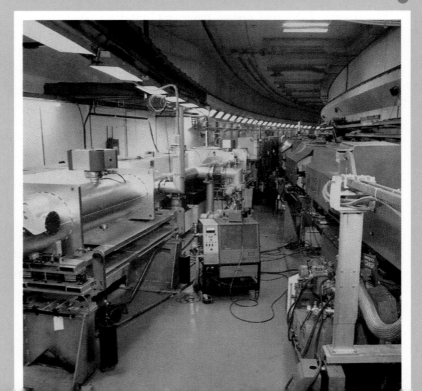

✓ In ancient swamps, plants died and fell to the bottom. Over the years they were covered by rocks and changed to coal.

✓ In ancient oceans, the bodies of tiny plants and animals changed to petroleum and natural gas. Today we burn such fossil fuels to meet many of our energy needs.

✓ Most fossil fuels pollute the air. ■ They are becoming more and more expensive as well. Sooner or later our supplies will run out.

✓ The atom is another source of energy. In a nuclear reactor, uranium atoms break apart during fission. Part of the matter of the uranium is lost. At the same time, nuclear energy is released.

✓ This leads us to another important concept:

In a nuclear reactor, matter can be changed to energy, but the total sum of matter and energy remains the same.

✓ People are looking for new and cleaner sources of energy. Wind and water can spin a turbine and generate electricity. ●

✓ We use the energy of the Sun to help heat our homes. ▲ Geothermal energy beneath the Earth can also be tapped. Scientists are testing these and other new sources of energy.

✓ You have your job, too. People must be more responsible in their use of energy. When it comes to conserving energy, it seems your work and the work of scientists are one and the same.

A. CHOOSE THE BEST ANSWER.

1. A substance that releases energy when burned is
   a. a gas   b. water   c. a fuel

2. The first ground vehicle that was not pulled by animals was powered by
   a. peat   b. steam   c. solar energy

3. An atom with six protons is
   a. carbon   b. hydrogen   c. boron

4. To find the atomic number, we count the
   a. electrons   b. protons   c. neutrons

5. The fission of one atom releases a neutron, causing the fission of a second atom. This is called
   a. an explosion   b. a chain reaction
   c. nuclear energy

6. Heavy road-building equipment often burns
   a. natural gas   b. diesel oil   c. heating oil

7. A black, cementlike petroleum product is
   a. asphalt   b. diesel oil   c. kerosene

8. Most solar cells are made of a layer of
   a. plastic   b. silicon   c. steel

9. Heat deep below the Earth is called
   a. volcanic energy   b. geothermal energy
   c. geyser energy

10. The statement that fits the *main* concept of this unit is:
    a. People have come to find ways to use the many different sources of energy on Earth.
    b. Whatever energy sources we come to rely on, there will always be pollution.

B. ANSWER THESE QUESTIONS.

1. Why are coal, oil, and gas called fossil fuels?

2. The energy from coal was once the energy from sunlight. Explain what this statement means.

3. What are the advantages and disadvantages of using either coal or oil as a fuel?

4. Why is shielding so important at a nuclear power plant?

5. Other than fuels, what other petroleum products do we use?

6. Are wind, water, and solar power sources of energy for the future? Why? Why not?

Find Out More

The wastes from these chickens can be used to manufacture gas. ■ Such manufactured gas is called a *synthetic fuel.* See if you can find out more about the different synthetic fuels we can produce. *Hint:* Some can be produced when we change coal into coke.

Challenge Your Thinking

A piece of shale is burning. ● How can a rock burn?

Genes – Units of Heredity

Walk down the aisle of a large supermarket or a small grocery store. You see canned foods, bottled foods, frozen foods, and fresh foods. You may wonder why there is such a wide variety of foods to choose from. However, chances are you don't often think about where these foods come from before they are picked, processed, and packaged. You just enjoy eating them.

Farmers, along with scientists, develop better varieties of plants and animals. They develop foods that taste better, grow faster, and feed more people. They even look for ways to produce entirely new kinds of plants and animals.

How can we improve common plants and animals, or get a new kind of plant or animal? Turn the page and begin your search into some "Prize Genes."

343

1 ▶ A Garden Grows

Barbara and Joseph want to plant a garden in the spring. They begin their plan for the garden during the cold days of winter, long before the ground is ready for planting. First, they look at many seed catalogs. They are surprised at the different kinds of plants they can grow. Some plants are suited to dry climates. Others are suited to climates where there is a lot of rain. Finally, they find two that are well-suited to the area they live in. These are the seed packages they send for. ■

Barbara and Joseph plant their seeds at the proper time. They follow all the directions on the seed package. The seeds soon sprout. After a while, tiny green peppers and cucumbers begin to develop in their garden. ● Barbara and Joseph are not surprised, of course. They knew they would get cucumbers and green peppers from their seeds. They also knew the green peppers and cucumbers would look like the ones on the package.

Green peppers are not all the same, are they? Some are bigger than others. Some may be darker, too. Yet you can always tell a green pepper from a cucumber. All green peppers share certain physical characteristics. They share certain **traits** (TRAYTS). All plants and animals that are of the same kind share traits. *ACTIVITY*

Traits

You can use: several groups of fruit such as green peppers, cucumbers, bananas, and apples; a small kitchen knife

1 Pick one group of fruit such as the bananas. Make a list of all the traits you can see that the bananas share. ■ For example, they are probably all yellow bananas. Make a second list of the ways they are different.

2 Now do the same for all the other groups of fruit. Compare your lists. Do some fruits share similar traits with other kinds of fruits? Do any share all the same traits?

3 There are traits other than those you see on the outside. Carefully cut open two of each kind of fruit. ● Continue your list of traits. For example, you may find that bananas all have seeds in the same place.

4 Are there any traits inside the fruits that different fruits share? What are they?

Heredity

Look at these young animals. ■ Here are the adults. ● You have no trouble matching the young to the adults, do you? Young and parents do not always look exactly alike, of course. Yet it is easy to see they share many of the same traits. Both plants and animals pass on their traits to their offspring. We say the offspring inherit the traits.

You, too, inherit traits from your parents. Study yourself in a mirror. What is your eye color? What is your hair color? These are among the traits you inherited from your parents. What are some of the other traits you inherited?

The traits that a living thing inherits form what is called its **heredity.** How are traits passed on? What controls heredity?

Chromosomes

These are radish seeds. ▲ Right now they might look like any kind of seed to you. When we plant one, the cells in the seed begin to divide and make new cells. Some of the new cells form roots. Some of the new cells form leaves, and still others form the stem. In time, we have a new radish plant. The new plant has inherited the traits that make it a radish from its parents.

Every time we plant a radish seed we get a radish plant. We never get a squash or pumpkin instead. Somehow the parents of the radish provide instructions for the seed to develop the traits of a radish. The parents provide a kind of blueprint for the growing radish seed.

Plants and animals inherit chromosomes from their parents. **Chromosomes** (KROH-muh-somes) are rod-shaped structures found in the nucleus of cells. Each plant and animal cell has a set of chromosomes. You can see the chromosomes clearly in the cells from the growing tip of an onion root. ◆

Chromosomes, then, control the heredity of an organism. They carry the blueprint that determines what kind of organism will develop.

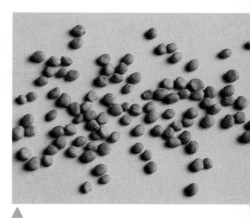

▲

◆

347

The Genetic Code

Plants and animals have many traits. In the chromosomes a large molecule called **DNA*** provides the blueprint for each of these traits. We say that DNA carries a code for an organism's heredity.

DNA in a chromosome is divided into smaller parts called **genes.** Each gene or group of genes contains the code for a certain trait. One group of genes in the banana, for example, contains the code for its yellow color. Another group contains the code for the banana's shape. All the genes combined contain the **genetic code** that controls heredity.

The genetic code on this hen's chromosomes determines that it will lay brown eggs. ■ While this hen looks quite similar, it isn't. ● Its genetic code causes it to lay white eggs. The hens have inherited many similar traits, but their genetic codes are not completely alike. How can you tell?

The genetic code helps determine what an organism looks like, and how it grows. However, there are other factors involved as well. *ACTIVITY*

*DNA is short for deoxyribonucleic acid.

Environment and Living Things

You can use: a potato with at least 4 "eyes," 4 small flowerpots, garden soil, water, small kitchen knife

1 Carefully cut the potato into four pieces of equal size. Make sure each piece has an "eye." The "eye" is a bud from which a new potato plant can grow.

2 Label the pots, 1, 2, 3, and 4. Fill each pot with soil. Plant a piece of potato under the soil in pots 1, 2, and 4. Trim away almost all the potato from the last bud. Plant this small piece in pot 3.

3 Water the soil in each pot so that it is moist. Put pot 1 in a dark closet. Water it regularly. Put pots 2, 3, and 4 where they will get light. Do not water pot 2 again after the first watering. Water pots 3 and 4 regularly.

4 Make a chart on a separate sheet of paper. Show the different conditions for each bud. ■ The information for pot 4 is already filled in.

5 Watch your plants develop and record your observations. Here is what one student saw. ● How can you explain these results?

Pot	Food	Water	Light
1			
2			
3			
4	yes	yes	yes

Heredity and Environment

We can grow new plants from the buds of one potato. Since each bud comes from the original plant, each bud has exactly the same chromosomes. So each new plant has the exact same heredity. Yet if we change the conditions in the environment, the plants do not all develop in the same way. A lack of food, or water, or sunlight changes the way the plant develops. The coast redwood trees in California, for example, are among the tallest in the world. However, without the proper environment they could not grow to their full height.

Organisms with the same heredity may develop differently in different environments. Here is evidence, then, that heredity is not the only thing that affects a plant's development. The environment also has an important effect. The genetic code on the chromosomes determines a plant's traits. The same is true for animals. But genes do not act alone. The development of an organism is also influenced by the environment.

On a separate sheet of paper, write each statement with the best ending.

1. As a radish seed grows, its cells
  a. combine   b. divide
  c. lose half their chromosomes

2. Plants and animals that are of the same kind share
  a. parents   b. food   c. traits

3. Giving a plant no water changes its
  a. heredity   b. environment
  c. chromosomes

4. A radish seed grows into a radish. The blueprint for the growing seed is found in its
  a. traits   b. chromosomes
  c. environment

5. The statement that fits the *main* concept of this section is:
  a. The way a plant or animal looks is controlled by its heredity.
  b. A living thing is a product of its heredity and environment.

YOU CAN DISCOVER

This patch of watermelons is growing in a hot, sunny environment. ● In the northern United States, summers can be quite hot and sunny, but watermelons do not grow outdoors there. Can you find out why? *Hint:* How long does it take to grow a watermelon from a seed?

A potato grown from a bud has only one parent. The new plant inherits traits from the parent. These flowers, as well as many other plants, have two parents. ■ How do flowering plants pass on traits?

Flowering Plants

If you can, remove the petals from a large flower like this tulip. ● Now you will be able to see the parts of the flower easily. ▲ Do you see the **stamen** (STAY-mun) of the flower? The stamen produces tiny grains of **pollen** (PAHL-un). Each grain of pollen contains a sperm cell. Within the sperm cell are chromosomes. The sperm cell has one-half the normal number of chromosomes for a tulip plant.

A pollen grain may be picked up by an insect. It is transferred to the **pistil** (PIS-tul) of another tulip flower. The pollen grows a long tube toward an egg cell deep inside the pistil. The egg cell also contains chromosomes. It, too, has one-half the normal number of chromosomes for a tulip plant.

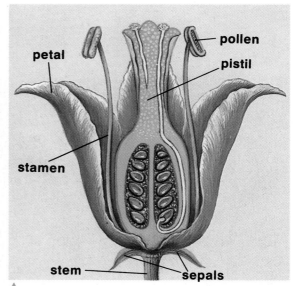

The sperm cell from the pollen tube unites with the egg cell. This union of sperm cell and egg cell produces the beginning of a new plant. The new plant is the **embryo** (EM-bree-oh). The embryo has inherited the proper number of chromosomes for a tulip plant, half from each parent.

A seed soon forms around the embryo. Later the seed falls to the ground. The seed protects the embryo. In the spring, when the soil is warm and moist, the seed provides food for the embryo. The seed begins to grow. The new tulip will have the traits it inherited from the chromosomes of both parents.

Pure-Breeding Plants

Another flowering plant is the garden pea. Some garden pea plants grow tall. Others remain short. Tallness and shortness are inherited traits carried by genes on chromosomes.

When a plant only has genes for a certain trait, it is called a *pure-breeding plant*. A plant that has genes for tallness only is a pure tall plant. A pure short plant has genes for shortness only.

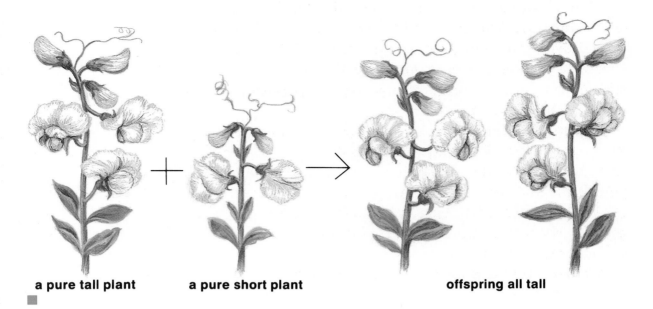

a pure tall plant   **a pure short plant**   **offspring all tall**

Suppose you are growing pea plants. You want to cross a pure tall pea plant with another pure tall plant. That is, you plan to put pollen from the stamen of one pure tall plant on the pistil of another pure tall plant. You expect all the offspring to be tall as well, and they are.

Now suppose you cross a pure tall plant with a pure short plant. You expect that some of the off-spring will be tall. Some will be short. Perhaps some will be in-between. Yet when you try it, all the off-spring are still tall. ■

Dominant and Recessive Genes

It is curious, is it not, that all the offspring are tall? Over 100 years ago, a man named Gregor Mendel also grew pea plants. He observed the plants very carefully. Pure tall plants produced only tall plants. Pure short plants produced only short plants.

Mendel investigated. He crossed pure tall plants with pure short plants many times. Mendel saw the same results you saw. The offspring were always tall!

Mendel studied the results. He called tallness a **dominant** trait. The genes for tallness dominated, or "ruled over," the genes for shortness. Mendel called shortness a **recessive** trait. The recessive genes were still present in the new plant, the offspring. However, only the dominant trait showed.

Suppose we let **T** stand for the gene for tallness. We use a capital letter since tallness is a dominant trait. A pure tall plant must have two genes for tallness (**TT**). One gene was inherited from each parent. Now suppose we let the small **t** stand for the recessive gene for shortness. A pure short plant must have two genes for shortness (**tt**).

We can cross a pure tall plant (**TT**) with a pure short plant (**tt**). ● The pure tall plant passes on one gene for tallness (**T**). The pure short plant passes on one gene for shortness (**t**). So all the offspring must have one gene for tallness and one gene for shortness (**Tt**). Since the tall gene is dominant, all the offspring are tall.

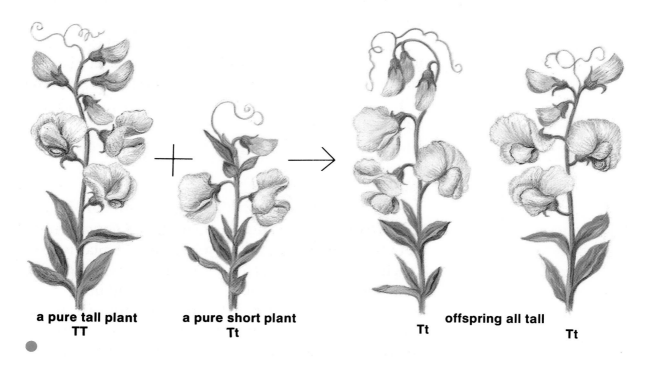

a pure tall plant
TT

a pure short plant
Tt

offspring all tall

Tt   **Tt**

Crossing Flowering Plants

Some garden pea plants have white flowers, but others have red flowers. In garden pea plants the trait for red flowers is dominant. We let (**R**) stand for the dominant gene for red flowers. The trait for white flowers is recessive. We let (**r**) stand for the gene for white flowers.

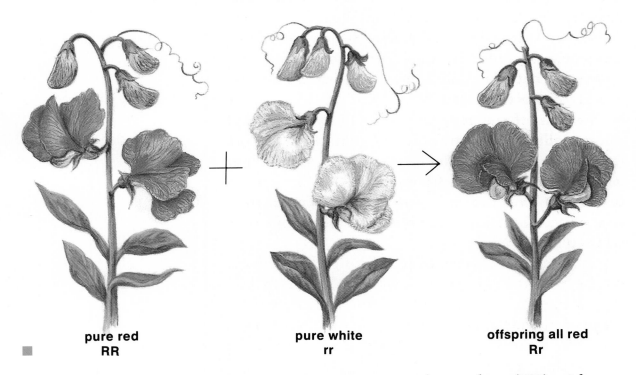

pure red
RR

pure white
rr

offspring all red
Rr

We can cross a pure red pea plant (**RR**) with another pure red plant (**RR**). The offspring are all red, of course. When we cross a pure white pea plant (**rr**) with another pure white plant (**rr**), the offspring are all white. Now suppose we cross a pure red (**RR**) with a pure white (**rr**). ■ The offspring get one gene from each parent. They are all (**Rr**). Since red is dominant, they all have red flowers.

You might not expect farmers to be interested in the color of a garden pea plant, but they are. Pea plants with white flowers produce the bright green peas that most people like to buy. Pea plants with red flowers often produce a gray pea. The gray pea tastes just as good, but it doesn't look as good. Naturally, farmers want to sell all their peas. So they prefer to plant only white-flowering pea plants.

Imagine you are a farmer and want to grow only white-flowering pea plants. It might seem like a good idea to collect and plant only seeds from pea plants with white flowers. If you planted those seeds, however, you might be in for a surprise. The flowers may be red or white. How can seeds from a white-flowering pea plant produce red flowers?

Recall that pea seeds are the product of two parents. Suppose the pollen from a red pea plant lands on the pistil of a white pea plant. ● The sperm cell in the pollen carries the dominant gene (**R**) for red flowers. The seeds forming within the white pea plant will then carry the gene for red flowers. The offspring will be red, even though the seeds came from a white pea plant. How, then, are you going to grow only white plants?

Commercial growers grow seeds to sell. The label on the packet says "white-flowering." Farmers buy that packet. They expect only plants with white flowers to grow from those seeds. So scientists have found a way to make sure that the seeds will produce the plants expected.

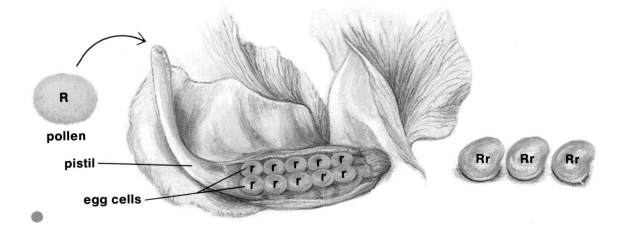

pollen

pistil

egg cells

Cross-Pollination

Seed companies want to produce pea seeds that only grow white-flowering plants. To do so they must cross white-flowering plants only with other white-flowering plants. They first take the pollen from one white flower. ■ Then they place the pollen on the pistil of another white flower. ● This process is called **cross-pollination.**

The people at the seed company know that pollen from a red flower can be blown by the wind onto a white flower. They know that bees and other animals may carry pollen from a red flower to a white flower. So they place a paper bag over the flower. ▲ The bag prevents accidental cross-pollination by a red flower.

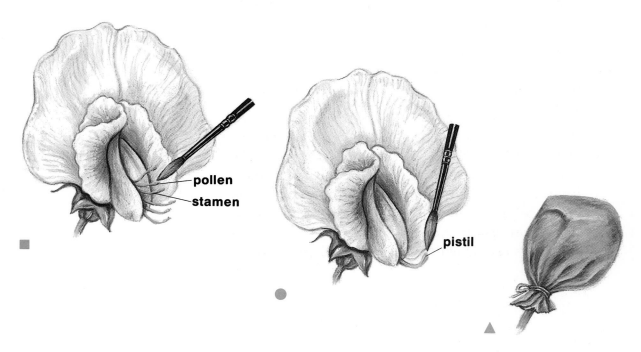

pollen
stamen

pistil

The seed company uses cross-pollination to produce seeds that are sure to grow white flowers. The people who buy the seeds know what kind of plant will grow from each seed. You can cross-pollinate plants at home as well. *ACTIVITY*

Cross-Pollinating Petunias

You can use: tweezers, small scissors, small paper bag, small paintbrush, red-flowered petunia in pot, white-flowered petunia in pot

1 You can cross a white-flowered petunia with a red-flowered petunia. First, select an unopened flower bud on the white petunia. Carefully open the bud with the tweezers. Then cut off all the stamens. ■ Why you must do so?

2 Cover the bud with a paper bag. Once a day, open the bag to check the bud. When the white flower opens, you are ready to cross-pollinate.

3 Use the brush to remove some pollen from the stamen of a red flower. Immediately, brush the pollen onto the pistil of the white flower. ● Then place the bag over the flower again.

4 When the flower has dried out, cut the seed cases from the base of the pistil. Each case contains several tiny seeds, each produced by cross-pollination. Save the seeds in a dry place until the next spring. Plant the seeds and care for them until they grow into new plants. Will the offspring be red or white? What is your prediction?

■

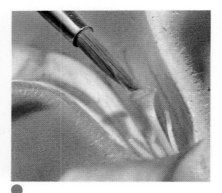
●

Blending Traits

After Mendel had written about his pea plant experiment, it was thought that all genes were either dominant or recessive. Tallness in garden peas, you will remember, is dominant over shortness. Red flowering in garden pea plants is dominant over white flowering.

All of this seemed very clear. Then a German scientist, Carl Correns, made a discovery. Correns was studying another common garden flower, four-o'clocks.

Correns started growing and crossing pure red and pure white four-o'clocks. The results were surprising. When Correns crossed pure red four-o'clocks with pure white plants, the offspring were neither red nor white. The offspring were pink. ■ This outcome could not be explained using Mendel's theories alone.

Today we know that many genes are neither dominant nor recessive. Instead, these genes act together to produce a blend of certain traits. In four-o'clocks, neither the gene for red flowers nor white flowers is dominant. When we cross a red with a white four-o'clock, the traits blend to make pink flowers.

PARENTS

RR   WW

OFFSPRING

RW

The color genes in a red four-o'clock could be written as **RR.** How will we write those in a white four-o'clock? Write them as **WW** since they are neither dominant nor recessive to the red. Notice that in this case we use capital letters for both red and white genes. ● Small letters are used only to stand for genes that are recessive.

A pure red four-o'clock crossed with a pure white four-o'clock results in a pink plant. One gene (**R**) must have come from the red plant. One gene (**W**) must have come from the white plant. The new plant must be **RW,** pink.

Hybrids

We can cross a pure tall plant (**TT**) with a pure short plant (**tt**). The offspring have one (**T**) gene and one (**t**) gene. We call an organism that has two unlike genes for the same trait a **hybrid** (HY-brid). In this type of hybrid, one gene is dominant over the other.

When we cross a pure red four-o'clock with a pure white one, we get another kind of hybrid (**RW**). In this case, neither gene is dominant over the other.

Genetic Disorders

Some diseases affecting people are caused by bacteria and viruses. Other diseases are caused by abnormal genes. Diseases caused by abnormal genes are called *genetic disorders.* Geneticists, the scientists who study genes, have learned a great deal about genetic disorders in recent years. They have found some of the abnormal genes that are associated with particular disorders.

A serious genetic disorder among white Americans is cystic fibrosis (SIS-tik fy-BRO-suhs). This disorder causes very thick mucus to interfere with breathing. Recently, a team of scientists discovered a peculiarity in the DNA of people who have cystic fibrosis. This finding now enables doctors to identify people who carry the gene for cystic fibrosis.

Sickle-cell disease is a blood-related genetic disorder that affects mostly blacks. Scientists have discovered that people who have one gene for the sickle-cell trait do not show any symptoms of the disease. Those who have two genes for the sickle-cell trait develop sickle-cell disease. Some die within the first 20 years of life. Doctors are beginning to treat victims of sickle-cell disease with gene therapy.

Today's powerful microscopes make it possible for scientists to actually see human DNA. That is one reason why geneticists are learning so much more about genetic disorders.

On a separate sheet of paper, write each statement with the best ending.

1. A pure tall pea plant crossed with a pure short pea plant will produce
   a. all tall plants
   b. tall and short plants
   c. all short plants

2. A hybrid plant may have the genes
   a. **RR**   b. **RW**   c. **WW**

3. Pollen in a flower is produced in the
   a. pistil
   b. seed
   c. stamen

4. A pure green plant is crossed with a pure red plant. All the offspring are green. For this plant, the gene for green
   a. is recessive
   b. blends with the gene for red
   c. is dominant

5. The statement that fits the *main* concept of this section is:
   a. Genes for a trait are either dominant or recessive.
   b. Although many genes are dominant or recessive, others act together to blend their traits.

YOU CAN DISCOVER

White flowers and red flowers are two varieties of pea plants. Other organisms have different varieties as well. Here are just a few of the many varieties of apples. ■ See how many other varieties of different plants and animals you can discover.

3 ▶ New Types of Plants and Animals

Farmers and scientists often cross similar organisms that have desirable traits. In this way, they hope to produce offspring with genes for the best traits of both parents. For example, they may find a particular fruit that tastes good, but it won't grow in cold weather. Another variety of the fruit does grow in cold weather, but it doesn't taste very good.

Suppose the scientists cross both fruits. They cannot control what traits are passed on, of course. So they may obtain a plant that not only doesn't taste good, but won't grow well either. Then finally, perhaps after many years of trying, they obtain a variety that tastes good and grows in cold weather. The new fruit will be better for farmers. It will be better for consumers as well. It has what we might call "prize genes."

Now let's look into some of the ways scientists help develop new varieties of plants and animals.

New Varieties of Plants

The sugar beet is an important source of sugar, second only to sugar cane. The sugar comes from the large fleshy part of the root. However, besides the large root, sugar beets also have another root system that spreads throughout the nearby soil. When you pull the sugar beet out of the ground, these roots pull out almost half a kilogram of soil. For many years, varieties of sugar beets were crossed. Finally a sugar beet with the desired trait was developed. This scientist is holding the new sugar beet. ■ When it is pulled from the ground, it comes out cleanly. This saves soil, time, and eventually saves the consumer money.

As you know, wheat is a very important food crop. The small colored spots on this wheat plant are caused by a disease called wheat rust. ● Once a plant develops wheat rust, nothing can be done to save it. There are some varieties of wheat with genes that make them resistant to wheat rust. Yet these may not be the varieties that produce the best kind of wheat for baking bread. By crossing the two, we produce a variety of wheat that makes good bread and is resistant to rust. Today we have also developed varieties of corn and oats that are resistant to rust.

Many food crops, such as the tomato, are killed each year by insects. ▲ So we cross a tomato plant that is resistant to beetles with a tomato plant that produces good-tasting fruit. The new plant produces fine tomatoes and will not be easily killed by an insect attack.

The development of new varieties of plants has helped us in a great many ways. By crossing plants with different desirable traits, we develop varieties that need less fertilizer. We develop plants that can

grow in dry areas with less water. We develop varieties that grow so much faster that we can get two harvests in a single growing season. We also develop varieties that grow in climates that are very different from those they are used to. In all these ways we help feed many people faster, inexpensively, and with more healthful foods.

The next time you go to the supermarket, look for plants in the fruit and vegetable department. You may see boxes of giant red strawberries, or blueberries as big as marbles. Look at the bin of large, mild Bermuda onions and the firm, green cabbages. All the fruits and vegetables you see came from plants with prize genes. ■

New Varieties of Animals

We can also cross animals with different traits to produce new varieties of animals. For example, cattle ranchers have always been searching for ways of improving their cattle—to produce a larger quantity and better quality of beef.

About 60 years ago, ranchers began crossing Brahman bulls from India with American shorthorned cows. The Brahman bull could stand hot, dry weather, and its thick skin could resist insect-borne diseases. ● However, it was not as good a beef producer as the American shorthorned cattle.

In 1920 after repeated crossings of Brahman and shorthorned cattle, a very special offspring was born on the famous King Ranch in Texas. The offspring, named Monkey, had prize genes. Monkey was one of the ancestors of this herd of Santa Gertrudis cattle developed by the ranchers. ▲ The Santa Gertrudis bull is strong. It can endure a dry, hot climate. It is also a very good beef producer. It has inherited the most desirable traits of each parent.

The Santa Gertrudis cattle are only one type of new variety of animal. Scientists have crossed many other animals to obtain offspring with the best traits of each parent. These turkeys, for example, were developed through the repeated crossing of many turkeys. ◆ These turkeys have more meat than other varieties, and the meat is more tender as well.

EXPLORING SCIENCE AND TECHNOLOGY

A Change in Chickens

About 100 years ago, chicken farms were quite small. Fresh eggs and fresh chicken meat were expensive. Today eggs and cooking chickens are plentiful. They are usually inexpensive as well. What happened to cause the change?

In the past, chickens were raised mainly for their eggs. When a chicken grew old and stopped laying many eggs, it was sold for meat. Now, however, farmers raise two different kinds of chickens. One variety, the Leghorn chicken, is raised for its ability to produce eggs. Over the years, farmers have chosen Leghorn hens that have produced the largest numbers of eggs. These hens are used to breed other chickens. Through such breeding, farmers have developed flocks of chickens that can lay remarkable numbers of eggs. In fact, a common Leghorn can lay an egg a day.

When raising chickens for meat, farmers want chickens that gain as much weight as possible while eating the least amount of food. By crossing the Plymouth Rock chicken with other kinds of chickens, they have developed just such a variety. Today cooking chickens are ready for market only eight weeks after hatching. In that time their body weight increases over 40 times!

On a separate sheet of paper, write each statement with the best answer.

1. One way to produce new varieties of plants and animals is by
   a. making cuttings
   b. crossing
   c. adding fertilizer

2. Farmers developed a sugar beet that
   a. tastes better
   b. is resistant to rust
   c. pulls cleanly out of the soil

3. An undesirable trait in tomatoes is
   a. easily damaged by insects
   b. resistance to insects
   c. good-tasting fruit

4. Crossing Brahman bulls and short-horned cows produced
   a. longhorned cattle
   b. Santa Gertrudis cattle
   c. Leghorn cattle

5. The statement that fits the *main* concept of this section is:
   a. When we cross two organisms, the best traits of each are passed on to the offspring.
   b. By crossing organisms with desirable traits, we sometimes obtain offspring with desirable traits from each parent.

YOU CAN DISCOVER

1. The mule is an animal produced from the cross of two different animals. ■ What animals produce a mule? What advantages does the mule have over its parents? Does it have disadvantages as well?

2. These tangelos are a variety of fruit produced by crossing two different kinds of fruit. ● Find out how tangelos are produced.

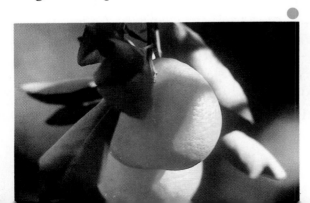

4 ▶ Mutations

It may take farmers years of crossing before they can produce a variety of plant or animal with the traits they desire. Yet sometimes an organism may suddenly appear with an entirely new trait. The trait is not caused by crossing different varieties.

The code for all our traits, remember, is passed on by the genes from parent organisms. So if a new trait appears, it follows that the code on the gene or a group of genes has been changed. These sudden changes in the genes are **mutations** (myoo-TAY-shuns). Genes that mutate, change suddenly, are mutant genes.

A Sudden Change in Oranges

Suppose you have a grove of orange trees. ■ All the oranges you grow have seeds in them. ● Then one day you pick an orange from a tree. When you cut it in half, you can't believe your eyes. There are no seeds in this orange. ▲ Some of the genes in the orange have mutated to produce an orange without any seeds.

An orange without seeds has a very desirable trait. People are usually willing to pay more for seedless oranges. They are easier to eat. The mutated gene, it seems, is a prize gene. Most orange growers would like to have many seedless orange trees. However, seedless oranges present a problem. How can we pass on these prize genes and grow more mutant orange trees if there are no seeds?

Growing Oranges Without Seeds

Here is a clue. Recall that you could plant a piece of potato containing an "eye." If the environment is right, it will take root and grow. If you plant a small branch, or twig, from a plant such as a geranium, you can get a new plant. You can grow a plant, you see, without using a seed! ◆

Farmers use a similar process to grow seedless orange trees. First they cut a small twig from the

geranium plant

cutting in damp soil

new geranium grows from the cutting

371

branch from
seedless
orange tree

rooted
lemon tree

mutant tree. Notice the shape of the cut. ■ The trunk of a young, healthy lemon tree is cut in the same way. ● The grower then joins the seedless orange twig to the rooted lemon tree. ▲ This joining is called a **graft.** The grower wraps cloth around the graft to protect it, and seals it with a special wax. The new tree will grow seedless oranges.

A New Variety of Potato

Mutations that cause desirable traits occur in many plants from time to time. When they do, we try to breed the mutant plant and produce more mutants with the desired trait. For example, mutant potatoes have been discovered. Their genes have changed so that they are resistant to some diseases.

Scientists and farmers wanted to preserve this resistance to disease in potatoes. To do so, they crossed the original mutant potatoes many times. Finally they got what they were looking for.

The new variety of potato—the Katahdin potato—is resistant to diseases. ◆ It also looks and tastes better than older types of potatoes. The Katahdin potato is another prize package of genes.

It might appear as if genes that mutate always produce desirable new traits. This is not the case. Many mutations do not produce any obvious changes. Many more are actually harmful. In those cases, the mutation may damage the development of the organism, or even cause it to die. *ACTIVITY*

Growing Mutated Corn Seeds

You can use: mixture of albino and normal corn seeds, flower box (or several flower pots), potting soil

1 Sometimes corn plants can mutate to produce albino corn seeds. Albino plants have no green chlorophyll.

2 Fill the flower box with rich potting soil. Plant the mixture of normal and albino corn seeds. Place each seed about 1 centimeter below the surface.

3 Place the box where it will get sunlight. Keep the soil moist. Here is what one student saw after the seeds sprouted. ■ Do the mutant albino seeds sprout as well as the normal seeds? Can you explain why?

4 Continue to water the corn plants. Observe their growth every few days. What happens to the mutant plants? Here are a student's results after several weeks. ●

Ancon Sheep

The genes of animals can also mutate and produce new traits. Consider the story of one mutant lamb.

In 1791, a strange lamb was born in Mississippi. Instead of long legs, it had short legs. These short legs were an advantage to the farmer. This lamb could not do something others could do—it could not jump over fences! This lamb, it seemed, had prize genes.

The farmer waited for the mutant lamb to grow up. Then the farmer crossed it with a sheep with long legs. The farmer made many such crosses. There was no way to know when an offspring would be short-legged. The farmer could only wonder and wait.

Finally, after many years, the farmer developed a flock of sheep with short legs. The sheep were known as Ancon sheep.

For over 75 years, Ancon sheep were bred in New England. Then they died out. Many years later another mutant sheep with short legs was born in Norway. From that sheep, breeders produced another flock of Ancon sheep. You can compare the photograph of a regular sheep with the short-legged Ancon to see how much a simple mutation can change an animal. ■

A New Breed of Cattle

Here is another example of a mutant gene. This is a longhorned Texas bull. ● One day a shorthorned animal such as this was born to longhorned parents. ▲ The gene for long horns had mutated into a gene for short horns. Ranchers liked the shorthorned mutant. Shorthorned cattle are easier to handle. In shipping, they do not hurt one another when loaded into close quarters.

Luckily, in this case, the prize genes for shorthorns are dominant over the genes for longhorns. The offspring of a cross between a longhorned bull and shorthorned cow is another shorthorn.

Today, many ranchers prefer to raise the shorthorned cattle. They cross only shorthorned cattle with other shorthorned cattle to develop a herd of pure shorthorns. By breeding only pure shorthorns, they can be sure that all the offspring will also be shorthorned.

The mutant sheep and cattle have traits we consider desirable. So we breed them. Like those of plants, many mutations in animals damage the organism and are not favorable. That is why we are so careful to preserve and breed plants and animals when favorable mutations do occur.

375

On a separate sheet of paper, write each statement with the best ending.

1. The seedless orange was the result of a
   a. change in the environment
   b. mutation   c. hybrid cross

2. An advantage of the Katahdin potato is its
   a. better taste   b. larger size
   c. resistance to disease

3. Albino corn is an example of a
   a. helpful mutation
   b. harmful mutation

4. If we cross a shorthorned cow and a longhorned bull, the offspring will all have
   a. short horns   b. long horns
   c. medium horns

5. The statement that fits the *main* concept of this section is:
   a. A mutation is passed along in the genetic code.
   b. Changes in the genetic code do not change living things.

YOU CAN DISCOVER

This fruit fly is pure for the trait of straight wings. ■ Yet its offspring has curly wings. ● Find out how this could happen. *Hint:* Look up Dr. Herman Muller and read about his work with X rays.

Farm Operator

In this country, there are large farms employing many hundreds of people. Also, there are small farms run by a few people. In both cases the farm is most likely managed by the farm operator.

The farm operator and helpers have many duties. They plan what crops to plant in a growing season. They prepare the land before planting. ■ At the proper time, they plant their seeds. Then they must keep conditions in the environment as close to perfect as possible. To do so, they water or irrigate the crops and add fertilizers to the soil. ● Finally, when the crops are full grown, they must be harvested, packed, and sent to market. ▲

If the farm raises animals, farm operators are in charge of their care and well-being. They must make sure the animals are fed properly. They must clean the barn, pens, and milking areas to prevent disease. Very often they may have to build fences to keep farm animals in and keep hungry, wild animals out.

The tasks of the farm operators often never seem to end. They wake early and work much of the day. Their reward is a field full of healthy crops.

✓ Plant the seed of an oak tree, an acorn. ■ How well the plant grows depends on the kind of soil and the minerals in the soil.

✓ Plants also depend on water and sunlight to grow. The growth of a plant, then, depends on the environment.

✓ The kind of plant that develops—an oak tree, or some other kind of tree—depends on the genes on the chromosomes in its cells. ●

✓ Genes pass on a plant's traits. Genes set the shape of its leaves, the color of the bark, and so on. The genes carry the code of heredity.

✓ This leads us to an important concept in science: **An organism is the product of its heredity and the environment in which it develops.**

✓ We can cross organisms with different traits to produce offspring with the most desirable traits of both parents. By crossing such organisms with prize genes we can develop new and better varieties of plants and animals.

✓ Sometimes a gene may change or mutate. If the mutation provides a new and better trait, we may cross the mutant with other such organisms to produce new varieties of plants and animals. ▲

A. CHOOSE THE BEST ANSWER.

1. All the traits a living thing inherits are called its
   a. chromosomes   b. heredity   c. genes

2. A pure short plant crossed with a pure short plant will produce
   a. all tall plants   b. tall and short plants
   c. all short plants

3. Pea plants with white flowers produce
   a. green peas   b. gray peas
   c. both green and gray peas

4. Pollen grows a long tube toward an egg cell inside the
   a. stamen   b. pistil   c. petal

5. In a plant, the union of a sperm cell and an egg cell produces
   a. a gene   b. an embryo   c. chromosomes

6. The trait for red feathers is dominant over white. When pure red-feathered roosters are mated with white-feathered hens, the results are
   a. only red-feathered chickens
   b. only white-feathered chickens
   c. rust-feathered chickens

7. An organism that has unlike genes for the same trait is a
   a. mutant   b. hybrid   c. pure breed

8. A fruit tree that produces only seedless fruit can be reproduced by
   a. planting the seeds
   b. grafting
   c. planting the fruit

9. An advantage of the Ancon sheep is that they
   a. cannot jump over fences
   b. have high quality wool
   c. eat little food

10. The statement that fits the *main* concept of this unit is:
    a. By crossing organisms with desirable traits and allowing them to grow in the right environment, we can develop varieties with prize genes.
    b. The environment determines whether an organism will live or die. Heredity determines what an organism will look like.

B. ANSWER THESE QUESTIONS.

1. Why are some organisms often thought of as having prize genes?

2. When we plant a corn seed, we always get a corn plant. Why?

3. Explain why a plant with red flowers can produce seeds that grow into plants with white flowers.

4. Mendel's theory of dominant and recessive genes doesn't explain the results of Correns' experiments. Why?

5. A farmer crosses pure tall plants with pure short plants. All the offspring are short. Diagram this cross showing the genes for both parents and the offspring. Which gene is dominant in this plant?

6. Why is it important to preserve and breed plants and animals with favorable traits?

Find Out More

This is one of the world's largest banks. ■ No, there is no money on deposit here. It's a government seed bank located at Fort Collins. Seeds of plant varieties from all over the world are stored here. Why is such a seed bank necessary? What services does the bank provide?

Challenge Your Thinking

Cross a fish with a bird? ● Cross a bee with a lizard? ▲ Not likely. However, this *liger* is the result of one unusual cross between two different animals. ◆ What is a liger?

Glossary

Certain science words are in darker print in your textbook. They are listed in this glossary with their definitions and page numbers. The page numbers tell you where to find more information about the words.

Some of these words have a pronunciation in parentheses. The pronunciation shows you how to say the word. The key below will help you pronounce some common word sounds.

a as in cat
ay as in late
air as in bear
ah as in father
aw as in ball
e as in egg
ee as in team
i as in sit
y as in ice

oh as in boat
oi as in toy
or as in born
oo as in pool
ow as in cow
yoo as in use
u or **uh** as in sun

amplifier, a device that increases the strength of an electric signal from a microphone, 170

animal kingdom, one of three kingdoms into which all living things can be classified, 74

antibiotic, a substance which, when introduced into the body, controls many bacterial infections, 110

antibody, a substance, made by special body cells, that acts against specific disease-causing organisms or other foreign bodies, 105

antiseptic, one kind of substance that slows down or stops the growth of bacteria outside the body, 108

atomic number, the number of protons in the nucleus of an atom. It is also the index of the properties of the atom, 318

bacilli (buh-SIL-y), **bacillus** (singular), rod-shaped bacteria, 83

bacteria, bacterium (singular), microscopic organisms that are found just about everywhere on Earth. Some bacteria cause disease, 82

binary stars, a pair of stars circling around a common center, 250

biomes (BY-ohms), areas with similar geography and climate. Similar plants and animals live in similar biomes, 45

black hole, an area, surrounding a dead star, that has such a strong gravitational pull that light is trapped inside it. 288

carnivore (KAHR-nuh-vohr), an animal that eats only other animals, 26

chain reaction, a process in which neutrons from the fission of one atomic nucleus cause fission of other nuclei, 321

chlorophyll (KLOR-uh-fil), a green substance in green plant cells that allows photosynthesis to take place, 4

chromosome (KROH-muh-sohm), a structure inside the nucleus of a cell that contains substances which determine the characteristics of new organisms, 347

cilia (SIL-ee-uh), tiny hairs that line the inside of the nose and the tubes to the lungs, 102

circuit-breaker, a switch that automatically stops the flow of electric current when there is a short circuit or an overload, 160

cocci (KAHK-sy), **coccus** (singular), sphere-shaped bacteria, 84

colony, a group of many bacteria, 82

community, a group of living things in one place, 25

concave lens, a lens that is thicker near the edges than in the middle. It forms an image by spreading out light in an orderly way, 196

concave mirror, a mirror that is curved inward like the inner surface of a spoon, 191

conductor, a substance through which an electric current can flow easily, 138

coniferous (ka-NIF-ur-us), bearing cones. Coniferous trees have needlelike leaves that fall all year long, 48

constellation, a pattern of stars seen with the unaided eye in a small region of the sky, 243

consumer, a living thing that cannot make its own food but must instead find food and eat it, 9

control, that part of an experiment that includes all conditions (variables) except the one being studied, 37

convex lens, a lens that is thicker in the middle than near the edges. It focuses light at a point, 194

convex mirror, a mirror that is curved outward like the outer surface of a spoon, 192

cross-pollination, the transfer of pollen from the stamen of one flower to the pistil of another, 358

current electricity, an electric charge that is moving from one place to another, 132

deciduous (di-SIJ-oo-us), shedding leaves annually. Common deciduous trees are maple, oak, and beech, 46

decomposer, a living thing that feeds on dead matter. Decay bacteria are the most common decomposers, 10

DNA, the substance in chromosomes that determines the characteristics of an organism, 348

dominant, a trait that always appears in the offspring if it is carried by a gene, or genes, in the cells, 355

ecology (i-KOL-uh-jee), the study of the relationship between living things and their environment, 12

ecosystem (EE-koh-sis-tum), the relationship between living things and the nonliving environment, 21

egg cell, a specialized cell in a plant or animal which, when united with a sperm cell, can develop into a new organism, 352

electric charge, bits of electricity carried by electrons and protons, 128

electric circuit, a closed path electrons take, 134

electromagnet, a magnet made up of a coil of wire wound around an iron core in which the magnetic field is produced by electric current flowing through a coil, 147

electron (i-LEK-trahn), a tiny, negatively-charged particle revolving around the nucleus of an atom, 128

embryo (EM-bree-oh), the living organism in a seed (before germination), in an egg (before hatching), and in a mammal (before birth), 353

enamel, the hard, outer layer of teeth, 114

energy, the ability to do work; the ability to set matter in motion, 4

environment (en-VY-run-munt), all the surroundings of an organism, including all matter and all forms of life with which an organism is interdependent, 12

epidemic, a disease that spreads rapidly and affects many people, 99

fission, the splitting of the nucleus of an atom, 319

flagella (fluh-JEL-uh), the thin, hairlike structures extending from some single-celled organisms, such as certain bacteria. By beating flagella like whips, bacteria can move about, 85

fluorescent (flohr-ES-unt), giving off light as a result of ultraviolet light photons being released by excited mercury atoms, 224

focal length, the distance from the lens to the focal point, 194

focal point, the point at which light rays are brought together, or focused, 191

food chain, a series of organisms, usually starting with a green plant, in which each organism is used as food by the next one in the series, 13

food web, all the possible connected food chains in an ecosystem, 17

fossil, the preserved remains or imprint of a plant or animal that lived long ago, 301

fuel, a substance that releases energy when burned, 298

fuse, a protective device that prevents short circuits or overloads by breaking the circuits, 160

fusion (FYOO-zhun), the combining of atoms to form a new atom, 282

galaxy, a large group of stars, as well as the planets, gases, and other objects around those stars, 251

gene, a part within the DNA molecule that is basic to the development of a certain trait, 348

generator, a device that converts mechanical energy into electric energy, 147

geothermal (jee-oh-THUR-mul) **energy,** heat deep inside the Earth, 335

glucose (GLOO-kohs), a sugar made in the process of photosynthesis, 5

graft, the joining of two plants so that they grow together as a single plant, 372

herbivore (HUR-buh-vohr), an animal that eats plants, 25

heredity, the passing of traits from parents to offspring, 346

hibernate, to spend the winter in a deep sleep, 47

hybrid (HY-brid), an organism that results from the mating of two organisms, each pure for a different given trait, 361

immune, having conditions within the body unfavorable to disease-causing microorganisms, 105

immunity (i-MYOO-ni-tee), the ability of a body to recognize invading microorganisms and fight off an infection, 103

incandescent (in-kun-DES-unt), hot enough to give off light. A glowing tungsten filament in a bulb produces incandescent light, 223

infection, invasion of an organism by harmful bacteria or other microorganisms, 92

infrared (in-fruh-RED), the invisible band of light below the red band in the visible spectrum, 205

insulator, a substance that does not allow an electric current to flow easily, 138

interdependent, being dependent on one another, 18

invertebrate (in-VUR-tuh-brayt), an animal that does not have a backbone, 77

laser beam, a special beam of light that is only one color and travels in one direction in a narrow beam, 230

lens, a piece of glass or plastic shaped in a special way to bend rays of light, 194

light-year, a unit of length in astronomy that is equal to the distance light travels in one year, 264

lines of force, the pattern of the magnetic field showing the amount and direction of force around a magnet or a conductor of electricity, 145

mass, the amount of matter in an object, 280

meltdown, too much heat builds up in the core of a nuclear reactor, 323

microorganism (my-kroh-AWR-guh-niz-um), an organism that can be seen only with a microscope, 82

microphone, a device that converts sounds into an electric current, 170

microwave, a kind of radio wave that can pass through glass or paper but is reflected by metal. Special ovens use microwaves to cook food, 227

migrate, moving from one area or climate to another, 48

mucus (MYOO-kus), sticky fluid given off by special cells that line the mouth, nose, and other places in the body, 101

mutation (myoo-TAY-shun), a new characteristic resulting from a change in the genes. The new characteristic can be inherited, 370

natural gas, gas produced from the remains of plants and animals. It is used as a source of fuel, 314

nebula (NEB-yuh-luh), **nebulae** (plural), a huge cloud in space made up of dust and gases. New stars may form from a nebula, 253

neutron (NOO-trahn), a particle in the nucleus of an atom that has no electric charge, 128

neutron star, a star whose mass is pulled into a dense core as a result of supernova explosion, 288

niche (NICH), the role an organism plays in its community, 31

nitrogen-fixing bacteria, bacteria that take nitrogen gas from the air and combine it with other substances, 89

nuclear energy, energy inside the nucleus of an atom that is released when the nucleus is split or fused with another nucleus, 318

nuclear reactor, an apparatus in which a nuclear chain reaction is started and controlled, so that energy is produced, 323

omnivore (AHM-ni-vohr), an animal that eats both plant and animal life, 26

parallel circuit, an electric current in which the current has two or more paths to follow, 135

paramecium (par-uh-MEE-see-um), a single-celled, foot-shaped organism, often classified as a protist, 74

peat, the beginning stage in the formation of coal when layers of plant matter have hardened, 301

permafrost, soil that stays frozen throughout the year, as in the tundra, 65

petroleum (puh-TROH-lee-um), the thick, dark liquid pumped from the ground from which gasoline and oil are derived; crude oil, 310

phosphor (FAHS-fur), a substance that gives off light after absorbing certain kinds of energy, 225

photon (FOH-tahn), a tiny bundle of radiant energy that an atom may give off one at a time, 208

photosynthesis (foh-toh-SIN-thuh-sis), the process by which green plants use light energy to make food, 4

pistil (PIS-tul), the part of a flower that contains the egg cells at its base, 352

plant kingdom, one of three kingdoms into which all living things can be classified, 74

plaque (PLAK), a sticky, colorless substance found on teeth. It is made up of saliva and dead cells, 114

pollen (PAHL-un), a powdery grain on the stamen of a flower. It contains the plant's sperm cell, 352

population, a group made up of one kind of living thing in an ecosystem, 24

producer, a plant that makes its own food and upon which other living things depend; a green plant, 2

protist (PROH-tist), a microscopic, usually single-celled organism. Protozoans, bacteria, algae, and fungi can be classified as protists, 74

protista kingdom, one of three kingdoms into which all living things can be classified. This kingdom includes organisms that have both plant and animal characteristics, 74

proton (PROH-tahn), a particle in the nucleus of an atom, with an electric charge, 128

protozoans (proh-tuh-ZOH-unz), a group of single-celled organisms with some animallike characteristics. They can be classified as protists, 74

pulsar (PUL-sahr), a star that gives off radio waves in pulses at regular intervals, 257

quasar (KWAY-zahr), a very distant object in space that is a powerful source of light and radio waves, 258

radar, a method of detecting faraway objects and finding their exact positions with the use of radio waves, 233

radiant energy, energy given off by an excited atom, in a bundle called a photon, 208

radiation, the energy given off by the decay of certain atoms, 325

radio telescope, an antenna, often dish-shaped, used to collect and focus radio waves from space, 255

radio waves, a stream of photons below the band of infrared light. These photons have less energy than the photons of visible light, 209

receiver, the part of a telephone that converts electrical impulses back into sound, 167

recessive, a trait that only appears in an organism when the organism has two identical genes for the trait, 355

red giant, an aging star that has grown larger and glows with a red light, 284

reflected, bounced off an object, as light off a mirror, 188

reflecting telescope, a telescope that uses concave mirrors, 247

refracting telescope, a telescope that uses lenses instead of mirrors, 247

refraction (ri-FRAK-shun), the bending of light, 193

respiration (res-puh-RAY-shun), the breakdown of food to release energy, 8

retina (RET-un-uh), the lining of the back of the eyeball that senses light, 196

scavenger (SKAV-in-jur), an animal that feeds, in part, on dead plant and animal matter, 12

series circuit, an electric circuit in which the current follows a single path through the entire circuit, 135

solar energy, energy that comes directly from the Sun, 331

spectroscope (SPEK-truh-skohp), an instrument that separates white light into its spectrum. It is used to analyze light from glowing objects, 271

spectrum (SPEK-trum), **spectra** (plural), the series of colors seen when white light is refracted, 203

sperm cell, a special cell in a plant or animal that, when united with an egg cell, can develop into a new organism, 352

spirilla (spy-RIL-uh), **spirillum** (singular), bacteria that are shaped like corkscrews, 84

stamen (STAY-mun), the part of a flower that produces pollen, 352

static electricity, an electric charge that builds up on an object, 130

supernova (soo-pur-NOH-vuh), a star that collapses in a tremendous explosion, giving off great amounts of heat, 286

telegraph, an instrument used to send messages through a wire, 165

toxin (TAHK-sin), a poison produced by an organism, such as bacteria, 92

trait (TRAYT), a characteristic of an organism, 344

transmitter, the part of a telephone that converts sounds into electrical impulses that are sent over wires, 167

ultraviolet (ul-truh-VY-uh-lit) **light,** invisible band of light above the violet band in the visible spectrum, 205

vaccine, a substance containing dead or weakened bacteria or viruses introduced into the blood to develop immunity to a disease, 111

variable, a condition that changes as the conditions upon which it depends change, 36

vertebrate (VUR-tuh-brayt), an animal that has a backbone, 77

virus, a particle smaller than a bacterium. A virus can reproduce only inside a living cell. A virus can cause disease, 94

wavelength, the distance between the top of one wave and the top of the next, 215

white blood cell, a special kind of cell in the blood that can engulf and destroy bacteria, 103

white dwarf, a star that collapses when its helium fuel is used up completely, 285

X rays, a stream of photons that are beyond the band of ultraviolet light. These photons have more energy than the photons of visible light, 209

Index

abacus, 180

acid rain, 303

Acquired Immune Deficiency Syndrome, 106

AIDS, 106

air, 3, 5, 8, 19, 38, 85, 89, 210; disease-causing microorganisms in, 96–97

air pollution, 32, 303, 313, 325, 339

Alexandria, lighthouse of, 232

algae, 75

Algol (star), 250

Alpha Centauri (star), 250, 264, 267

aluminum, 138

amber, 126, 129

ameba, 75

amphibians, 77, 78

amplifier, 170–71

Ancon sheep, 374

Andes Mountains, 25

Andromeda galaxy, 266

Animal Kingdom, 74, 77–78

animal populations, 24–25

animals, 10, 12; in biomes, 44–45; breeding of, 366–68, 374–75, 378; carnivores, 26; classification of, 77–78; of coniferous forest, 50, 67; of deciduous forest, 47; desert, 59, 61–62; as disease carriers, 97–99; in ecosystem, 21–26, 28–31; energy stored in, 307–08, 339; environmental effect on development, 19, 350; in food chain, 13–14, 17–19; as food consumers, 2–3, 9, 13–14, 38–39; of grasslands, 58; herbivores, 25–26; hereditary traits, 346–48, 350; omnivores, 26; reproduction of, 78; tropical rain forest, 52, 53–54; tundra, 66

Antares (star), 275, 277

anteater, 54

antenna: radio, 174, 175, 233, 255; television, 176

antibiotics, 110, 121

antibodies, 104–05, 106, 111, 121

antiseptics, 108–09, 113, 118

appliances, electric, 134, 138, 141, 158

apprentices, science, 35

Arizona, 63

armadillo, 78

asphalt, 314–15

astrolabe, 245

astronomy, 242–53, 256–57; radio, 255–59; see also stars; Universe

atmosphere, 210, 249; see also air

atomic bomb, 322

atomic number, 318

atoms, 128, 207–08, 282; excited, 208–12, 218–19, 236–37, 255; fission of, 318–19, 321–22, 338, 339; fusion of, 282–86; structure of, 128, 317

bacilli, 83

backbone, in animals, 77

bacteria, 29, 75, 82–92, 94, 96, 101, 120; antibiotics and, 110; antiseptics and, 108–09; benefits of, 89–90, 120; colonies of, 83; decay, 10, 17, 18, 75, 86, 89, 120; defenses against, 101–04, 105, 108–11, 121, 228; disease-causing, 86, 89, 90, 92, 98, 113, 114–15, 120; infected by virus, 95; intestinal, 90; movement of, 85; nitrogen-fixing, 89, 120; reproduction of, 86–87; soil, 18, 82, 89, 92; types and shapes of, 83–84

390

hydrogen as, 283, 284, 327; kerosene, 311; oil, 223, 307, 311–13; peat, 301–02; synthetic, 341; uranium, 322; wood, 298, 300, 302

Fundy, Bay of, 289

fungi, 75

fuse, electric, 160

fusion, nuclear, 292, 327; of carbon atoms, 286; helium to carbon, 284–85; hydrogen to helium, 282–83, 327

galaxies, 251–53, 258, 266, 291; distances of, 266; movement of, 278, 292; radio, 257, 266; sizes of, 265; spiral, 252

galvanometer, 144, 146

garbage, as energy source, 336

gas, 273; drilling for, 308–09; as fuel, 223, 307, 314, 316, 336; from garbage, 336; natural, 314, 339; from organic wastes, 341; in space, 286–88, 293; *see also* nebulae

gas-discharge lighting, 224–25

gasoline, 311–12

gasoline engine, 143, 311–12, 316

geese, 66

geiger counter, 325

generators, electric, 147, 149, 150–51, 302, 331

genes, 348, 350, 353, 360–61, 378; dominant and recessive, 354–57, 360–61; mutant, 370–75, 378; prize, 364, 366, 367, 371, 372, 374–75, 378

genetic code, 348, 350, 370

genetic diseases, 362

geothermal energy, 335, 339

German measles, 111

geysers, 335

giant stars, 277; red, 284

giant tube worm, 29, 86

glaciers, 49; meltwater as power source, 330

glasses, eye, 198

glucose, 5

gold, 138

graft, of plants, 372

grasses, 8, 25, 46, 58, 66

grasshoppers, 58

grasslands biome, 45, 56, 57–58, 71

gravitation, 280–82, 284, 286, 288; and tides, 289

grazing animals, 58, 66

Great Plains, 57

Greenland, glacial meltwater power, 33

grizzly bear, 55

ground squirrel, 50, 67

growth, factors in: environment, 19, 349–50, 378; heredity, 347–48, 350, 378

Gulf Stream, 329

Hale telescope, 246–47

halophytes, 63

hare, snowshoe, 50, 66

hawks, 58

health, 113–17

heat, 207, 210–11, 298

heating, 207, 302; kerosene, 311; natural gas, 314; oil, 312–13; solar, 332–33

helium, 273, 282–83; fusion to carbon, 284–85

hemlock, 48

herbivores, 25

heredity, 346–48, 352–61, 378; chromosomes and, 347–48, 352–53; and environment, 350, 378; *see also* genes; traits

Helens, Mount St., 81

Hero, 298, 300

Herschel, William, 204, 226

hibernation, 47, 50, 67

hickory, 46

High Speed Surface Transport, 154

hoofed mammals, 78

moose, 50

mosses, 49, 76

moths, 54

motors, electric, 155–57, 161, 183

mouth, 101–02; bacteria in, 114–16

movie projector, 195, 200, 236

movies, special effects, 235

mucus, 101–02, 121

mule, 369

multiple stars, 250

mumps, 94, 111

muscle power, 143, 298, 300

mushrooms, 3, 10, 75

musk oxen, 67

mutations, 370–75, 378

NASA, 249, 276

natural gas, 307, 314, 339; *see also* gas

nearsightedness, 198

nebulae, 253, 260, 282, 287–88, 291

neon: lights, 225; spectrum of, 273

Neptune, 276

neutrons, 128, 317–19; as fission "bullets," 318–19, 321

neutron stars, 288–89, 293

niche, 30–31, 71

Nile River, 28

Nimbus 7 weather satellite, 220

nitrogen, 89, 286

nitrogen-fixing bacteria, 89, 120

Northern Hemisphere, 245

northern lights, 187, 210

North Star, 245, 265

nose, 101–02

nuclear energy, 317, 318–19, 321–25, 339; problems of, 325

nuclear reactions, 292; *see also* fission, nuclear; fusion, nuclear

nuclear reactors, 322–24, 327, 339; Chernobyl, 325; meltdown of, 323, 325;

power plants, 317, 324, 325, 326; Three Mile Island, 325

nucleus, atomic, 128, 317–18, 321–22

oak tree, 46

observation, 35–36

ocean: food chain, 14; food producers in, 75; as power source, 329, 330

octopus, 77

oil, as fuel, 223, 307, 311–13; crude, 310; drilling for, 308–09; heating, 312–13; pollution, 313, 325; refining, 310–11

Oklahoma dust bowl, 56

olives, 7

omnivores, 26

operations, surgical, 113, 118; laser, 231

opossums, 53

optic nerve, 197

optics, 199

oranges, seedless, 370–72

orangutan, 78

orchids, 53

Orion (constellation), 244, 274

otters, 13

owls, 17, 58

oxygen, 19, 85, 286; atom, 317–18; release in photosynthesis, 5, 10, 18; use in respiration, 8, 9, 10

oysters, 77

Palomar, Mount, 246

panda, giant, 15

panthers, 54

parallel circuit, 135–37, 182

paramecium, 74

parasites, 34

parrots, 53

particle accelerator, 338

particle physicist, 338

viral diseases, 94–96, 98, 104–05, 111, 121

viruses, 94–96; defenses against, 104–05, 110–11, 121

vitamins, 90; B, 90; D, 228

volcano: Mount St. Helens, 81

volvox, 75

Voyager spacecraft, 258, 276

walkie-talkie, 174

warblers, 30–31

Washington, George, 307

water, 3, 8, 11, 19, 38, 85, 378; disease organisms in, 97, 123; in photosynthesis, 5; *see also* drinking water water animals, 77

water birds, 66, 67

water cycle, 11

water flea, 3

Water Lilies (Monet), 51

water plants, 14, 75

water pollution, 32; oil spills, 313; treatment of, 90, 97

water power, 329–30, 339; electric power plants, 150–51, 155, 313, 329–30

water tubes, plant, 76

water wheels, 329

wavelength, 215–17, 237

waves, 212–13, 237; nature of, 215

wave theory of light, 212–14, 216–17, 219

weasels, 50

weather prediction, 220, 233

weather satellites, 220

Westward (research ship), 331

wheat, rust-resistant, 365

white blood cells, 103

white dwarfs (stars), 284–85, 289, 293

whooping cough, 92, 111

wildflowers, 46, 51, 58

Wilson, Mount, 295

windmills, 331

windpipe, 102

wind power, 143, 331, 339

winter, 44–45, 46, 48, 50, 52, 65

wiring, electric, 134–37; in homes, 137, 138, 158–160, 181

wolves, 30, 50, 58, 66

wood, as fuel, 298, 300, 302

woodchuck, 47

woodpecker, 21

worms, 47, 77; *see also* earthworm; giant tube worm

wounds, 103–04, 108, 114

X rays, 209, 211, 237; from space, 260; uses of, 228–29; wavelength, 217

X-ray telescope, 260, 291

yeasts, 75

Yellowstone National Park, 81

yogurt, 90

zebras, 24

zodiac, signs of, 254

Phil Dotson/DPI, (b) G. D. Plage/Bruce Coleman; **79,** Clara Aich.
UNIT 3: 80(l), Roger Werth/Woodfin Camp & Assoc., (r) Tom Zimberoff/Sygma; **81**(t), George Holton/Photo Researchers, (b) H. Gritscher/Peter Arnold; **82**(t), Clara Aich, (b) William E. Ferguson; **83**(l), Martin M. Rotker/Taurus, (r) Manfred Kage/Peter Arnold; **84**(tl), A. M. Siegelman, (tr) Manfred Kage/Peter Arnold, (b) Grant Heilman; **85,** A. M. Siegelman; **86,** Mangred Kage/Peter Arnold; **88**(l), Metropolitan Museum of Art, (r) Michael Melford/Image Bank; **89**(t), Kirtley-Perkins/Photo Researchers, (b), Dan Guravich/Photo Researchers; **90**(t), Clara Aich, (b) Lizabeth Corlett/DPI; **91,** EPA; **92**(t), courtesy Dr. McClurg, (b) Jack Parsons/Omni-Photo Communications; **93**(l), Clara Aich, (r) Martin M. Rotker/Taurus; **94**(tl), J. F. Gennaro, Jr./Photo Researchers, (r) T. F. Anderson, E. L. Wollman & F. Jacob/Photo Researchers, (bl) Charlton Photos; **96,** Alec Duncan/Taurus; **98**(l), Phil Dotson/DPI, (r) L. Mulvehill/Photo Researchers; **99,** Culver Pictures; **100, 102,** A. M. Siegelman; **103,** G. Cox/Bruce Coleman; **104**(all), @ Lennart Nilsson BEHOLD MAN/Little Brown & Co.; **106**(t), John Giannicchi/Science Source/Photo Researchers, (b) David Pollack/Stock Market; **107,** NASA; **108**(both), **109**(both), Clara Aich; **110,** Martin M. Rotker/Taurus; **111,** Ken Karp/Omni-Photo Communications; **112,** Granger Collection; **113,** Harry Hartman/Bruce Coleman; **114**(t), Clara Aich, (b) Manfred Kage/Peter Arnold; **115**(l), Paolo Koch/Photo Researchers, (r) Clara Aich; **116**(t), Clara Aich, (b) John Lei/Omni-Photo Communications; **117**(tl), F. Lisa Beebe/DPI, (tr) Eric Kroll/Taurus, (cr) John Lei/Omni-Photo Communications, (b) Clara Aich; **118,** Bettmann Archives; **119**(t), Martin M. Rotker, (b) HBJ/Haynes; **120,** J. Alex Langley/DPI; **121,** Tom Pantages; **123**(t), August Upitis/Shostal, (b) Alec Duncan/Taurus.
UNIT 4: 124(l), Michael Melford/Peter Arnold, (tr) Henry Grossman/DPI, (br) Wil Blanche/DPI; **125**(t), E. R. Degginger, (b) Joel Greenstein/Omni-Photo Communications; **127**(both), **131,** Clara Aich; **132**(t), William Koplitz/DPI, (b) Kennedy International Stock Photo; **134**(both), **135**(both), **136**(both), Clara Aich; **137**(l), G. Leavens/Photo Researchers, (r) John Lei/Omni-Photo Communications; **138**(both), **139**(all), **140**(both), **141**(all), Clara Aich; **142,** Michael Melford/Peter Arnold; **143**(t, bl), Granger Collection, (br) Clara Aich; **144**(both), **145**(both), **147**(both), Clara Aich; **149,** Grant Heilman; **150**(tl), John Blaustein/Woodfin Camp & Assoc., (r) DPI, (bl), Grant Heilman; **151,** William R. Wright/Taurus; **153,** Bill Pierce/Rainbow; **154,** Graig Davis/Sygma; **155**(both), Clara Aich; **157,** White Pite/International Stock Photo; **158**(both), Clara Aich; **159**(tl), Clara Aich, (r) A. B. Joyce/Photo Researchers; **160**(tl, tr), Clara Aich, (c) John Lei/Omni-Photo Communications, (b) Lizabeth Corlett/DPI; **161**(tl), Paul Stephanus/DPI, (tr) Alan Reininger/DPI, (bl) Alec Duncan/Taurus, (br) J. Alex Langley/DPI; **162**(tl), L. L. T. Rhodes/Taurus, (tr) Grant Heilman, (bl) Sylvia Johnson/Woodfin Camp & Assoc., (br) Richard W. Tolbert/DPI; **163,** Clara Aich; **164,** Bettman Archive; **166**(t), Granger Collection, (b) Bettmann Archive; **167,** AT&T; **168**(t), Clara Aich, (b) AT&T; **169,** AT&T; **171**(l), Granger Collection, (r) John M. Roberts/Stock Market; **172**(both), Clara Aich; **173,** Lowell Georgia/Photo Researchers; **174**(t), George Hall/Woodfin Camp & Assoc., (c) Noel L. Brooks/DPI, (b) Clara Aich; **175,** AT&T; **177**(t), Vance Henry/Taurus, (c) Grace/Focus on Sports; **178**(tl), Frank Fisher/After Image, (tr) Malcolm S. Kirk, (c) Science Museum, England; **179**(t), Hank Morgan/Rainbow, (c) Chuck O'Rear/West Light, (b) Heathkit/Zenith Educational Systems; **180,** John Lei/Omni-Photo Communications; **181**(l, tr), Chris Reeberg/DPI, (br) George Dodge/DPI; **182,** Bill Bridge/DPI; **183,** AT&T; **185**(t), Russ Kinne/Photo Researchers, (b) Ann Hagen-Griffiths/Omni-Photo Communications.
UNIT 5: 186(l), E. R. Degginger, (r) Jon Feingersh/Stock Market; **187,** Jeff Apoian/Photo Researchers; **188,** Grant Heilman Photography; **189,** Clara Aich; **190,** Scala; **191**(t), Tim Eagan/Woodfin Camp & Assoc., (b) Gazuit/Photo Researchers; **192**(both), **193**(both), Clara Aich; **194**(t, c), Clara Aich, (b) Shelley Rotner/Omni-Photo Communications; **197,** Clara Aich; **199**(t), Richard Fukuhara/West Light, (c) Jeff Zaruba/After Image, (b) Dale Clark; **200,** Clara Aich; **201,** C. B. Jones/Taurus; **202**(both), Clara Aich; **203,** DPI; **204,** Clara Aich; **207**(t), Bettmann Archive, (b) J. Alex Langley/DPI; **210**(l), Ira Block/Woodfin Camp & Assoc., (r) Ned Haines/Photo Researchers; **211**(t), Dale Brown/DPI, (bl, br), Clara Aich; **212**(both), **214**(both), Clara Aich; **215,** Mimi Forsyth/Monkmeyer; **216, 219**(both), Clara Aich; **220,** NASA, (tr) NOAA; (b) Clara Aich; **221,** Richard Wood/Taurus; **222,** Marvin Newman/DPI; **223**(l), Bettmann Archive, (r) John Lei/Omni-Photo Communications; **224,** Clara Aich; **225,** Ken Karp; **226,** Clara Aich; **227**(tl), Dan McCoy/Rainbow, (tr) Dan McCoy/Rainbow, (b) Clara Aich; **228,** Clara Aich; **229,** Van Bucher/Photo Researchers; **230,** NASA; **231**(t), Anthony Howarth/Woodfin Camp & Assoc., (b) Naval Photo Center/Photo Researchers; **232**(t), Granger Collection, (bl) Joel Greenstein/Omni-Photo Communications, (br) Manfred Kage/Peter Arnold; **233,** Randy Taylor/Sygma; **234,** Ken Biggs/DPI; **235**(t), Lucas Film, Ltd., (bl) Lucas Film, Ltd., (br) Granger Collection; **236**(t), DPI, (b) Vance Henry/Taurus; **239**(t), courtesy Psychological Corp., (b) Clara Aich.
UNIT 6: 240, Ned Haines/Photo Researchers; **241,** Finley Holiday Film Corp.; **242,** W. H. Hodge/Peter Arnold; **243,** Ira Victor/DPI; **245**(t, c), Granger Collection, (b) Tom Mareschal/Image Bank; **246**(t), Hansen Planetarium, (bl) Kitt Peak National Observatory, (br) Hale Observatory; **247,** Smithsonian Institution Whipple Observatory; **248**(both), Clara Aich; **249**(t), NASA, (b) Hank Morgan/Rainbow; **251,** Kitt Peak National Observatory; **252**(t), Lund Observatory, (b) Cerro Tololo Inter-American Observatory; **253**(t, br), Kitt Peak National Observatory, (bl) Hale Observatory; **254,** Granger Collection; **255**(l), Bell Labs, (r) National Radio Astronomy Observatory; **256**(t), Dan McCoy/Rainbow, (b) National Radio Astronomy Observatory; **258**(t), Kitt Peak National Observatory, (b) NASA; **259**(l), NASA, (r) Dan McCoy/Rainbow; **260**(both), **261,** NASA; **264,** Hansen Planetarium; **266,** Cerro Tololo Inter-American Observatory; **267, 268,** Hale Observatory; **269**(l), NASA, (r) W. Wilberforce/Shostal; **270**(all), HBJ; **272**(both), **274,** Clara Aich; **276**(tl, b), JPL/NASA, (tr) NASA; **279**(l) Ken Biggs/DPI, (r) NASA; **280,** Mike J. Howell/Leo de Wys; **281, 283,** NASA; **286,** National Optical Astronomy Observatory; **288,** Hale Observatory; **289**(both), Russ Kinne/Photo Researchers; **290**(t), Dan McCoy/Rainbow, (tr) Chuck O'Rear/West Light, (bl) Digital Art/West Light, (br) Gabe Palmer/Stock Market; **291,** Palomar Observatory; **292, 293, 295,** Hale Observatory;
UNIT 7: 296(l), Granger Collection, (tr) Clara Aich, (br) Bettmann Archive; **297**(t), E. R. Degginger, (b) Cecile Brunswick; **298,** American Museum of Natural History; **299**(both), HBJ/Haynes; **300**(all), Granger Collection; **301**(t), Grant Heilman, (b) Dan Brunswick/Woodfin Camp & Assoc.; **303**(t), Grant Heilman, (b) Cary Wolinsky/Stock, Boston; **304**(t), Olive Rebot/Stock, Boston; (bl), Collier Condit/Stock, Boston, (br) Wally McNamee/Woodfin Camp & Assoc.; **305**(tl), DPI (tc) Dick Durrance/Woodfin Camp & Assoc., (tr) Tim Eagan/Woodfin Camp & Assoc., (b) Guy Gillette/Photo Researchers; **306, 307,** Grant Heilman; **308**(both), Clara Aich; **309**(l), Grant Heilman, (tr) Mi. Seitelman/Woodfin Camp & Assoc., (br) Sepp Seitz/Woodfin Camp & Assoc.; **310**(t, bl) Propix/Monkmeyer, (br) Craig Aurness/Woodfin Camp & Assoc.; **311**(t), Grant Heilman, (c) Irving Schild/DPI; (b) Henry Ford Museum/Edison Institute, Dearborn, Michigan; **312**(tl), Sepp Seitz/Woodfin Camp & Assoc., (tr) Maratea/International Stock Photo, (b) Panuska/DPI; **313**(t), Sam Falf/Monkmeyer, (bl) Pete Saloutos/Stock Market, (br) Block/Monkmeyer; **314,** Clara Aich; **315**(t), Bob Straus/Woodfin Camp & Assoc., (c) Bill Gillette/Stock, Boston, (bl) HBJ, (br) Clara Aich; **316,** John Lei/Omni Photo Communications; **317,** Dan McCoy/Rainbow; **320**(all), Clara Aich; **322,** J. Alex Langley/DPI; **324**(t), Naval Photographic Center/Photo Researchers, (b) George Hall/Woodfin Camp & Assoc.; **325,** Michael Collier/Stock, Boston; **326**(l), Martin M. Rotker/Taurus, (r) Grant Heilman; **327,** Property of Livermore Labs; **328,** William Hubbell/Woodfin Camp & Assoc.; **329,** Frederick D. Bodin/Stock, Boston; **330,** Van Bucher/Photo Researchers; **331**(l), Westward, (tr) Vance Henry/Taurus, (cr) George Dodge/DPI, (br) Bernard Wolf/DPI; **333,** Guichar/Sygma; **334**(all), Peter Menzel; **335**(t), Jerry Cooke/Photo Researchers, (c) John Zoiner/Peter Arnold, (b) George Dodge/DPI; **336**(l), Paolo Koch/Photo Researchers, (r) Dept. of Sanitation, NY; **337,** Randa Bishop/DPI; **338**(l), Dan McCoy/Rainbow, (r) Brookhaven National Laboratory; **339**(t), Daniel Brody/Stock, Boston, (c) George Dodge/DPI, (b) Richard Choy/Peter Arnold; **341**(t), Cary Wolinsky/Stock, Boston, (b) Dick Durrance/Woodfin Camp & Assoc.;
UNIT 8: 342(l), Craig Blouin/Taurus, (tr, cr) Grant Heilman, (br) Tana Hoban/DPI; **343**(t), Pictor/DPI, (b) Maurice D. Spector/DPI; **344**(l), R. F. Head/Earth Scenes, (r) Anne Gordon/Taurus; **345**(both), Clara Aich; **346**(tl, tr), Stephen J. Krasemann/Peter Arnold, (bl) Lanstour Photographers/DPI, (br) Lou Niznik/DPI; **347**(l), Photo Researchers, (r) HBJ; **348**(l, r), Grant Heilman; (l inset, r inset), Clara Aich; **349**(all), HBJ; **350,** Tom McHugh/Photo Researchers; **351,** Grant Heilman; **352,** Frank & Dora Lambrect/DPI; **353**(t), Grant Heilman, (b) Charlton Photo; **360,** Russ Kinne/Photo Researchers; **362**(l), Dan McCoy/Rainbow, (r) HBJ/Haynes; **364,** Grant Heilman; **365**(l), USDA, (r) Grant Heilman; **366,** HBJ; **367**(tl), R. F. Head/Animals Animals, (tr,.b), Grant Heilman; **368**(both), Grant Heilman; **369**(l), Corri Barrs/DPI, (r) Grant Heilman; **370,** Leverett Bradley/DPI; **371**(both), Clara Aich; **372,** Grant Heilman; **373**(both), HBJ; **374,** Herb Gehr, Life Magazine @ 1947 TIME, Inc.; **375**(l), Phil Dotson/DPI, (r) Grant Heilman; **376**(both), Grant Heilman; **377**(l, tr), Grant Heilman, (br) Peter Menzel/Stock, Boston; **378**(all), Grant Heilman; **381**(l), Hogle Zoological Gardens, (r) USDA.

D 9 0 1
E 2
F 3
G 4
H 5
I 6
J 7